Compliments
of your chef

Best Luck

Ciao

To Bellissimo Sherry
"Mamma mia"
With Love

La Cucina di

Andrea's

NEW ORLEANS May 23-2001

To Great Cooking
Great Friends

[signatures]

Ciao Bella arrivederci

I've only
known you for
a short period in
my life (1 year) but
you are indeed a special
person. We miss you. May
God always bless you. Never stop SMILING
Diana

Sherry, thanks
for inviting me
to your shower!
good luck in Austin,
I am sure you'll
do great! Sorry
I didn't get a
chance to work w/
you longer.
Cathy Piett

Best of luck to you
in all you do. I thank you
for having faith & confidence
in my work and opening the
door for me to transplant.
I am sorry to see you go &
can only hope that we
will keep in touch.
Best of Wishes
Valerie

Thanks for welcoming
me in & for all
your advice, especially
when my mom was so
ill! — I will always
remember you & I hope
your life is full & wonderful!
God bless you.
— Amy

Sherry, I wish you a
wonderful future!
for you! it has been
a privilege and an
honor to work with you!
good luck.
Joanne

You are as pungent
as the fresh mozzarella
& as sweet as tiramisu!
No, seriously, I am
really, really, gonna miss
you! This wasn't how
things were supposed to
work out! I wish you all
the happiness in the world!
I will love
Tortola.
xoxo,
Lisa

La Cucina di

Andrea's

NEW ORLEANS

Extra-Virgin Recipes

*From One of America's Best
Northern Italian Restaurants*

Chef Andrea Apuzzo

Edited by Tom Fitzmorris

Cucina dell'ART, Inc., Publisher
Andrea's Restaurant
3100 Nineteenth Street
Metairie, Louisiana 70002

New Orleans, Big Bend & Pacific Company, Co-Publisher
P.O. Box 51831, New Orleans, Louisiana 70151

Library of Congress Cataloging-In-Publication data:
Apuzzo, Andrea. De Angelis, Roberto. Fitzmorris, Tom
La Cucina di Andrea's New Orleans:
Extra-virgin recipes from one of America's best Northern Italian
restaurants/Andrea Apuzzo, Roberto de Angelis, and Tom Fitzmorris.
Includes index.
I. Cookery, Italian. I. Title
89-63780

The type is set in 10-point ITC Tiffany, a modernized version of a Baskerville-inspired typestyle of the 19th Century. The headings are set in Belwe Inline, an attractive slab-serif face.—T.F.

A la mia cara mamma
Regina De Angelis Apuzzo
Che mi ha sempre inspirato nella mia carriera
e passione per la cucina, la gente, e la vita
di buon mangiare e bere.

Foreword

One of my favorite cities is famous for one of my favorite pastimes—eating. New Orleans is known to connoisseurs around the world for the virtuosity and refinement of its palate. New Orleanians know and expect good food.

So, when one of my knowledgeable friends in the Crescent City wanted to introduce me to a new restaurant, I naturally leaped at the chance.

I have been thanking my friend ever since.

In this city of great dining experiences, Andrea's stands alone at the top. Owner and chef Andrea Apuzzo prepares a peerless Italian cuisine with superb delicacy of touch and a creative nuance of flavor. He serves sensible portions artistically presented in a gracefully tasteful atmosphere. And that atmosphere is permeated by the man himself. Andrea is warm, charming and dedicated to seeing that his patrons enjoy a memorable evening of dining.

Andrea, I'll be back as soon as I can.

—Lee Meriwether

Introduction

First-class Northern Italian cooking—made with ingredients of the spectacular quality one finds in Italy, and served with attention to details—was a most elusive commodity around New Orleans until Andrea's opened. The very fact that most Orleanians had never experienced the kind of cuisine and service envisioned by Andrea Apuzzo and Roberto De Angelis meant that the two Capri-born cousins had a battle before them. It looked as if they had to educate most of their customers before they would be able to serve them.

Well. While there is nothing easy about starting a new restaurant, at least this adjustment was easy. Orleanians took to Andrea's like a crawfish to soft mud. With a long history of enthusiastic eating, the city knows a good thing when it tastes it.

And something equally gratifying happened. The classic Italian cooking styles which Chef Andrea had practiced since he was seven years old picked up a few cues from the New Orleans cuisine. What emerged was an Italian taste with Louisiana ingredients. Olive oil and crushed red pepper met soft-shell crabs and Tabasco. Red beans and rice got a Caprese accent. And gumbo became the first course of a meal that went on to include linguine al pesto, osso buco, tirami su, and espresso.

Andrea's is a very deep restaurant. Beyond the fascination provided by the Creole-Caprese synthesis we find layers and layers of excellence. Two in particular have impressed me. The first is the chef's obsession with freshness. Very few restaurants in America find it worth the trouble to buy all their fish whole and perform all the trimming themselves; Chef Andrea says that it is essential to look into the fish's eyes for him to be satisfied. For the same reason, the kitchen manufactures many raw materials—pasta, cheese, and bread, among other things—that lesser restaurants would buy already prepared from outside.

The second practice that strikes me as uniquely delightful is the incredible amount of work that went into the development of Andrea's wine list. Co-proprietor Roberto De Angelis is one of the two or three most knowledgable people I have ever met when it comes to Italian wine. But in New Orleans, it was almost as if Italy didn't make anything but Frascati and Soave, and Roberto couldn't find the wines he wanted locally. He dealt with importers all over the country, then struck deals with local wholesalers so the wines could pass through the complex legal maze built by the state for the alcohol trade. The result is without question the most distinctive wine list in New Orleans, replete with joyful discoveries for the connoisseur of Italian wine.

No explanation for the success of Andrea's is as convincing as the enthusiasm both Chef Andrea and Roberto show for their work. They set their own standards higher than any that had been set for them before, and they worked with abandon to achieve them.

Chef Andrea seems to be either tireless or to have the ability to be in several places at once. He both orchestrates the kitchen activities and spends lots of time in the dining room lovingly expostulating the night's menu for his guests. He is always there for any civic or charitable organization that asks for his dazzling, delicious presence. Meanwhile, Roberto's imagination and sense of style when it comes to finding new ways to delight his guests know no bounds.

Chef Andrea and I disagree on whose idea it was to do this cookbook. We each claim to have brought it up first after lunch one day. But that doesn't matter much. What is important is that we completely agreed on the essence of the book: that it should contain all the recipes for which Andrea's is celebrated, and that all the recipes had to be tested and measured exactly.

Our approach to writing the book was simple. Andrea cooked each dish while I stood by with a portable computer, typing in everything I saw. We measured absolutely everything that went into each dish—including salt, pepper and water. Whenever I saw any technique that I didn't understand or thought would be confusing, I asked Andrea what he did and why he did it.

Although we worked with restaurant equipment, all the recipes were prepared in small batches. You will find that most recipes serve four to six people. The only exceptions are things like soups or sauces that can be kept for a few days. This is critically important. I am sick of restaurant cookbooks that obviously were written by merely dividing bulk recipes by some number. (When you see measurements like one and one-fifth tablespoons of an ingredient, you can bet that's what happened.) That shortcut simply doesn't work. The chemistry of cooking is different for a small batch than for a large one, and the recipe must be worked from scratch for a smaller quantity.

Not all of our recipes were immediate successes. There were quite a few that we had to cook two or even three times to discover the right way.

The proof came in my own kitchen. I am not a bad cook but you couldn't call me a professional. I own no professional equipment. I cooked over half the recipes in this book at home and discovered only the smallest and rarest departures in taste from what we had come up with in the restaurant. I feel secure in telling you that these recipes will also come out deliciously in your own kitchen.

I cannot resist telling you which were my favorite dishes. (Of course, we ate everything we cooked.) I call your attention, then, to Insalata Andrea, Ostriche Andrea, Lumache Barolo, Vitello Tonnato, Zuppa Di Pasta e Fagioli, Cannelloni Ai Frutti Di Mare, Ravioli Ai Funghi Porcini, Gamberi Tommaso, Pompano Al Pesto, Pollo Della Nonna, Vitello Michelangelo, Vitello Abruzzese, Vitello Tanet, Trippa Milanese, Melanzane Parmigiana, Torta Al Formaggio and Tirami Su. (I can hear the chef now. "What's the matter? You didn't like the Gamberi Caprese?" I did, Andrea. If I had disliked anything we put in this book, I would have tried to talk you out of it.)

I hope you enjoy this great food as much as I have.

—Tom Fitzmorris

A Few Notes from the Chef

Mia casa e tua casa. My house is your house. That is how I try to present Andrea's Restaurant to every guest that walks through the door. Although both Roberto and I have trained all our lives to learn the right ways to do everything in a restaurant, the first rule we keep in our minds always is: Whatever the guest wants is our pleasure to give him.

You will read in many places in this book about my feelings concerning freshness. If there is one thing that makes Italian cooking the best in the world, it is the availability, freshness, and excellence of the foods we have to work with. My philosophy is simple: if the fish, vegetables, or meats I need to make a certain dish are not available fresh, then I forget that dish and make something else. For example, I would never substitute frozen or five-day-old fish for fresh, whole fish with clear eyes and red gills. This may seem picky to you, but such tiny details separate a five-star restaurant from the also-rans.

Sharing some of the thousands of dishes I've created over the years in a cookbook is a dream I've had for many years. Putting it together has been, in a way, a miniature version of creating a restaurant. Like a restaurant, it involves the advice and participation of trusted colleagues. First among these is my cousin and partner Roberto De Angelis. Our major goal—to please the guest—is the same. But we don't always have the same idea about how best to do that. We are a great team because we can recognize when the other cousin has the better idea. Two heads are better than one—especially when their experience and areas of expertise overlap, but don't cover one another totally.

My wife Cathleen has also been a major force behind this book—mainly in that she has been pushing me to do it for years. Week after week, she got me out of bed on Saturday mornings at 9 a.m. when I hadn't left the restaurant till 3 a.m. the night before, so we could spend a whole day working on the cookbook recipes. Her patience with me throughout the entire process of running a restaurant, and her indispensable help at the restaurant itself is a great gift from her to me. Being the wife of a chef is not easy.

Third, I thank Lonnie Knisley, one of the finest bakers I have ever met. Lonnie and I have worked together for over ten years, since my days at the Royal Orleans Hotel. Most of the recipes in the **Desserts** section are his own creations—and a master baker does not share his recipes easily. Andrea's would not be the same without Lonnie's daily output of outstanding bakeries.

I don't know anything about writing a book. I couldn't have put this volume in your hands without the help of Tom Fitzmorris, who stood with me for hundreds of hours at the stove. He asked many questions to dig out important procedures that I probably would have forgotten to tell you about, and made many valuable suggestions as to how the recipes best could be presented for home use. He then spent hundreds more hours at his keyboard, making sure the recipes are easily understandable and interesting to read. Throughout the entire process, I have been most impressed by Tom's taste and knowledge of food. There is a reason why he is the number one restaurant critic in New Orleans.

I knew from the very beginning that I wanted excellent color photographs in this book. That required an excellent food photographer. I found one in Glade Bilby II, who I consider to be nothing less than an artist. His technical ability and sense of style provided us with stunning pictures. His stylist, Martha Torres, also contributed greatly to the photos you see herein.

Many suppliers were instrumental in letting us have or use furnishings for the photographs. La Cuisine Classique, a great kitchen store, loaned us many pieces for the shots and were very helpful. So was Mediterranean Tile Company, which provided us with lots of interesting marble slabs to use as background texture in the photos. Diane Burke and Leigh Zollinger at the store Antiques Magazine provided us with beautiful china and silverware. Jerry Landry and Roussel's Antiques of Laplace were also very helpful. The Central Grocery loaned us a magnificent giant jar of marinated vegetables for our photograph on the back cover.

Whether they knew it or not, the entire staff of Andrea's had a hand in writing this book. While we were testing recipes, I had everybody in the place running around fetching ingredients and equipment. Even the clean-up and dishwashing staff had extra work to do as a result of our cookbook experiments. I thank them all.

Finally, I would like to thank all the guests of our restaurant, past and future, for inspiring us to create the kind of food you'll find in this book.

—Chef Andrea Apuzzo

About Chef Andrea Apuzzo, Roberto De Angelis, and Andrea's

Andrea Apuzzo and Roberto De Angelis were born and grew up on the island of Capri, a resort just off the west coast of Italy near Naples. Although Andrea and Roberto are cousins and both worked in hotels from an early age, it was not until much later and in a different land that they brought their marvelously complementary talents together.

Andrea was born in the early Fifties. Italy, like the rest of Europe, was well on its way to recovering from the war, through an enormous amount of work and industriousness on the part of the population. It was not uncommon for Europeans to start working very young, and at the tender age of seven and a half Andrea was working in a bakery. He went to school at the same time; since Capri's main economy is tourism, it was natural for him to go to hotel school.

But Andrea didn't choose his career merely because it promised him a good living. "As soon as I started working in kitchens I knew that I wanted to become a good cook and then a great chef," he says. "I knew that reaching my goal would take lots of patience and sacrifices, but it seemed very much worth it."

At age 16, Andrea left Capri on a tour of duty that saw him cooking in hotels in Switzerland, Germany, France, Bermuda, Mexico, and Argentina. In 1975, he arrived in America—fulfilling another dream he'd had since he was young. His first big assignment was in Atlanta, where he worked for the Omni Hotel. There he opened the Bugatti Restaurant, which became an immediate hit: it was the first time Atlantans had a chance to explore Italian cuisine with the same sort of elegance and creativity as the French places.

Andrea came to New Orleans in 1977 as executive chef of the celebrated Royal Orleans Hotel. Several things happened to him there. He discovered that he liked New Orleans. New Orleans discovered it liked Andrea. And he worked with Ronald Pincus, general manager of the hotel. Pincus, who Andrea calls the most professional gentleman he ever worked for, encouraged Andrea to spare nothing to make his operation the best.

"Working in a five-star hotel with a man like Pincus made me believe that only the freshest and best fish, produce, and meat was good enough for our guests," says Andrea. "It made me believe that you couldn't take shortcuts in the kitchen. You have to make your stocks and sauces and pasta and bread and pastry fresh from scratch if you wanted to be the best. That is the philosophy that I brought with me when I opened Andrea's."

But before we get to opening day, let's find out what Roberto was doing all this time. His family owned a chain of the most exclusive hotels in Capri, and although he worked with them in his early years he broke away to establish a career as a hotelier on his own. "I told my father that I would be the general manager of a major hotel by the time I was 30," Roberto says—and, indeed, his climb up the ladder was extremely rapid. His first assignment was the Sheraton Hotel in London, where he divided his time between formal and practical training in his business.

Roberto came to America to work at the Hyatt in New York. In the early

Eighties, he moved to the newly-opened Ritz-Carlton in Atlanta, where he was hired by a man he calls one of the most brilliant in the worldwide hotel business — Horst Schulze, who expanded the Ritz-Carlton chain to its present magnificence in America. Roberto was in charge of service at the hotel, and created the look and style of the flagship restaurant in the Ritz-Carlton.

"Horst Schulze introduced me to an idea that I have practiced ever since and that is the rule at Andrea's," explains Roberto. "He told me that we were not servants, but that we were ladies and gentlemen serving other ladies and gentlemen. This meant that all the table service personnel had to act with the most class and intelligence. They couldn't say something like, 'Can I get you a cocktail from the bar,' because the customer already *knows* that a cocktail comes from the bar."

Two other men are inspirations for Roberto. The first is his father, Aniello De Angelis, who showed him that there's never anything to be lost by maintaining the highest standards. The second was Tony May, generally conceded to be the finest Italian restaurateur in New York. Tony May befriended Roberto and demonstrated that one didn't have to dilute one's native culture in America.

Roberto shortly thereafter became head of the fine-dining division for all the Ritz-Carlton hotels. He was still in his mid-twenties. His goal of general manager by 30 was within sight when he was interviewed for the food and beverage director's position at the new Laguna Miguel Hotel, an exclusive property near San Diego. While in the offices of the hotel, he ran into somebody else who was being interviewed: Andrea Apuzzo. Cousins Roberto and Andrea agreed to meet for drinks later that night to talk about Capri and other things.

Andrea's Restaurant was born that night. The midwife was a bottle of Cognac, which lasted almost as long as the two cousins did — late, late into the night. The upshot was that on May 4, 1984, Roberto traveled to New Orleans, fell in love with the city, and started working with Andrea to open their restaurant.

The careers of both men had been overwhelmingly inside the hotel industry, whose restaurants live by different rules than those governing an independent restaurant. But each obstacle was overcome, a step at a time. An interesting story concerns how they acquired the building Andrea's occupies. Roberto found it in Metairie, a nearby suburb of New Orleans, and he thought it perfect. It was then occupied by its builder, Etienne de Felice, a long-time New Orleans restaurateur. When Roberto and Andrea approached the old man to ask about buying his restaurant, he threw them out.

Roberto asked his father to come to New Orleans to look over their plans. During the visit, Roberto drove by Etienne's with his father and told him the story. Aniello De Angelis asked, "Is this the place you really want?" Roberto answered that it was perfect. They stopped the car and the father went inside. He was about the same age as Etienne, and apparently there was a good chemistry between the two men. A half hour later, the property had been bought.

Andrea and Roberto took over the building on the first day of 1985, and started serving 21 days later. "The secret of our early success was what we did when we opened," says Roberto. "The first week, we accepted only 30 people a day for dinner. The second week, only 50. When we reached the number we wanted, we turned down all requests for reservations and walk-in customers. Soon everybody in the city was talking about a great new Italian restaurant in Metairie where it was impossible to get a reservation. And then we did fantastic."

Contents

Basics

How To Use These Recipes, And Other Tips

I have attempted to keep the language and techniques of the recipes as consistent as possible. Here is what we mean by three very frequently used items in the recipes:

tsp. is the abbreviation for **teaspoon**. Use a measuring teaspoon with solid contents level with rim of spoon. (Note lower-case "t".)

Tbs. is the abbreviation for **tablespoon.** A tablespoon is three teaspoons. (Note capital "T".)

Water is not included in the lists of ingredients. Since many recipes call for the addition of water several times during the cooking process, we give the quantity at each point where it's used in the instructions.

I've tried to limit myself to easily-available foodstuffs and standard cooking techniques in this book. There are, however, a few advanced or unusual recipes. In most of those, I describe the hard-to-find ingredient or specialized utensil in the instructions for the particular recipe.

Despite all that, you may find some ingredient or technique in a recipe that may be confusing or new to you. This chapter, which is arranged alphabetically, lists everything we could think of that might cause problems.

CUTTING, CHOPPING, ETC. Consider a medium onion. When the ingredient list calls for the onion to be **cut up**, that means to cut it into eight chunks. **Cubed** means about 16 chunks. **Coarsely chopped** means cut into pieces about the size of your fingernail. **Chopped** refers to small chips about the size of rice. It's the same idea for all other vegetables for which these terms are used.

Sliced usually means that the vegetable or meat should be cut into slices about the thickness of two stacked nickels. When it should be thinner or thicker than that, we'll say so. **Julienne** slices are about the size of kitchen matchsticks.

CALAMARI. See "Squid," below.

EGGPLANT. The eggplant is a unique and delicious vegetable. Our favorite serving of it is in various kinds of antipasti. But we also like to saute it, stuff it, and include it in sauces. The only drawback that eggplants have is that they can be bitter. There is no easy way to tell whether this is the case, although if you cut into an eggplant and find that it has a green tinge on the inside, it will almost certainly be bitter.

We have a method for extracting the bitterness from eggplant before we start cooking. We use this method for almost every dish we make involving eggplant. Here's how it works:

1. Slice the eggplants to the size called for by the recipe. Put the slices into a bowl and sprinkle 1 Tbs. salt over the eggplant. Toss well to coat all the eggplant with salt. Don't worry whether this is too much salt; it will be washed off later, and very little of it will make it to the final dish.

2. Put the eggplant slices into a colander. Array them in a relatively uniform layer up the sides. Put a bowl the same size as the colander inside the colander, and weigh it down with three or so pounds of weight. Put this entire unit into the sink. A great deal of water will drain from the eggplants for about 45 minutes. This will remove the bitterness.

3. Rinse the salt off the eggplant with cold water. Drain it well, then squeeze it dry. The eggplant is now ready for you to proceed with the next step in your recipe.

FAVA BEANS. Fava beans are large, flat, brown-skinned beans. They are relished by all Italians. In New Orleans, they are most often seen on St. Joseph's Day, when they are given out as "lucky beans." The are always available dried, but in the springtime you can occasionally get fresh fava beans. They are in large pods that have to be removed.

FRESH HERBS. Except in stocks, we use fresh herbs in all our cooking at Andrea's. The supermarkets are catching up with the demand, and the important herbs are now usually available fresh. The most important of them as far as our cooking is concerned—basil—can be grown easily in a flowerpot in your back yard. Just pick off the tops; the plants grow back like weeds if watered well and kept in direct sunshine.

If you must substitute dried herbs for fresh, remember that in most cases you would use half as much as if the herb were fresh. Here are some rough equivalents for herbs whose measurement in the recipes is usually given by the sprig or leaf:

2 sprigs fresh oregano equals ½ tsp. dried
3 sprigs fresh thyme equals ¼ tsp. dried
1 sprig fresh rosemary equals ½ tsp. dried
5 leaves fresh sage equals ¼ tsp. dried, rubbed
8 leaves fresh basil equals ½ tsp. dried
1 Tbs. fresh tarragon equals 1 tsp. dried

In some cases, there is a great flavor difference between fresh and dried herbs. For example, I don't find much in common between fresh and dried tarragon. My advice it to seek out the fresh herbs whenever possible. They make the dish more vivid in flavor and appearance.

OLIVE OIL. We use two kinds of olive oil in our cooking. Both are of superb quality, imported from Italy. The more expensive is *extra virgin olive oil*, a light, flavorful oil from the first pressing of the olives. I recommend it for all salad dressings, for substituting for butter in low-cholesterol sauces, and in a few dishes where subtlety of flavor is a main theme. Extra virgin olive oil is specified in recipes when I think it makes a difference. When not specified, use the regular *100 percent pure olive oil*, which is considerably less expensive but still a fine product. There is also such a thing as *virgin olive oil*, which is somewhere between the extra virgin and the standard in lightness and flavor. The brand we use in our restaurant and that I would recommend to you is Colavita.

Two techniques for which you would not use olive oil are deep frying or dishes in which the oil must stay extremely hot for a long time. In such cases, use a good vegetable oil (preferably one made from cottonseed oil).

OVEN PREHEAT. It is extremely important that your oven be preheated to the right temperature *before you put the food in*. All the cooking times in the recipes are based on the assumption that the oven is already hot. It is critical for many—if not most—of the dishes to receive a full blast of heat immediately, otherwise they may not crust over and will dry out as a result. (This is especially true of bakery items.) In our restaurant's kitchen, the ovens are kept hot—at around 300 degrees at least—all the time we are open.

A frequent source of problems when recipes are followed at home is the great variation in the accuracy of oven thermostats. The best course is to have an oven thermometer, and to place it on the shelf where you'll be putting the food. This assures you of the right temperature. (You may be amazed at how far the actual temperature in the oven deviates from what you set on the dial.)

PANCETTA. Italian-style bacon, taken from the leaner part of the pork belly and mildly smoked. Unlike ordinary bacon, it is ususally rolled, so that slices of it form a circle. It has a distinctive flavor that I like. If pancetta is unavailable, you can substitute bacon.

PARMESAN CHEESE. There is a wide range of cheeses made in the style common around the city of Parma, but the one we refer to here is the hard cheese which is grated to fine crumbs and sprinkled atop pasta and anything else that seems appropriate. It is also delicious eaten by the chunk. The most famous and expensive Parmesan cheese is *Parmigiano Reggiano.* In our restaurant we use *Grana Padano,* which is only slightly less well known and whose flavor I especially love. I recommend that you grate the cheese at the time of serving.

PEPPERS, BELL. Any bell peppers for any purpose must have the stem, seeds, and white inner membrane removed. That's easily enough done, and is the first step if you are adding raw peppers to a recipe. However, some recipes call for **roasted bell peppers**. The easiest way to do this at home is under the broiler on maximum temperature. Place the peppers on the rack and roast, turning them as the skin blackens, until about 75 percent of the outer surface of the peppers is black. Don't be shy about this; it will look like you're burning and ruining them, but you're bringing out the flavors of the peppers. This can also be done by holding the peppers above the open flame on your stove with a fork. After the peppers are charred, let them cool. Then peel off the outer skin—both the charred parts and those that aren't. Pull off the stem end, which will have a lot of the seeds attached; try to get most of them out. Split the pepper open and remove the rest of the seeds.

PINE NUTS. *Pinoli* come from the cones of pine trees, and they're delicious in salads. They're also indispensable for pesto sauce. Pine nuts should be lightly toasted before you use them in most recipes. To do this, put the pine nuts in a small ovenproof pan one nut deep, and toast the nuts under a broiler about three inches from the heat. You can also do this in a toaster oven. When a few of the nuts start to brown—this will happen in 30 seconds or so—take them out. Careful! A few seconds too much, and pine nuts turn black on you!

SPINACH. You cannot cook Italian for long without using spinach. Indeed, so much spinach is used in the cuisine from around Florence that the term "florentine" ("Fiorentina" in Italian) has come to be applied to almost any dish with spinach in the sauce.

I strongly recommend you use fresh spinach. It is easily available and inexpensive. It does, however, require a bit of work on the part of the cook to get it ready. The first step is to pick off the coarse parts of the stems. This is somewhat time-consuming, but I find it a calming activity.

Even more important is that the spinach be properly cleaned. Fresh spinach always carries an incredible amount of dirt. To get rid of this, dunk the spinach in a big bowl or sink of water and stir it around. Then pull the spinach out of the water and drain the water. *Never* pour the water out of the bowl with the spinach still in it—the leaves will just catch all the dirt again. Keep washing the spinach with fresh changes of water until you see no more dirt. This may take five, six, seven washings. But there are few things worse than gritty dirt in an otherwise perfect dish.

The way we usually cook spinach is by poaching. Bring a pot of water to a boil and drop the spinach into it. When the water resumes boiling—about two minutes later, usually—the spinach is cooked. Remove it and immediately wash it with cold water to stop the cooking. Another way to cook spinach is to simply put it into a covered pot over low heat. The water that sticks to the leaves from the washing is enough to steam the spinach.

You can almost not overestimate the amount of spinach you need to cook. A pound of fresh spinach shrivels down to a tiny amount when cooked.

SQUID. The most important step when cooking *calamari* (unfortunately, it's the one which is most often neglected by cooks) is cleaning them properly. Here's how that goes:

1. Pull the tentacled part of the calamari off the body, tearing right behind the eyes. This will usually take with it the very small entrails, which can be pulled off and discarded. A small gray-silver part of this is the ink sac, which you might want to save to make some recipes elsewhere in this book that call for squid ink.

2. Cut the part of the tentacle section including the eyes away from the tentacles. Then halfway turn the ring of tentacles inside out, which will eject the beak and a small ball of inedible tissue. Also pull away any loose membranes. The tentacles are what you want, not the stuff in the middle.

3. Insert your finger into the body of the squid and remove everything you find inside. One of these items will be the "pen" or bone, which looks like a thin piece of flexible, clear plastic.

4. The body will be covered by a rather tough exterior skin, and that has to be removed. It comes off fairly easily most of the time. Occasionally, you will have to plunge the squid into boiling water for a minute (followed by a quick cold water bath, so it won't keep cooking) to loosen this skin.

5. Most of the time, we leave the tentacle section in one piece, and slice the body into rings about an inch wide—less than that if they're to be deep-fried.

4

WHERE TO BUY WHAT YOU NEED. The New Orleans area is blessed with many resources for buying the best foodstuffs and utensils for doing the kind of cooking in this book. Not only are there many gourmet specialty shops, but the supermarkets are stocking more interesting and fresher products.

The first store to know about is the **Central Grocery**, across from the French Market. It is full of magnificent imported Italian groceries, and its deli has great salamis, prosciutto, mortadella, and the like, as well as a superb cheese selection. The **Progress Grocery,** two doors away, is also very good.

The two best stores for beef, lamb, and veal are **Dorignac's** in Metairie and **Langenstein's** in the Uptown area. Both stores have the best quality and very good butchers. **The Real Superstore** also has superb prime beef. Dorignac's and Langenstein's carry very good fresh seafood. So does **Schwegmann's,** which differs from most large supermarkets in having a large selection of fresh whole fish. The Real Superstore's seafood department displays a good variety, although most of it is filleted.

The best stores for produce are The Real Superstore, the **Winn-Dixie Marketplace** stores, and **Canal-Villere**. You can still find good vegetables at the French Market, but don't count on finding a particular item.

For cheeses, sliced meats, pates, exotic seasonings (like saffron) and other deli items I recommend The Real Superstore, **Whole Food Company, Macy's, Martin Wine Cellar,** Dorignac's, and **Magazine Cuisine.** Magazine Cuisine also carries lots of unusual condiments and herbs. Martin Wine Cellar is without a doubt the city's leading wine shop, and the place to look for Italian wines. Jim Walsh, who manages Martin Wine Cellar's Metairie store, is one of the most knowledgeable retailers in the city when it comes to the wines of Italy.

For cooking gear I recommend **La Cuisine Classique,** which carries an enormous variety of very fine and often very exotic cookware. Also good are the kitchen stores of Macy's and **Maison Blanche.**

If all you need is advice, I would highly recommend that you listen to the daily radio show hosted by my co-author Tom Fitzmorris. You can call in on the show and ask him anything about cooking, dining, or wine, and get a good answer. He's on WSMB Radio, 1350 AM.

Oh, yes. . . I would be happy to discuss anything in the book with you next time you come in for lunch or dinner at Andrea's. Meeting my guests is something that always makes me feel good.

Fondi

Stocks

When I begin a recipe, I insist on building upon a strong foundation. That's where stocks come in. I would sooner run my kitchen without stoves than without stocks that I made myself. I never have used commercial stocks or bases and never will. I feel that strongly about the contribution a homemade stock can make to the flavor of a dish.

A soup or a sauce will reveal many more layers of complex flavors when made with the right stock than if made with just water. Your guests may not know exactly why the flavor is much better, but they will taste the difference — this I guarantee.

A stock is a simple thing, really. It's made by simmering meat, poultry, or seafood in water for a long time with seasonings, and then straining out the solid parts and skimming the fat. What's left is an essence of flavor and aroma.

You can make a large quantity of stock at a time and keep it in the refrigerator for up to a week. Or freeze it and keep it for a long time, using it as you need it.

To infuse an extra measure of flavor and aroma into our stocks, we put in what we call a "sacchetto," or little bag. (It's the same thing that the French call a "bouquet garni.") We make a bag from two layers of cheesecloth and put various dried seasonings in — typically black peppercorns, thyme, marjoram, parsley, and bay leaves, although the composition may change from stock to stock.

There are many different kinds of stocks for many different purposes. Here are the main ones we use at Andrea's.

Fondo Bianco di Vitello

Veal Stock for White Sauces

This stock, like many others we use, is made from veal bones. It used to be that you could get veal bones free from the butcher. But these days, you usually have to buy them — or save them yourself from other recipes. For this stock we do not brown the veal bones, nor do we add anything like carrots that would color the stock. This is because you will be using this veal stock in light-colored sauces.

4 lbs. veal bones
2 ribs celery
½ large onion
8 cloves
½ leek, pulled apart and washed well

Sacchetto: Put these dry seasonings into a small cheesecloth bag:
1 tsp. black peppercorns
1 tsp. thyme
1 tsp. marjoram
1 tsp. rosemary
¼ cup fresh chopped parsley with stems
4 bay leaves

1 Remove the leaves from the celery (reserve for some other use) and cut celery ribs into one-inch pieces. Stud the onion half with the cloves. Clean the leek very well (it can contain a lot of sand) and chop off the roots.

2 Put all the ingredients into a large stockpot with three gallons of water and bring to a boil. Lower to a simmer and allow to simmer for three to four hours — until you have about half the original amount of water. (The longer you simmer, the stronger the stock will get, but reducing it by half gives the strength of stock we will be using in all the other recipes in this book.) Skim the scum off the top of the pot as it simmers (this is mostly fat).

3 When the stock has reached the right concentration, strain it through a large sieve or a "china cap" (a big, cone-shaped strainer used by professional cooks). Refrigerate the stock in a large open container. Any fat that remains will float to the top and congeal, so you can remove it easily. Store the stock in closed containers.

Makes a gallon and a half of stock.

Fondo Bruno di Pollame

Chicken Stock

Chicken stock is an absurdly useful thing to have around the kitchen. We use it by the gallons in our kitchen. It finds its way into all kinds of dishes, from soups and sauces to casseroles and vegetables. Once you see what a difference it makes in your cooking you'll make it regularly and always have it on hand.

4 lbs. chicken (either whole chickens or leftover pieces like backbones, etc.)
2 ribs celery
½ onion
4 cloves
4-5 leeks (green tops only)
1 tsp. salt

Sacchetto: Put these dry seasonings into a small cheesecloth bag:
1 tsp. black peppercorns
1 tsp. thyme
1 tsp. marjoram
1 tsp. rosemary
¼ cup fresh chopped parsley with stems
4 bay leaves

The procedure is exactly the same as for the veal stock, except use only two gallons of water. You will note that the chicken stock will throw off a lot less scum but a lot more fat. This should be thoroughly removed.
Makes one and a half gallons of stock.

Fondo Bruno di Carne

Beef Stock

This is a more robust stock that we use in bean and onion soups. Once again, the essential ingredient—beef bones—will have to be begged or bought from your butcher.

6 lbs. beef bones, not cut or broken
1 medium onion
6 cloves
6 ribs celery
1 large carrot
Stems only from one bunch parsley
8-10 bay leaves
1 tsp. dried thyme
½ cup tomato, chopped

Sacchetto: Put these dry seasonings into a small cheesecloth bag:
1 tsp. black peppercorns
1 tsp. thyme
1 tsp. marjoram
1 tsp. rosemary
¼ cup fresh chopped parsley with stems
4 bay leaves

1 Boil four gallons of water in a large stockpot. Meanwhile, slice the onion (don't peel it) in half, and place the halves cut side down in a hot black iron skillet or on a griddle. Leave them there until the downside of the onion gets black. This will caramelize the sugars in the onion and also lend a little color. Stud the onion with the cloves.

2 Put all the ingredients into the stockpot and proceed as instructed for the veal stock. You will note that this stock will take on a light brown color as it simmers, in contrast to the very pale color of the other two stocks.

Makes one and a half gallons of stock.

Salsa di Base Bruna

Demi-Glace

Demi-glace is the most concentrated essence of veal, a sort of super-concentrated stock. It is an extremely valuable ingredient to have on hand; it adds an incomparable depth of flavor to sauces for meats. It takes a very long time to prepare — two days, if you do it right. Fortunately, you don't have to constantly attend to it. It is a badge of excellence for a chef to make his own demi-glace; there are not many restaurant kitchens that do. When you achieve your own demi-glace, you have the right to be very proud of yourself.

6 lbs. veal bones
1 large carrot, coarsely chopped
1 medium onion, coarsely chopped
4 ribs celery, leaves removed, coarsely chopped
6 cloves garlic, coarsely chopped
¼ cup tomato paste
1 qt. dry red wine
1 cup all-purpose flour

Sacchetto: Put these dry seasonings into a small cheesecloth bag:
1½ Tbs. black peppercorns
1½ Tbs. dry rosemary leaves
1 tsp. dry sage
1 Tbs. thyme leaves
1 Tbs. marjoram

6 cherry tomatoes, cut in half (or one regular tomato, cut up)
10-12 parsley stems

1 With a heavy cleaver, split bones into two-inch pieces (you can ask your butcher to do this for you). Load bones into a baking pan. Put the pan on top of the stove over high heat first to heat the bones up quickly. Then put the pan of bones into a 500-degree oven. Every 10 minutes, shuffle bones around in pan.

2 Meanwhile, make a mirepoix by chopping the carrot, celery, onion, and garlic coarsely and mixing together.

3 When the edges of the meat start to turn black (about 25-30 minutes), lower oven to 450 degrees and scatter the mirepoix around in the pan. Mix the bones and the mirepoix well, and return to the oven.

4 After about five minutes, mix tomato paste into pan. Return to oven another five minutes, then add red wine. When wine has reduced to about half the original quantity, add one quart of water and stir pan well.

5 After the bones have been in the oven for about an hour total, sprinkle flour over pan and stir contents well. Immediately load contents of pan into a large stockpot.

6 Pour half a gallon of water into the pan, scraping the bottom and sides. Pour this water from the pan, along with another three and a half gallons of water, into the stockpot. Add the sacchetto. Put the stockpot over a hot fire and bring to a boil. Skim top of pot occasionally to remove scum and fat.

7 After about three hours, add tomatoes and parsley stems to pot. After stock is reduced by half, add two more gallons of cold water. Continue to simmer and skim. You can even let the pot simmer over a low fire all night long. (Make sure the kitchen has adequate ventilation and smoke alarms, and observe other common-sense safety precautions.)

8 Reduce to half or even more, depending on the intensity of the demi-glace you want. Strain the demi-glace through fine cheesecloth. Skim off any remaining fat.

Reserve demi-glace in refrigerator until ready to use; it will keep from a week to two weeks. It can also be frozen.

Makes two quarts.

Fondo Bianco di Gamberi

Shrimp Stock

This stock is an essential ingredient for a wide range of soups, sauces, and casseroles, and uses parts of the shrimp that you would ordinarily throw away. Note: if you use the peelings from New Orleans-style spicy boiled shrimp, rinse them off first and leave out the salt at the end.

1 lb. shrimp shells and heads
1 medium carrot, peeled and cut into chunks
½ medium onion, cut up
2 sticks celery, cut up
1 Tbs. salt

Sacchetto: Put these dry seasonings into a small cheesecloth bag:
1 Tbs. black peppercorns
1 Tbs. dried thyme
1 Tbs. dried oregano
1 Tbs. dried basil
5 stems of fresh dill or 1 tsp. dried
½ tsp. dried sage
4 bay leaves
1 tsp. marjoram
2 sprigs parsley

1 Put the shrimp shells, onion, carrot, and celery into a soup pot with two gallons of cold water. Over medium high heat, bring to a boil. Add the sacchetto.

2 Boil the stock gently for one hour, then add the salt and remove from the heat.
Makes one and a half gallons of stock.

Fondo Bianco di Pesce

Fish Stock

I'll warn you ahead of time: this gets to looking pretty nasty as it's simmering. You will find that using fish stock in appropriate recipes will greatly amplify the flavors.

5 lbs. fish heads, skins, backbones, etc. (omit livers)
2 ribs celery, coarsely chopped
1 whole medium onion, cut into chunks
2 bay leaves
1 whole leek, cut up
1 Tbs. salt

Sacchetto: Put these dry seasonings into a small cheesecloth bag:
1 tsp. black peppercorns
½ Tbs. dried thyme
½ Tbs. dried oregano
½ Tbs. dried marjoram

1 The fish bones throw off a lot of scum, so I always pre-boil them before starting the stock. Put the fish bones in a stock pot and cover them with water. Bring the pot to a boil for five minutes. Then drain off all the water and rinse the fish bones with cold water. Drain that water off, too.

2 Now add two gallons of water to begin really making the stock. Put in all the vegetables and seasonings and bring to a boil. Let the pot boil briskly for five minutes, then lower the fire to medium. Simmer for 90 minutes, or until you have a little more than half the volume you started with. Skim the foam now and then during the cooking. When the reduction is complete, strain the stock through a large sieve or china cap.

This stock has the flavor strength I find most useful in my kitchen. Of course, you can continue to reduce it to make it stronger. It will keep in the refrigerator for about a week. You can also freeze it for use as needed.

Makes one and a half gallons of stock.

Antipasto

The Very First Course

When we first opened Andrea's, Roberto and I agreed that a display of antipasti would be a distinctive and important part of our dining room. It is just inside the door: a large marble-topped table completely filled with dishes designed to make your mouth water, to let you know that food is the primary element of atmosphere in our restaurant.

Antipasto is served before any other course. It awakens your palate with a light, fresh taste. You don't even have to wait for a menu to get it. You just tell the waiter that you want this or that antipasto, or — better yet — an antipasto misto, including a little of everything we made that day. On a summer day, you can make a very refreshing meal of antipasti.

What I like about antipasto is that it can be just about anything. Some of the most common elements require no preparation — cold meats such as prosciutto, salami, bresaola (a fascinating dried, salted beef with an intense taste), and cheeses.

Antipasti generally involve only minimal preparation. (Certainly this is true of the meats and cheeses, which need only to be sliced.) Most antipasti can be prepared well ahead of time. Indeed, some of them *have* to be prepared in advance, and gain their flavor by marination over days or weeks. Here are the dozen antipasti our guests have enjoyed most — a small fraction of the different antipasti we have displayed over the years.

If there is one piece of advice I'd give you about antipasto, it's this: use vegetables in the peak of their seasons. In Italy, we look forward to the never-ending succession of seasonal vegetables, because freshness and vividness of taste are of paramount importance. Besides, who wants to eat the same things year-round?

Peperonata Marinata

Marinated Bell Peppers

The combination of nutty sweetness and mild peppery sharpness, mellowed by the sauce, makes this a palate-perking first course. Pretty, too.

3 medium-large red bell peppers
3 medium-large green bell peppers
1 medium-large yellow bell pepper
3 small black bell peppers*
½ cup extra virgin olive oil
3 cloves garlic, sliced (not chopped)
¼ tsp. crushed red pepper
4 sprigs Italian parsley, chopped
½ tsp. salt
Pinch white pepper

*Optional; these are grown by specialty farmers and are occasionally available in very good produce departments.

1 Roast peppers under a hot broiler, turning to blacken about 75 percent of the outer surface of the peppers. (This can also be done by holding the peppers above the open flame on your stove with a fork.) Don't be shy about this; it will look like you're burning and ruining them, but you're bringing out the flavors of the peppers. After they are charred, let them cool.

2 Peel off the outer skin—both the charred parts and those that aren't. Pull off the stem end, which will have a lot of the seeds attached; try to get most of them out. Split the pepper open and remove as many seeds as possible. Slice the peppers into strips about a half-inch wide.

3 Heat the olive oil very hot in a saute pan. Cook the garlic until browned around the edges. Lower the heat and add the crushed red pepper, parsley, salt, white pepper, and the bell peppers. Cook for about 15 seconds, combining the ingredients thoroughly and making sure the peppers are well-coated with the oil.

4 Remove the contents of the pan to a bowl and allow to cool. Serve at room temperature as an antipasto.

Serves eight to ten.

Suggested wine: Vino Nobile Di Montepulciano

Carciofini Sott'Olio d'Oliva

Marinated Artichokes

If you can think ahead about a week or two, you can serve your family or guests these eminently tender, succulent baby artichokes. After marinating for a long time, the leaves become completely edible. With all the oil, this is messy to eat, but good.

2 cups white vinegar
6-8 baby artichokes
2 cups extra virgin olive oil
½ tsp. crushed red pepper
1½ tsp. chopped garlic
½ tsp. salt
Pinch white pepper
2 sprigs fresh oregano
1 broken bay leaf

1 Boil one gallon of water with the vinegar.

2 Trim the outer two layers of artichoke leaves. (Reserve these for making artichoke soup).

3 Put the artichokes in the boiling vinegar-water. Boil for about 20 minutes, or until the inner surfaces of the artichoke leaves are tender. Plunge artichokes into cold water to cool.

4 Cut off the top end of the artichoke, along with any excess stem. (The first half-inch or so of the stem is good to eat.) Slice in eighths from top to bottom.

5 Put the artichokes and all the other ingredients into a large jar or airtight container. Make sure there is enough olive oil to completely cover the artichokes. Gently shake the container to distribute all ingredients evenly.

6 Store the container in the refrigerator for one week to marinate. (It gets even better if it marinates two or even three weeks.)

Serves six to eight.

Suggested wine: Vino Nobile Di Montepulciano

Peperoni Rossi e Verde Farciti

Stuffed Bell Pepper

After over 15 years in this country, I am still not familiar with all the intricacies of the law. I understand that there is a federal statute which requires all cookbooks to contain a recipe for stuffed bell peppers. I am told by the people who order this at Andrea's that they find it both very good and very different from any other they've eaten. We serve these peppers with tomato-basil sauce with pasta on the side. It's also delicious cold and sliced as an antipasto.

1 lb. fresh ground inside beef round
¼ cup extra virgin olive oil
3 sliced pancetta or bacon, chopped
½ cup chopped onions
¼ cup chopped celery
10 medium fresh mushrooms, chopped
¼ cup sliced, pitted black olives
1 Tbs. chopped garlic
1 tsp. salt
¼ tsp. white pepper
1 Tbs. chopped fresh basil
1 Tbs. chopped fresh oregano
1 Tbs. chopped Italian parsley
4 anchovies, chopped
8 oz. mozzarella, shredded
2 eggs
1 cup grated Parmesan cheese
½ cup bread crumbs
6 bell peppers, red or green
⅓ cup olive oil
2 eggs, beaten

   Preheat oven to 450 degrees.
   1 In a skillet over medium heat, brown the ground beef, stirring it constantly to keep it loose. When lightly but completely browned, remove from the skillet and set aside.
   2 In the same skillet, heat the olive oil over medium heat and saute the pancetta, celery, and onions until transparent. Add the mushrooms and cook another minute; then return the beef to the pan with the olives, garlic, salt, pepper, basil, and oregano. Stir and saute until heated through.
   3 Remove the skillet from the heat and add the anchovies. Let the mixture cool for five minutes, then add the mozzarella, eggs, cheese, and bread crumbs — blending each one in at a time.
   4 Cut off the tops of the bell peppers and pull out all the seeds and membranes. Stuff ½ cup of the meat mixture into each pepper. Brush the top of each bell pepper generously with egg, then pat a thin layer of bread crumbs on top.

16

5 Heat the ⅓ cup olive oil in a skillet, and place the bell peppers top down in the hot oil. Cook for two minutes, until tops are crusty. Turn the peppers on their sides and put the whole skillet into preheated 450-degree oven for 18-20 minutes.

6 Put the skillet back on the stove and brown the sides of the peppers slightly on all sides.

Serves six entrees or 12-15 antipasto appetizers.

Suggested wine: Verduzzo Collio Orientali Del Friuli

Insalata di Fagiolini Verdi

Green Bean Salad

The shape and color of green beans make them a lovely addition to our antipasto table. Watch for nice, crisp beans when they come into season. The smaller they are, the better.

1 lb. fresh green beans
½ cup extra virgin olive oil
1 Tbs. chopped garlic
1½ Tbs. chopped onion
6 sprigs Italian parsley, chopped
¼ tsp. crushed red pepper
½ tsp. salt
1 tsp. balsamic vinegar
Pinch white pepper
1 Tbs. dry white wine

1 Boil a gallon of water with about 1 tsp. salt in a large saucepan. Drop in the beans. When the water returns to a boil, boil the beans for 15 minutes. Remove and plunge immediately into ice water to cool. Drain well.

2 In a bowl, combine all other ingredients. Add the beans and marinate overnight. Serve as antipasto or as a salad. Garnish with leaves of red lettuce.

Serves eight.

Suggested wine: Orvieto Secco

Insalata di Finocchi

Fennel Salad

Fennel—also called (incorrectly) anise—is a member of the celery family, but it has a highly distinctive, anise-like flavor. The crisp stems of the plant, particularly the large bulb-shaped base, provide a fascinating flavor and texture contrast in an antipasto assortment.

2 bunches fresh fennel
¼ onion, sliced
¼ cup extra virgin olive oil
Juice of one lemon
3 cloves garlic, crushed or pressed
2 sprigs Italian parsley
½ tsp. salt
Pinch white pepper
2 tsp. white vinegar

1 Cut out the root core of the fennel and almost all of the stems. Pull the bulbs apart and wash very well. Chop into strips.

2 Add all other ingredients and mix well.

3 Cut off, wash, and dry small sprigs of the feathery fennel leaves to garnish the salad.

Serves eight as an antipasto or small after-entree salad.

Suggested wine: Prosecco Di Conigliano (Sparkling)

Carote alla Menta

Carrots With Mint

There's almost always a plate of fresh carrots on our antipasto table at Andrea's, and it's one of the things that our guests specify we make sure is on their antipasto assortments. If you follow this recipe closely, you'll get all the vivid color and crunch.

3 large carrots
4 sprigs fresh mint leaves, chopped
3 leaves fresh basil, chopped
1 Tbs. chopped onion
½ tsp. chopped garlic
⅓ cup extra virgin olive oil
¼ tsp. Tabasco
½ tsp. Worcestershire
1 sprig oregano leaves, chopped
1 Tbs. balsamic vinegar
1 tsp. white vinegar
½ tsp. salt
Pinch white pepper

1 Peel carrots and cut off tops. Slice carrots on a slight diagonal into coins about 1/8 inch thick.

2 Bring a gallon of water with 1 tsp. salt to a boil. Put the carrots in and cook for seven to ten minutes, until they're somewhat tender but still have a raw-carrot taste. As soon as you remove the carrots from the boiling water, plunge them into ice water.

3 Combine all other ingredients in a bowl. Add the carrots and toss well with the sauce. Let carrots marinate overnight, and serve with a garnish of lettuce or fresh herbs.

Serves six to eight.

Suggested wine: Lacrima Christi

Melanzane Sott'Olio d'Oliva

Marinated Eggplant In Olive Oil

This excellence of this simple dish comes from what the wine-lovers would call bottle age. The eggplant is marinated in oil and seasonings—the longer, the better. When I make it for myself, I store it six months before I eat it.

4 medium eggplants (about 3½ lbs. total)
½ cup salt
1 quart white vinegar
1 cup extra virgin olive oil
3 cups olive oil
¼ cup chopped garlic
1 tsp. crushed red pepper
1 Tbs. dried oregano
½ tsp. salt

1 Slice the skins off the eggplants, and slice them about ¼ inch thick from top to bottom. Then slice across to get pieces the size of French fries. Put the eggplant strips in a bowl and toss with the salt.

2 Move the eggplant strips into a colander, arraying them in a relatively uniform layer up the sides. Put a bowl the same size as the colander inside the colander, and weigh it down with three or so pounds of weight. Put the entire apparatus in the sink to drain for 45 minutes. This will remove the bitterness from the eggplant.

3 Rinse the salt off the eggplant with cold water. Drain it well, then squeeze it dry. Put the eggplant in a bowl with the vinegar, and marinate it for 30 minutes.

4 Drain the vinegar from the eggplant and squeeze it dry again. Put the eggplant into a bowl with all the other ingredients.

5 Pour the contents into a canning jar. Make sure there is enough olive oil to completely cover all the eggplant about ½ inch deep. Tightly seal and refrigerate the jar. Marinate the eggplant for at least a week; the ideal time is actually three months, and the eggplant will keep getting better even after that.

Serves four to eight.

Suggested wine: Muller Thurgau

Melanzane a Fungitelli

Eggplant Caponata Andrea

Many people write off caponata after tasting that awful stuff in cans and jars. But they'd change their minds if they ate caponata made with good fresh eggplant. The flavor is outstanding as an appetizer. It's also more than a little good as a side vegetable, served hot—or even tossed with pasta.

1 cup cottonseed oil
3 medium ripe eggplants, well washed
½ cup salt
1 lb. fresh plum tomatoes
¼ cup extra virgin olive oil
3 cloves garlic, lightly crushed
¼ tsp. crushed red pepper
8 leaves fresh basil, chopped
Salt and pepper to taste
1 sprig Italian parsley, chopped

1 Cut eggplants into one-inch dice. Put the eggplant dice into a colander, arraying them in a relatively uniform layer up the sides. Put a bowl the same size as the colander inside the colander, and weigh it down with three or so pounds of weight. Put the entire apparatus into the sink to drain for 45 minutes. This will remove the bitterness from the eggplant.

2 Rinse the salt off the eggplant with cold water. Drain it well, then rinse again. Shake excess water off, then dump eggplant onto a large dry towel. It is very important that you get the eggplant as dry as possible, to avoid spattering when you saute.

3 Heat oil very hot in a large, deep skillet. (Extra care must be taken with hot oil to avoid spilling; this can be a fire hazard.) Brown garlic lightly, and then add about half the eggplant. Saute till golden brown—about two minutes. With a skimmer, remove first batch and drain on paper towels. Keep the garlic in the pan and saute the remainder of the eggplant.

4 Cut the stem ends off the tomatoes, and cut tomatoes in half. Squeeze the seeds out. Chop tomatoes coarsely.

5 Heat extra virgin olive oil very hot in the same skillet you used to saute the eggplant. Saute garlic to a light brown in hot oil; add crushed red pepper and tomatoes and saute over medium-high heat for about a minute. Add ½ cup water and lower flame to medium. Reduce contents of skillet by half.

6 Add basil, a pinch of salt, and parsley to pan and stir in. Add eggplant and heat through. Remove from fire and allow to cool. Serve at cool room temperature.
Serves eight to twelve.

Suggested wine: Regaleali from Sicily

Scarole alla Scapece

Escarole With Raisins And Olives

Escarole is a member of the lettuce family. It has a texture and a slightly bitter taste that gets your mouth ready for the rest of the meal. It's good both as a room-temperature antipasto and as a warm side dish. It is sometimes even baked into a pie. You may be tempted to add some kind of liquid during the cooking process, but resist this—the escarole will throw off enough water of its own.

3 heads escarole
½ cup extra virgin olive oil
½ tsp. red crushed pepper
4 cloves garlic, crushed
¼ cup raisins
¼ cup black olives, pitted and crushed
1 tsp. salt
Pinch white pepper
8 anchovy fillets, chopped
¼ cup pine nuts

1 Cut the heads of escarole into eight pieces top to bottom and pull apart. Put the leaves into a large bowl and wash three times with cold water. Escarole often has a lot of dirt in it. Drain well and spin or towel dry.

2 Heat the olive oil very hot in the largest skillet you have. Saute the garlic with the crushed red pepper until garlic is lightly browned. Add the escarole (Careful! Hot oil may spatter!) and saute over low heat until leaves are limp but stemmy parts are still crisp. Add all the other ingredients and cook until warmed through.

Serves eight to ten.

Suggested wine: Tocai

Insalata di Fave

Fava Bean Salad

A wonderful antipasto that we frequently feature on the table just inside our entrance. The big fava beans are especially delicious in the springtime, when we get them fresh.

1 lb. fava beans
½ cup dry white wine
½ cup extra virgin olive oil
1 Tbs. balsamic vinegar
4 bay leaves
1½ tsp. garlic
½ small red onion, slivered
6 sprigs Italian parsley, stems removed, chopped
½ tsp. salt
Pinch white pepper

1 Soak fava beans overnight. Drain and put into a pot with one gallon of cold water. Simmer for two hours or so, until beans are tender but not breaking apart.

2 Drain and allow to cool. Remove skins from beans.

3 In a bowl blend wine, olive oil, and vinegar with a wire whisk. Add bay, garlic, onion, parsley, salt, pepper, and fava beans. Toss ingredients well. Give the beans an hour or two to absorb the sauce, then serve as an antipasto at room temperature.

Serves eight.

Suggested wine: Malvasia Di Brindisi Secco

Zucchini Ripieni Farciti Regina

Stuffed Zucchini

This is a rather elaborate, somewhat filling, and very satisfying antipasto; I have been known to make a lunch out of it. The hardest part is hollowing out the zucchini. A thin-bladed fruit knife is perfect.

8 oz. ground veal
4 oz. ground pork
3 medium zucchini
2 Tbs. extra virgin olive oil
1 Tbs. chopped onions
1 Tbs. chopped garlic
10 leaves fresh basil, chopped
3 sprigs fresh oregano
½ tsp. crushed red pepper
6 sprigs Italian parsley, chopped
5 slices white bread, crusts removed
1 cup milk
¼ cup grated Grana Padano cheese
1 egg
½ tsp. salt
Pinch white pepper
½ cup plain bread crumbs
Flour for dusting
1 egg, beaten, for dipping
½ cup vegetable oil

Preheat the oven to 400 degrees.

1 Cut off the ends of the zucchini, then cut each zucchini in half (to get a round cross-section—not end-to-end). With a long, thin knife, hollow out the zucchini until walls of zucchini are about a quarter-inch thick. Discard insides.

2 In a skillet, saute the onions, garlic, parsley, oregano and crushed red pepper in the olive oil until onions turn translucent. Put this into a food processor container along with the ground meat.

3 Soak the bread in the milk until very soft. Squeeze the excess milk out of the bread, and add the bread to the food processor, along with the egg and the grated cheese. Process on high speed until mixture is well blended. Stir in salt, white pepper, and bread crumbs.

4 Fill the zucchini with the stuffing. (We use a pastry bag, but a spoon works well.) Dip each end of the stuffed zucchini in flour, then in egg, then in bread crumbs.

5 Heat vegetable oil in a skillet. Carefully dip the coated ends of each zucchini in the oil for about ten seconds each, to sear and seal the ends. Then place the zucchini on their sides in the skillet and put the whole skillet into a preheated 400-degree oven. Bake for about 20 minutes, or until they are tender when squeezed.

6 Cool until zucchini reach room temperature. Then cut into half-inch-thick slices and serve as antipasto.

Serves twelve.

Suggested wine: Capri Bianco

Mozzarella di Bufala Capricciosa

Buffalo-Milk Mozzarella Antipasto

Many people find it hard to believe, but there really are buffalo in Italy. They are true water buffalo, not the bison of America. Their milk produces the best imaginable mozzarella, with a creamy taste and a rubbery texture. This great cheese is just now becoming available in this country; if you find some, try eating it this way. You can add sliced ripe tomatoes as a contrast.

8 oz. buffalo-milk mozzarella
1 leaf chopped fresh basil
1 Tbs. extra virgin olive oil
¼ tsp. salt
Pinch white pepper
½ tsp. balsamic vinegar

Slice the mozzarella about ¼ inch thick, and fan the slices out on a plate. Combine all the other ingredients and pour over the cheese.

Serves two.

Variation: Dice the mozzarella, and include ½ tsp. chopped fresh garlic in the sauce. Toss the sauce with the cheese and garnish with a sprig of fresh basil.

Suggested wine: Terlano

Uova Sode al Pesto

Hard-Boiled Eggs With Pesto Sauce

These look like devilled eggs, but the unique flavor of the pesto sauce gives it an entirely new dimension. It both looks and tastes good on an antipasto plate.

6 eggs
*½ cup pesto sauce (see **Sauces**)*
2 Tbs. unsalted butter
Pinch salt
¼ tsp. Worcestershire
¼ tsp. Tabasco
½ tsp. lemon juice
Small basil or parsley leaves and strips of red bell pepper for garnish

1 With a skimmer, lower the eggs into boiling water gently, so as not to break them. Boil for 13 minutes (15 if the eggs are ice-cold right out of the refrigerator). When cooked, immediately immerse eggs in ice water to stop the cooking.

2 When the eggs are cool, remove shells. Slice eggs in half end to end with a sharp knife. Take the yolks out and put them in a food processor. Put the whites on a rack so that they drain completely. Slice off a little sliver of the round side of each egg white so it will stand steady on a plate.

3 Add the pesto, salt, Worcestershire, Tabasco, lemon juice, and the butter to the egg yolks in the food processor and puree together.

4 Put this mixture into a pastry bag with a star tip and fill the cavity of each egg white with the pesto-egg yolk mixture.

5 Garnish with small strips of bell pepper and basil leaves.

Makes eight small antipasti.

Suggested wine: Cinque Terre from Liguria

Primi Piatti

Appetizers

Having an Italian restaurant in New Orleans gives a chef many possibilities. This happy circumstance is realized most fully in the first course after the antipasto. Seafood, especially shellfish, is the prime raw material for creating memorable appetizers. I feel that there are no better shrimp, oysters, or crabs than those which come from Louisiana waters. And our area practically owns the exclusive rights for crawfish.

I think that I have absorbed more influence from the New Orleans Creole cuisine in first-course dishes than I have in any other part of my cooking. In these appetizers, you will find some pure Italian ideas and a few straight-ahead Creole tastes, but many combinations of the two. I think you'll find the synthesis very exciting to your palate.

Spiedino d'Ostriche

Oysters En Brochette

The pairing of oysters and bacon is a classic, one much appreciated around New Orleans. Most of the time, one finds the oysters wrapped with a bit of bacon, skewered, then deep-fried or broiled. At Andrea's, we have a way of cooking this old favorite that's quite different both in procedure and results. Tom thinks that the full slice of bacon I wrap around each oyster is too much—that a half-slice will do. But that's what he thinks.

24 large fresh oysters
1 leek
24 slices bacon
1 cup lemon cream sauce (see **Sauces***)*

Preheat the broiler.

1 In a saucepan, bring two quarts of water (including the water from the oysters) to a rolling boil. Add the oysters and poach very lightly—only until the edges curl, which should take a minute or less. Remove with a slotted spoon and drain.

2 Slice the leek in half and remove the roots and the ends of the stalks. Clean the leek well under running water (they usually contain a good deal of sand). Pull the leek apart and poach in the same water as the oysters for about one minute, or until they just start to become tender. Remove and slice leeks into pieces about an inch long.

3 Peel apart the slices of bacon and place them, just touching, in a rectangular pan. Put the pan under the broiler and broil the bacon until it just starts to curl and brown a little bit at the edges.

4 Top each poached oyster with a leek sliver or two. Roll up each oyster loosely with a piece of bacon, and secure with toothpicks. Drain the pan in which you broiled the bacon of any excess fat, and array the bacon-wrapped oysters in it. Put the pan under the broiler again and broil four to six minutes, until small black edges have formed on the bacon. Turn the oysters and broil another two or three minutes, until lightly brown all over.

5 Pour 1 Tbs. of lemon cream sauce on warm plates, and serve four oysters per person.

Serves six.

Suggested wine: Gewurztraminer Sudtirol from Trentino

Ostriche Andrea

Oysters Andrea

In New Orleans, almost every major restaurant uses the fabulous resource of fresh local oysters to create baked oyster appetizers on their shells. The two most common are oysters Rockefeller and Bienville. I took the latter idea as a starting point and reworked the dish with some Italian touches. I think you will find them to be a great improvement over oysters Bienville.

½ cup olive oil
½ cup chopped onions
2 Tbs. chopped garlic
3 slices pancetta, chopped
3 slices bacon, chopped
1 tsp. crushed red pepper
1 rib celery
1 cup mixed red and green bell pepper, chopped
1 cup dry white wine
1 tsp. salt
¼ tsp. white pepper
12 anchovies, crushed
1½ cups bread crumbs
½ tsp. Tabasco
½ tsp. Worcestershire sauce
2 sprigs fresh oregano, leaves only, chopped
6 leaves fresh basil, chopped
½ cup grated Parmesan cheese
¼ lb. butter, softened
8 sprigs Italian parsley, chopped
½ tsp. salt
Pinch white pepper
1 Tbs. lemon juice
2 egg yolks
36 fresh large oysters, drained, water reserved

1 Heat olive oil in a skillet over medium-high fire and add onions and garlic. Saute until onions turn translucent. Add pancetta, bacon, crushed red pepper, celery, and bell pepper. Saute over medium-high heat, stirring well. Cook until pancetta and bacon start to crisp slightly.

2 Add white wine, water from oysters, salt, and pepper. Reduce liquid contents of pan by one-third, then remove from fire.

3 Put the sauce into a food processor container with all the other ingredients except the oysters. Process into a coarse puree.

4 Place oysters on shells, in ramekins, or in small au gratin dishes. Top each oyster with a tablespoon of the sauce. If using shells, place them on a pie plate half-filled with rock salt. Bake oysters in preheated 450-degree oven for 10 minutes, or until tops are lightly browned.

Serves six.

Ostriche alla Fiorentina

Oysters Florentine

This dish is an Italian adaptation of a New Orleans classic, oysters Rockefeller. We use spinach, the favorite vegetable of Florence. The background flavor that makes this special is that of Sambuca, one of the most popular Italian liqueurs, which gives the dish a slight hint of anise.

2 lbs. fresh spinach, well washed and picked of large stems
10-12 sprigs Italian parsley leaves

White sauce:
¼ cup butter
⅓ cup all-purpose flour
1¼ cups milk

⅓ cup olive oil
1 Tbs. butter
½ green bell pepper, chopped
1 rib celery, chopped
5 cloves garlic, lightly crushed
1 large onion, chopped
1 cup fish stock
¼ tsp. cayenne
¼ tsp. nutmeg
2 tsp. salt
¼ tsp. white pepper
2 Tbs. oyster water
1 Tbs. Sambuca
36 oysters, drained, water reserved

Preheat oven to 450 degrees.

1 Boil two quarts of water in a large saucepan. In it poach the spinach for two minutes. Drain the spinach and wash with cold water. With your hands, squeeze the excess water out. In a food processor, chop the spinach and the parsley together until fine (but not pureed).

2 Melt butter in a medium skillet and, when bubbling, sprinkle in the flour while whisking constantly. Whisk milk in with butter and flour and bring to a boil. Lower to a simmer for five minutes, whisking frequently, to make a thick, smooth white sauce.

3 Heat the olive oil and the 1 Tbs. butter in a large skillet over medium-high heat. When bubbles appear, add bell pepper, celery, garlic, and onion. Cook until edges of onions begin to brown, stirring frequently.

4 Add fish stock. Bring to a boil and reduce by about one-third. Stir in spinach-parsley mixture from food processor. Add cayenne and nutmeg. Cook for three or four minutes over medium heat, stirring frequently, until excess liquid has been absorbed.

5 Stir in white sauce, salt, and white pepper. Cook until mixture begins to boil

30

again, then remove to the food processor container. Add oyster water, and process into a coarse puree.

6 Return sauce to skillet. Pour Sambuca over the top and carefully flame it. Heat sauce until bubbles well up, then remove from heat. Allow to cool to lukewarm.

7 Place oysters on shells, in ramekins, or in small au gratin dishes. Top each oyster with a tablespoon of the sauce. (For best visual effect, use a pastry bag fitted with a star tip.) If using shells, place them on a pie plate half-filled with rock salt. Bake oysters in preheated 450-degree oven for 10 minutes, or until tops are lightly browned. Serve with a warning to your guests about how hot they

Serves six.

Suggested wine: Nugola Bianco

Vongole in Umido

Steamed Clams

Clams are only rarely seen on menus in oyster-loving New Orleans. In fact, they are exotic to most of our diners, which explains why we sell so many of them. We cook clams in a variety of different ways, but I like to keep them simple. Steaming them with a light sauce like this one lets you see what they really taste like.

24 fresh clams, in shells
½ cup olive oil
¼ cup chopped onion
2 tsp. chopped fresh garlic
½ tsp. crushed red pepper
½ cup dry white wine
1 cup fish stock
2 tsp. chopped Italian parsley
¼ tsp. white pepper

1 Check the clams to make sure all of them are tightly closed. If you find one that's slightly agape, tap it lightly with a spoon; if it doesn't close, it's dead or worse. Throw it away.

2 Scrub clams well and rinse them with cold water.

3 In a large skillet, heat olive oil over medium heat and saute onion and garlic until onions are blond. Add crushed red pepper, wine, stock, parsley, and pepper. Bring to a boil.

4 Add clams in shell. Cover skillet and let clams steam for 10 minutes. Remove cover and agitate skillet to slosh sauce inside the clam shells, which will have opened.

5 Taste sauce and adjust seasonings. You probably will not need to add salt, since the clams are usually rather salty already.

Makes four appetizers or two entrees. If serving as an entree, accompany with cooked linguine tossed with extra sauce and garnished with chopped parsley.

Suggested wine: Soave Classico

Cozze in Umido

Steamed Mussels

Mussels are not found in any quantity in Louisiana waters, but they have become so easily available in recent years—alive and in in great condition—that we have been able to make them into several specialties at Andrea's. Remember that mussels cook very quickly.

24 mussels in shells
½ cup olive oil
¼ cup chopped onion
2 tsp. chopped fresh garlic
½ tsp. crushed red pepper
½ cup dry white wine
1 cup fish stock
2 tsp. chopped Italian parsley
½ tsp. salt
¼ tsp. white pepper

1 The most time-consuming part of cooking mussels is cleaning them. They must be washed extremely well, as they always contain more than a little sand. The "beard"—a mat of fibers with which the mussel attaches itself to its rock—must also be removed; sometimes this requires the use of a knife. Like clams, mussels should be closed when you receive them. Any open mussels should be tapped lightly with a spoon; if they don't close then, discard them.

2 In a large skillet, heat olive oil over medium heat and saute onion and garlic until onions are blond. Add crushed red pepper, wine, stock, parsley, and pepper. Bring to a boil.

3 Add washed mussels to skillet and cook, covered, until they open—about two minutes. Remove the mussels from the pan and wash them in a bowl of warm, salted water to remove the sand inside. Also remove any remaining beard.

4 Return mussels to skillet and continue to cook for two or three minutes more, sloshing the sauce inside the open shells. Mussels are cooked when the edges curl; don't overcook them or they'll become tough and tasteless.

5 Add salt and pepper to taste and serve very hot.

Makes four appetizers or two entrees. If serving as an entree, accompany with cooked linguine tossed with extra sauce and garnished with chopped parsley.

Suggested wine: Gambellara Bianco Superiore

Cozze o Vongole alla Marinara

Mussels or Clams Marinara

Marinara sauce is a simple tomato sauce named for the sailors who liked it a lot. I love to be at the table when we serve an order of our mussels or clams marinara — the first bite makes the eater's eyes really light up. This is delicious either as it comes off the stove or atop cooked linguine or other pasta. The preparation picks up from the end of the instructions for steamed clams or mussels.

2 tsp. chopped Italian parsley
1 Tbs. fresh oregano leaves
2 cups canned Italian plum tomatoes, chopped
1 cup juice from tomatoes
1 Tbs. chopped fresh basil
Salt and pepper

1 After preparing steamed clams or mussels according to the recipes above, remove them from the skillet and add all the marinara sauce ingredients. Bring the skillet to a boil, then lower heat and simmer for 15 to 20 minutes, until reduced by about one-third.

2 Return mussels or clams to the skillet, and toss with the sauce.

Makes four appetizers or two entrees. If serving as an entree, accompany with cooked linguine tossed with extra sauce and garnished with chopped parsley.

Suggested wine: Vernaccia Di Oristano

Carciofi Farciti al Grancevole

Stuffed Artichoke with Crabmeat Louisiane

Stuffed artichokes are much loved by New Orleans eaters. What makes ours different from most is that the center is stuffed with a great deal of seafood—crabmeat, oysters, and shrimp—instead of just bread crumbs.

12 small artichokes
½ tsp. salt
2 lemons, halved

Cut the stems and the brown tips off the artichokes. Put them into a gallon of boiling water with ½ tsp. salt and two halved lemons. Boil for 12 minutes (until leaves have just begun to get tender). Remove and cool.

Seafood stuffing:
½ cup olive oil
¼ cup chopped onions
1 Tbs. chopped garlic
1 rib celery, chopped coarsely
½ cup red and green bell pepper, chopped
8 anchovy fillets
6 medium shrimp, peeled and deveined, chopped
    OR ⅓ cup baby shrimp
2 scallops, chopped
2 oysters, chopped
½ cup lump crabmeat
½ cup dry white wine
5 sprigs fresh thyme leaves
2 sprigs chopped fresh oregano
2 chopped fresh basil leaves
3 sprigs chopped fresh Italian parsley
1/8 tsp. cayenne
¼ cup bread crumbs
¼ cup grated Parmesan cheese
½ tsp. salt
Pinch white pepper

Topping:
¼ cup extra virgin olive oil
2 anchovy fillets, chopped
2 sprigs fresh Italian parsley, chopped
1 cup chicken stock
½ tsp. salt
Pinch white pepper
Bread crumbs
Grated Parmesan cheese

Preheat oven to 400 degrees.

1 Heat the olive oil in a skillet and saute the onions, garlic, celery, green and red bell pepper and anchovies until vegetables are tender.

2 Stir seafoods in gently so as not to break up the crabmeat. Cook until bubbling.

3 Add the white wine and thyme, oregano, basil, and parsley, all chopped very fine. Cook until most of the liquid has been evaporated or absorbed. Add the cayenne, bread crumbs, and cheese.

4 Pull out the inner ten or twelve leaves from the inside of the artichoke and spread the other leaves apart. Salt and pepper the artichokes lightly and fill the center with about 2 Tbs. stuffing mixture.

5 Using the same skillet you used for the seafood stuffing, heat the olive oil and saute the anchovies and the parsley for 30 seconds. Add the chicken stock and the salt. Bring to a boil, then remove from heat.

6 Sprinkle artichokes with bread crumbs and cheese. Stand the stuffed artichokes in the skillet. Pour a cup of water around them and put the skillet into a preheated 400-degree oven for 10 minutes.

Serves twelve.

Suggested wine: Breganze Bianco

Gamberi Saltati "Bayou Lafourche"

Shrimp Saute Bayou Lafourche

Next time you find yourself with some big, good-looking fresh shrimp, try this robust approach. The cooking method is quick, the sauce is minimal, and it makes the flavors of the shrimp explode in your mouth. By the way, Bayou Lafourche is an abandoned ancient route of the Mississippi River, running along the eastern edge of the Cajun country.

6 shrimp, 21-25 count, peeled and deveined but with tails still on
1 Tbs. extra virgin olive oil
1 tsp. chopped shallots
1 tsp. chopped garlic
¼ tsp. crushed red pepper
1 Tbs. brandy
¼ cup dry white wine
¼ tsp. Worcestershire
Juice of ½ lemon
½ tsp. fresh rosemary leaves
¼ tsp. salt
Pinch white pepper
Pinch cayenne
1 Tbs. softened butter

1 Heat the olive oil in a saute pan. Saute the shallots, garlic, and crushed red pepper until onions are transparent. Add the shrimp, and cook, turning once, until shrimp are pink.

2 Add the brandy and flame it. Remove the shrimp and keep warm.

3 Add wine, Worcestershire, lemon juice, rosemary, salt, pepper, and cayenne. Lower the heat and simmer for ten minutes, until reduced by one-third. Return shrimp to the pan and cook for three or four minutes more, coating well with sauce. Take the pan off the heat and whisk in the butter.

Serves one.

Suggested wine: Pinot Grigio Collio.

Cappe Sante al Dragoncello

Scallops with Tarragon Sauce

The "head of the saint" is the scallop, so named for the halo-like shape of its shell. We love scallops at Andrea's and like to cook them as either appetizers or entrees.

1 Tbs. extra virgin olive oil
1 Tbs. chopped onions
1 tsp. chopped garlic
Pinch crushed red pepper
18 medium-large scallops (12 oz. total)
¼ cup dry vermouth
¼ cup dry white wine
½ cup fish stock
½ Tbs. fresh tarragon leaves
Dash Tabasco
¼ tsp. Worcestershire
½ tsp. salt
Pinch white pepper
1 Tbs. whipping cream
1 Tbs. softened butter

1 Heat olive oil in a saute pan over medium heat. Saute onions, garlic, and crushed red pepper until lightly browned.

2 Add scallops and saute for one minute. Remove the scallops and keep them warm. Add the vermouth, white wine, and fish stock. Bring to a boil and reduce the liquid by one-third.

3 Strain the sauce through a sieve into another skillet over medium heat. Return the scallops and add the tarragon, Tabasco, Worcestershire, salt, and pepper. When bubbles reappear in the sauce, add whipping cream. Cook for another minute or so. Don't overcook! The scallops should still bulge a bit when completely cooked.

4 Remove the scallops again and slice them into butterflies. Arrange them on the plates. Continue to reduce the sauce for another minute, then remove from heat. Whisk in the butter until incorporated, then spoon the sauce over the scallops.

Makes four appetizers or two entrees.

Suggested wine: Ribolla Gialla

Lumache al Barolo

Snails in Barolo Wine Sauce

We serve escargots in numerous preparations at Andrea's. This one is, I think, the most unusual. It pairs the rich flavor of Barolo wine—one of the best red wines in all of Italy—with the earthy snails and demi-glace sauce. It has a highly distinctive taste, and won a lot of friends at my co-author Tom Fitzmorris's wedding reception.

2 Tbs. extra virgin olive oil
1½ Tbs. chopped onions
2 tsp. chopped garlic
24 snails (largest you can find)
1½ oz. brandy
1½ cups Barolo wine
1½ cups demi-glace (see **Basics***)*
¼ tsp. salt
Pinch white pepper

1 Heat olive oil in a saute pan over medium heat. Saute onions and garlic until light brown.

2 Add the snails and saute for 30 seconds. Add the brandy and carefully flame it in the pan. When flames die down, remove the snails and keep them warm.

3 Add the Barolo and reduce by one-half. Add the demi-glace and return to a boil. Return the snails to the sauce and cook for about four minutes, until snails are thoroughly sauced. Add salt and pepper to taste.

Serves four.

Suggested wine: Gattinara

Lumache Andrea

Escargots Andrea

Snails and mushrooms were made for one another. Both have an earthy flavor and color, and both have an unusual texture. This dish looks as good as it tastes; it will be the most elegant serving of snails your guests will ever see. Great for cocktail parties.

24 medium fresh mushrooms, washed and stems removed
24 snails
¾ cup lemon juice
¾ cup dry white wine
¼ cup. extra virgin olive oil
1 Tbs. chopped onions
2 tsp. chopped garlic
1½ oz. brandy
¼ cup lemon cream sauce (see **Sauces***)*
¼ cup hollandaise sauce (see **Sauces***)*

Preheat the broiler to 500 degrees.

1 Heat an empty, medium-size skillet very hot. Toss the mushrooms in and immediately flood them with the lemon juice, wine, and 1 cup water. Cook the mushrooms, covered, for about three minutes until softened slightly but still firm.

2 Place six mushrooms top down on each serving plate or, better still, into six-pocket metal or ceramic snail dishes. Keep them warm.

3 In a separate skillet, heat olive oil over medium heat and saute onions and garlic until lightly browned. Add the escargots and saute for about 30 seconds. Add the brandy and carefully flame it.

4 When the flames die down, remove the escargots and place each one inside a mushroom. Nap each half-dozen mushrooms with 1 Tbs. lemon cream sauce and 1 Tbs. hollandaise.

5 Run the dishes under the hot broiler, three inches from the heat, until hollandaise begins to lightly brown in spots on top. Serve immediately.

Serves four.

Suggested wine: Gattinara

Lumache del Contadina

Snails in Garlic Butter Sauce

This is a somewhat more interesting version of what is known (inaccurately) around New Orleans as "escargots Bordelaise."

½ *cup extra virgin olive oil*
1 Tbs. chopped onions
1 Tbs. chopped garlic
Pinch crushed red pepper
24 snails
1½ oz. brandy
¼ *cup dry white wine*
¼ *cup fish stock (optional)*
2 tsp. lemon juice
1 tsp. salt
¼ *tsp. white pepper*
2 tsp. chopped Italian parsley
1 Tbs. butter

1 Heat olive oil in a saute pan over medium heat. Saute onions with garlic and crushed red pepper until light brown. Add escargots and saute for 30 seconds. Add the brandy and carefully flame it.

2 When the flames die down, add the wine, fish stock, lemon juice, salt, pepper, and parsley. Bring the pan contents to a boil.

3 As soon as pan boils, remove it from the heat. Remove the snails with a slotted spoon and place them on your serving plates (preferably snail dishes or, even better, snail shells). Whisk butter into the hot sauce, and spoon it over the snails. Serve with hot bread for dipping in the sauce.

Serves four.

Suggested wine: Gattinara

Animelle con Pasta

Sweetbreads with Angel Hair

Most veal sweetbreads are made into entrees—as we do elsewhere in this cookbook. But the delicate flavor and light texture of these thymus glands makes them interesting as a first course, too. Be careful with the portion; sweetbreads are more filling than you'd think, and you don't want to fill up your guests with the appetizer.

1 sweetbreads, poached and cleaned (see **Veal***)*
1 Tbs. extra virgin olive oil
½ tsp. chopped onion
½ tsp. chopped garlic
¼ tsp. crushed red pepper
1 Tbs. dry white wine
Juice of 1 medium lemon
2 sprigs Italian parsley, chopped
¼ tsp. salt
Pinch white pepper
4 oz. cooked angel-hair pasta

1 Slice two sweetbreads lobes about ¼-inch thick, and dust with flour.

2 Heat the olive oil to almost smoking temperature. Saute the onions, garlic, and crushed red pepper until onions are lightly browned.

3 Add the wine, lemon juice, parsley, salt, and pepper. Bring to a boil, then add the sweetbreads and cook for about two minutes on each side.

4 Add ¼ cup of water and bring to a boil. Lower the heat, add the pasta to the skillet, and toss all ingredients in the skillet. Serve hot.

Serves four.

Suggested wine: Traminer Collio Goriziano

Vitello Tonnato

Cold Roast Veal with Tuna Mayonnaise

When guests in our restaurant hear our description of this Tuscan specialty for the first time, they are sometimes mystified. But after they eat it, they never forget it. It is one of our most popular appetizers and makes an elegant, delicious first course.

1¼ to 1½ lbs. baby white veal round
1 tsp. salt
1/8 tsp. white pepper
3 Tbs. vegetable oil
¼ carrot, cut into coins
¼ onion, sliced
1 rib celery, chopped
2 garlic cloves, lightly crushed
1 cup dry white wine
1 bay leaf
½ tsp. dry rosemary

Sauce:
1 cup canned tuna, packed in water, well drained
  OR 4 oz. fresh tuna, poached
8 anchovies
2 Tbs. small capers
1½ tsp. minced garlic
1 Tbs. minced onions
1 cup freshly-made mayonnaise
1½ tsp. lemon juice
5 drops Tabasco
¼ tsp. Worcestershire sauce

Preheat oven to 450 degrees.
1 Make sure that the veal round is trimmed of excess fat and peeled of its "silk" (the butcher can do this for you). Sprinkle the salt and pepper on the outside of the veal.
2 Heat the oil in a skillet and saute the garlic until browned around the edges. Put the veal round in. Brown lightly on all sides. Put the entire skillet into a preheated 450-degree oven and roast, basting and turning the veal about every five minutes. After about ten minutes in the oven, add the carrot, onion, and celery, and continue to cook, baste, and turn for another ten minutes.
3 Add white wine, bay leaf, rosemary, and a cup of water. Cover skillet with aluminum foil and braise for 45 minutes, or until interior temperature is 140 degrees (measured with a meat thermometer pushed into the center of the veal).
4 Remove veal from oven and discard other skillet contents. Cool veal to room temperature.

5 Meanwhile, make sauce by blending all sauce ingredients in a food processor until anchovies and capers have been beaten into small bits. Do not puree.

6 When veal is cool, slice thinly at a 45-degree angle. Array five slices on a plate, and put two tablespoons of the sauce in the center of the plate. Garnish with strips of anchovy, individual capers, a sprig of rosemary, a wedge of lemon, and a slice of tomato. Serve cold.

Makes eight to ten appetizers.

Carpaccio

Invented at Harry's Bar in Venice and named after a 15th-century Italian painter, this raw beef dish has become one of the most popular first courses in Italian restaurants around the world. At Andrea's, we use only filet mignon, pounded until it's paper-thin and very tender. Serve it cold with a mustard sauce and a good Parmesan cheese for the classic style. But use your creativity to pair the tender tissue-thin beef with arugula, avocados, tomatoes, or whatever strikes your fancy.

4 slices of filet mignon, about ¼ inch thick (3 oz.)
¼ cup mayonnaise
1½ Tbs. Cremona mustard (or Dijon)
¼ tsp. Tabasco
¼ tsp. Worcestershire
1 Tbs. brandy
2 Tbs. whipping cream
¼ tsp. lemon juice

Garnish:
Extra virgin olive oil
Small wedges of Grana Padano cheese
1 large sliced mushroom
1 small lemon, quartered

1 Place the filets, one at a time, between two large sheets of heavy plastic. (A food storage bag works very well.) With the smooth side of a large meat mallet or the side of a heavy cleaver, pound the filets until they are about eight inches across and very thin. Carefully peel the meat away from the plastic, and arrange on a large serving plate.

2 Make the sauce by whisking together all the sauce ingredients. Spread extra virgin olive oil over the beef, then squeeze one lemon wedge over the beef, and top it with of the sauce, preferably poured on in a thin stream to form "strings" of sauce on the beef. Arrange slices of mushroom and wedges of Grana Padano cheese around the side.

Serves one.

Profiterole al Formaggio Principessa Anna

Princess Anne Cheese Puffs

I created this dish for a special banquet for Princess Anne of England, when she visited the home of Mr. Jimmy Coleman. Since then, this has been a very well-received tidbit at dinners for gourmet societies, weddings, and any place else they turn up. Warning: the cook will eat quite a few of these "testing" them.

The puffs are made from "pate choux," the same dough used for such things as eclairs and profiteroles.

Pate choux:
½ lb. butter
2 cups milk
1 Tbs. sugar
Pinch salt
2½ cups bread flour
8 eggs

Filling:
2 oz. mozzarella
1 oz. Bel Paese cheese
1 oz. Swiss cheese
1 oz. sour cream
1 oz. mascarpone cream cheese
¼ cup Reggiano Parmigiano cheese, grated
12 leaves fresh basil, chopped
2 sprigs fresh oregano leaves, chopped
2 tsp. chopped garlic
Pinch nutmeg
Salt and pepper to taste

1 Make the pate choux first. Combine butter and milk in a large saucepan and bring to a rolling boil.

2 Add all dry ingredients at once. Stir vigorously until the mixture breaks away from the side of the pan. Continue to cook and stir for about another minute, making sure the mixture doesn't burn.

3 Put the mixture into a mixer bowl with a paddle attachment and stir slowly until lukewarm.

4 Add eggs one at a time while continuing to stir. Wait until the mixture is smooth before adding another egg. Keep beating until completely smooth.

Preheat oven to 450 degrees.

5 With a pastry bag, squeeze out pate choux onto a baking pan lined with parchment; make each dot of pastry about as big around as a quarter.

6 Bake the pate choux in a preheated 450 degree oven until brown; about eight

44

minutes. Remove and cool.

7 Combine all filling ingredients in a food processor and blend into a smooth mixture. Load this into a pastry bag with a very thin tip. (A piece of paper made into a cone, with a very small opening at the tip, also works well.)

8 With a skewer, punch a small hole in the bottom of each puff pastry. Squeeze as much cheese as will fit inside the pastries; the inside is hollow, and will accept about ¼ tsp. of the cheese mixture.

9 Return the puffs to the oven for two to four minutes, until cheese in the center is hot. Pass around to your guests while still very hot.

Makes about 50 cheese puffs.

Soffiato di Trota

Trout Mousse

We make this mostly for our buffets, particularly during the cocktail hour of a gourmet banquet. It can be used as an elegant stuffing for a fish. It is also terrific when made with smoked trout.

1 Tbs. butter
1 cup flour
1 lb. trout fillets
⅓ cup whipping cream
Pinch nutmeg
¼ tsp. white pepper
1 egg yolk
4 egg whites

Preheat the oven to 400 degrees.

1 In a small saucepan, melt (but do not overheat) the butter. Add one cup of water and bring to a light boil. Remove the pan from the heat.

2 Sprinkle the flour into the saucepan, stirring as you go. This will result in a ball of dough that we call "pannata."

3 Pinch off 3 oz. of the pannata. Put it into food processor with the trout (run trout through a meat grinder first, if possible), whipping cream, nutmeg, white pepper, and egg yolk. Process into a smooth puree.

4 Beat the egg whites in a large bowl until stiff peaks form. With a rubber spatula, fold the trout mixture into the egg whites carefully until blended. Be sure not to break the egg whites.

5 Load the mixture into small ramekins and bake in a preheated 400-degree oven for 20 minutes. Serve with sauce hollandaise or lemon cream sauce (see **Sauces**). This is also outstanding with crawfish sauce—the same as for **Crawfish Ravioli** in the **Pasta** section.

Serves four.

Suggested wine: Verduzzo

Soffiato di Salmone

Salmon Mousse

This differs from the trout mousse in that it is served cold. It makes a polished first course, served on canapes and passed around during the cocktail hour.

1 sprig celery leaves
1 sprig parsley
1 Tbs. white vinegar
8 oz. salmon fillet
1 Tbs. fresh, snipped dill weed
½ tsp. chopped garlic
⅓ cup cream cheese
2 Tbs. sour cream
1 Tbs. chopped onions
½ tsp. salt
Pinch white pepper
½ tsp. Worcestershire
4 drops Tabasco

1 Put the celery, parsley, and vinegar into one gallon of cold water in a saucepan and bring to a boil. In it poach the salmon about 10 minutes, until firm but not falling apart.

2 Blend all the other ingredients together in a food processor. Crumble the salmon into the processor container and make into a puree with the sauce.

3 Load the puree into a pastry bag with a star tip. Squeeze out about 1 tsp. on canapes, Melba toast rounds, or croutons.

Makes about 20 canapes.

Suggested wine: Pigato

Zuppa

Soups

New Orleans, with its very small amount of cold weather, might be expected to consume less soup than in most other parts of the country. Not true. Not only are there lots of soups in the New Orleans cuisine, but they tend to be hearty and lusty. That suits me just fine, because I have a lot of hearty, lusty Italian soups to add to gumbo, turtle soup, crawfish bisque, and all the other Creole potages. We cook them all, at least five per day. My enthusiasm for the course is accurately reflected by the number of recipes in this chapter. I couldn't bear to leave any of them out.

Zuppa di Pasta e Fagioli

Pasta and White Bean Soup

This is one of the great soups of Italy. It has an irresistable aroma and a taste so heartwarming that you'll have to keep yourself from gobbling it all up. It is especially good during the cooler months, but any time of year it's worth more than the several hours it takes to make it. This is one of those soups that gets better the second day—so make plenty and enjoy.

4 oz. fagioli cannellini (Great Northern beans)
¼ cup olive oil
1 oz. (about 2 strips) pancetta or bacon
½ cup chopped onions
½ cup chopped carrots
¼ cup chopped leek, bulb only
2 tsp. chopped garlic
½ tsp. crushed red pepper
¼ cup dry white wine
½ cup peeled, seeded, and crushed tomato, with lots of juice
6 cups chicken stock
3 cups veal stock
Leaves from 2 ribs celery
1½ tsp. fresh oregano
1½ tsp. shredded fresh basil
2 cups tubetti or small shell pasta, cooked al dente (see **Pasta***)*

1 Sort through beans to pick out bad ones and foreign matter, and soak beans in water three hours to overnight.

2 In a large saucepan or Dutch oven, cook onions and pancetta in olive oil over medium heat until onions become tan. Add carrots, leeks, garlic and crushed red pepper and saute until tender.

3 Add beans and wine, and bring to a boil. As soon as bubbles appear, add tomato, three cups of the chicken stock, veal stock, celery leaves, oregano and basil.

4 Let soup simmer slowly for at least two hours, stirring every now and then. Add the rest of the chicken stock and three cups of water as needed to keep the soup liquid. Skim excess fat from top of soup, but don't be too thorough about this—a little fat adds richness. You will find that the soup will very quickly begin throwing off a superlative aroma that will make you very hungry.

5 When the beans in the soup begin to get tender, cook the pasta, drain it, and add it to soup. Stir well and serve with grated Parmesan cheese sprinkled over the soup at the table.
Serves eight.

Suggested wine: Bianco Piceno

Antipasto

Angel Hair Pasta with Smoked Salmon Andrea

Mussels Marinara

Crawfish Ravioli

Salad Andrea with Cheese in Filo Pouches

Seafood Gumbo

Gnocchi with Tomato and Pesto Sauces

Minestrone al Pesto

Stracciatella di Medici

Spinach and Egg Soup

This is my version of a classic Italian soup, named after the leading family of Florence during the Renaissance. It comes together very quickly; in fact, the most time-consuming part of the recipe is washing the spinach.

1 qt. beef stock
1 qt. chicken stock
½ lb. fresh spinach, washed and stems removed (see **Basics***)*
1 Tbs. chopped Italian parsley
4 eggs
½ cup grated Parmesan cheese
Pinch salt and pepper

1 Mix stocks and bring to a simmer in a large saucepan.

2 Bring about two cups of water to a light boil in a second saucepan. Poach the spinach for about 45 seconds. Remove and chop coarsely, and mix with parsley. Add that mixture to hot stock.

3 Beat the eggs in a bowl. Stir the Parmesan cheese into the eggs. Add egg-and-cheese mixture to stock and stir lightly, until egg and cheese are evenly distributed. Do not stir more than about 15 seconds.

4 Let soup return to a simmer. Stir soup again with kitchen fork to break up eggs, which will have congealed somewhat at top. Add salt and pepper to taste.

5 Serve hot with grated Parmesan cheese at the table.

Serves six.

Suggested wine: Zagarolo Secco from Lazio

Zuppa di Fave

Fava Bean Soup

Fava beans look like enormous lima beans, and they are an integral part of the Italian diet. In New Orleans, they most often turn up as "lucky beans" on St. Joseph's Day, which is celebrated with elaborate altars by the Italian population.

1 lb. fava beans
½ cup olive oil
1 cup chopped onions
1 Tbs. chopped garlic
½ tsp. red crushed pepper
3 slices pancetta or bacon, chopped
2 quarts chicken stock
2 medium white potatoes, peeled and diced
1 tsp. chopped Italian parsley
1 tsp. chopped celery leaves
2 shallots, peeled and chopped
½ tsp. salt
¼ tsp. white pepper

1 Soak fava beans overnight and remove the tough outer skins. (See **Basics**.)

2 In a large saucepan, heat olive oil over medium heat. Saute onions, garlic, crushed red pepper and pancetta until onions turn light brown.

3 Add beans and saute them about ten minutes over low flame. Add chicken stock. Bring the pot to a boil, then lower heat and simmer for about two hours.

4 When fava beans are tender, add potatoes, parsley, celery leaves, shallots, salt and pepper. Continue to simmer until potatoes are tender—about 15-20 minutes. Pasta can also be added to this dish if you like. Serve with a teaspoon of Parmesan cheese at the table.

Makes 8-10 servings.

Suggested wine: Albanello Di Siracusa Secco from Sicily

Crema d'Asparagi

Asparagus Soup

When we serve asparagus as a salad or side dish at Andrea's, we only use the tender top part of each spear. But the bottom, woodier third doesn't go to waste. We make a terrific soup with it, and so should you.

4 Tbs. butter
1 medium-large potato, peeled and chopped into cubes
1 rib celery, chopped
1 leek, well washed and chopped
1 medium onion, chopped
2 lbs. asparagus stem bottoms
1 cup white wine
2 qts. beef or chicken stock (we use a combination of the two)
2 cups whipping cream
Salt and pepper to taste
8 tender asparagus tips

1 Melt butter in a large saucepan. Add potatoes and saute briefly. Then add celery, leeks, onions, and saute until onions turn a translucent blond.

2 Add asparagus and white wine and bring to a boil briefly. Add stock and return to a boil. Reduce heat and simmer the soup until asparagus becomes tender—about an hour and a half.

3 Meanwhile, heat a small saucepan of water to a boil and poach the asparagus tips for four minutes, until just tender. Remove, wash with cold water, and reserve.

4 Strain soup. Put the solid parts in a food processor and puree. (This may take a few minutes, given the woody, stringy quality of asparagus.) Add the puree back to soup, and return soup to a boil.

5 After ten minutes of simmering, strain the soup through a sieve. Discard the solid parts and return the soup to a simmer.

6 In a skillet, bring cream to a boil and reduce by one-quarter. Whisk the cream into the soup.

7 Add salt and pepper to taste. Ladle soup into bowls, and top each bowl with one asparagus tip.
Serves eight.

Suggested wine: Muller Thurgau Emiliano

Zuppa di Broccoli

Broccoli Soup

The same is true of broccoli as for asparagus: after you cut off the good parts of your presentations, you are left with lots of stems which can be made into a delicious soup.

¼ cup butter
⅓ cup olive oil
2 ribs celery
1 medium onion, cut into chunks
½ Tbs. chopped garlic
4 oz. skin from a prosciutto, or pickled pork
8-10 broccoli stems, cut into chunks
1 medium-large potato, trimmed and cut into chunks
½ tsp. salt
Pinch white pepper
2 bay leaves
2 qts. beef or chicken stock, or a combination of the two
Florets from one stalk of broccoli
1 cup whipping cream

1 Melt butter in a large saucepan over medium heat, then add the olive oil and get it hot. Saute celery, onion, garlic and prosciutto skin until vegetables turn blond.

2 Add broccoli and potato to saucepan, and follow immediately with stock, bay leaf, salt and pepper. Bring to a boil and cook until broccoli is tender—about two hours.

3 Meanwhile, boil 2 cups of water in a saucepan. Break the broccoli florets into three, and boil for five minutes, until tender at the outside but still firm. Break into small pieces and reserve.

4 Strain soup. Remove pork and puree remaining solid parts in a food processor. Return puree to soup pot, and return pot to stove.

5 When soup returns to a boil, strain through a sieve. Stir in cream and simmer for five or ten more minutes. Ladle soup into bowls and top each with a few of the reserved florets.

Serves eight.

Suggested wine: Cortese

Crema di Carciofi

Artichoke Soup

This light, smooth soup is a great way to use parts of that highly distinctive vegetable that you otherwise would have thrown away. A very important step—as we discovered the first disastrous time we tested the recipe—is to soak the chokes in lemon juice and water overnight. Artichoke leaves have a natural bitter taste that has to be neutralized.

8 medium artichokes
½ cup lemon juice
1⅓ cups butter
2 ribs celery, cut up
1 medium onion, cut up
1 potato, peeled and sliced
½ cup dry white wine
3 qts. chicken stock
2 bay leaves
½ tsp. peppered salt
½ cup whipping cream

1 Soak the artichokes overnight in a gallon of water with the lemon juice.

2 From each artichoke, trim off and reserve the following: a half-inch to an inch off the top; a half-inch off the bottom, including the stem; and the outer two layers of leaves. The trimmings are what you use to make the soup. (Save the tender, trimmed artichokes for steaming, stuffing, or antipasto. To keep them fresh, store them covered with water with some lemon juice.)

3 In a large saucepan, heat the butter to bubbling and in it saute the celery and onions until the onions turn translucent.

4 Add the potatoes and artichoke trimmings. Cook over medium fire for about five minutes, until the artichoke leaves become tender. Add the wine and bring to a boil. Then add the stock, three quarts of water, and the bay leaves. Boil, then lower heat and simmer for two hours, or until everything is very tender.

5 Strain soup through a sieve. Remove the bay leaves. Put the rest of the soup solids into a food processor and make a coarse puree. Add this back into the strained soup. Strain the soup again through a coarse sieve to remove the stringy parts of the artichokes.

6 Return the soup to a simmer. Stir in whipping cream and add salt and pepper to taste. I prefer to keep my soups light in texture. However, you can thicken this soup by simmering it longer before the whipping cream is added.

Serves eight to ten.

Suggested wine: Ribolla Gialla

Crema di Cavolfiori

Cauliflower Soup

It might seem to you by now that if you know how to make soups with asparagus, artichokes, and broccoli, it shouldn't be hard to figure out how to do the same thing with cauliflower.

⅓ cup butter
¼ cup olive oil
1 med. white onion, cubed
½ leek, washed well and coarsely chopped
2 ribs celery, cubed
2 cloves garlic, chopped
1 head of cauliflower, cubed
2 potatoes, peeled and cubed
1 cup dry white wine
1 gal. chicken stock

Sacchetto: Put these dry seasonings into a small cheesecloth bag:
1 tsp. thyme
1 tsp. marjoram
3 bay leaves
1 tsp. black peppercorns
4 sprigs parsley
3 leaves fresh sage
1 sprig fresh oregano

2 cups whipping cream
½ Tbs. Tabasco
1 tsp. salt
½ tsp. white pepper

1 In a large saucepan, melt butter and heat olive oil over medium heat. Saute onion, leek, celery and garlic until browned lightly.

2 Add cauliflower and stir to coat well with the hot oil and butter. Then do the same thing with the potatoes.

3 When potatoes have warmed through (about two minutes), add the wine. Bring to a boil, then add chicken stock and two quarts of water. Return to a boil and, when the first bubbles appear, add the sacchetto, salt, and pepper.

4 Cook until reduced by about one-third—about 1½ hours. Strain through a sieve. Remove sacchetto. Put vegetables into a food processor and puree. Put the puree back into the pot with the strained soup and return to a boil.

5 Bring the whipping cream to a boil in a large saucepan. When you get a vigorous boil, whisk cream into soup. Strain soup again through a fine sieve. Add salt, pepper, and Tabasco to taste.

Serves eight to ten.

Zuppa d'Aglio

Garlic Soup

Garlic wears many hats. Most people think of it in its aggressive, green, aromatic, sharp form. Bit when garlic is cooked slowly for a long time, it takes on a sweet nuttiness that is every bit as interesting as its more raw flavors. The sweet side of garlic is exemplified by this soup.

3 heads fresh garlic
¼ cup olive oil
1 medium-large onion, cut up
2 ribs celery, cut up
1 cup dry white wine
¼ cup all-purpose flour
1 gallon chicken stock
1 medium potato, peeled and cut up
1 cup whipping cream
10 chopped fresh basil leaves
5 sprigs fresh thyme leaves
2 tsp. salt
½ tsp. white pepper
½ tsp. Tabasco
1 tsp. extra virgin olive oil
2 cloves garlic, sliced very thin, for garnish

1 Cut two of the garlic heads in half across and remove the papery outer skin. Put these cut side down on a very hot surface—a griddle or black iron skillet—until they're black. Peel all the garlic completely.

2 Heat the olive oil in a large saucepan and saute the onions, celery, and the garlic until lightly browned at the edges. Add the wine and bring to a boil.

3 Sprinkle in the flour and stir the pot thoroughly, but don't let it brown. Add the chicken stock, ½ gallon water, and the potato. Whisk the pot well and bring to a boil. Reduce to a rapid simmer and cook for about an hour and 15 minutes.

4 Strain out the solids from the soup, and puree them in a blender or food processor, along with enough broth to ease things along. Return the puree to the soup and restore the boil. Add the whipping cream, basil, thyme, salt, pepper and Tabasco.

5 Heat the extra virgin olive oil in a skillet very hot. In it toast the slivers of garlic until brown around the outside.

6 Ladle the soup into bowls and garnish with roasted garlic slivers. Float a toasted, garlic-buttered slice of French bread on top.

Serves eight to 12.

Suggested wine: Marinasco

Minestrone

Italian Vegetable Soup

When you ask most people to name an Italian soup, this is the one they will name. It is a classic of the cuisine, hearty and delectable and quite good for your health. And the aroma! We enhance it a little more by adding a dollop of pesto right before we serve it.

1 cup red beans
4 oz. fatty smoked pork
½ cup olive oil
1 cup chopped onion
1 Tbs. chopped garlic
1 cup chopped carrots
1 cup chopped celery
1 leek, white part only, washed well, chopped
2 Tbs. tomato paste
2 qts. chicken or beef stock (we use a combination of both)
2 bay leaves
1 large white potato, peeled and diced
1 large zucchini, chopped coarsely
1 tsp. salt
¼ tsp. white pepper
4 oz. green beans
¼ lb. fresh spinach, washed and large stems removed

Pesto Pastetta:
5 slices bacon, chopped
½ cup Italian parsley leaves
5 cloves garlic, peeled
8 fresh basil leaves
1 stem fresh oregano leaves

2 cups tubetti pasta, cooked al dente

1 Pick through the red beans to remove bad ones. Soak in cold water for several hours. Drain the water. Boil the beans for one hour in one gallon of fresh water. Pour off water and reserve beans.

2 In a large saucepan over medium heat, fry the pork to render some fat. Add the olive oil and get it hot. Saute onions, garlic, carrots and celery until onions turn blond.

3 Add leeks and tomato paste and saute for about a minute. Add stocks and bring to a boil. Add bay leaves and red beans, and continue to simmer for about 30 minutes. Then add the potato and zucchini and return to a simmer.

4 Meanwhile, bring two quarts of water to a boil in a saucepan. Add green beans and boil for five minutes. Remove green beans and wash with cold water. In the same boiling water, poach the spinach for about 45 seconds, and then wash it with cold water. Cut beans and chop spinach and add to soup pot.

5 Remove pork from pot and discard.

6 In the bowl of a food processor, combine bacon, garlic, parsley and basil, and puree. (The Italian word for this is "pastetta.")

7 When potatoes in soup pot are tender, add cooked pasta and pastetta. Stir in and serve immediately with grated Parmesan cheese.

Serves eight.

Suggested wine: Pinot Bianco Dell'Alto Adige

Crema di Castagne

Chestnut Soup

This is a Christmastime soup for two reasons: Christmas makes people think of chestnuts, and Christmastime is the only time you can get fresh chestnuts.

1 lb. fresh chestnuts (dried or canned okay but less desirable)
3 oz. butter
1 medium onion, chopped
1 rib celery, chopped
2 oz. dry white wine
2 qts. chicken stock
2 bay leaves
4 sprigs Italian parsley
Pinch nutmeg
Pinch dried sage
1 qt. milk
Salt & white pepper to taste
½ pint whipping cream

1 Shell the chestnuts, then boil for 12 minutes. Remove the soft inner skins. Save eight whole nutmeats for use later. Chop the rest coarsely.

2 Heat butter in a saucepan over low heat. Saute onion and celery until translucent. Add chopped chestnuts and wine; bring to a boil for a minute. Add chicken stock, bay, parsley, nutmeg and sage and return to a boil. Cook until chestnuts are very tender—about 25 minutes.

3 Strain soup through a sieve. Discard bay leaves and parsley. Puree remaining solid parts of soup in a food processor.

4 In a separate saucepan, boil the milk. Whisk in the puree a little at a time. Pour the contents of the milk pan into the soup pan and bring to a boil. Add salt, pepper and whipping cream. Cook on low heat for about ten minutes.

5 Cook the eight reserved chestnuts in boiling water until al dente. Ladle the soup into bowls and garnish each bowl with a chestnut. Serve with chopped Italian parsley.

Serves eight.

Crema di Funghi Coltivati

Cream of Mushroom Soup

Because mushrooms cook quickly, you can turn them into a great-tasting soup in very short order—at least if you have some chicken stock on hand. This is also a good end for mushrooms that are starting to look a little tired.

½ cup butter
1 medium onion, cut up
1 rib celery, chopped
1 leek, well washed, white part only (see **Basics**)
2 lbs. medium mushrooms, well washed, patted dry and sliced
1 medium potato, peeled and cubed
1 gal. chicken stock
1 cup whipping cream
1 cup milk
Salt and white pepper

1 Heat butter in a large saucepan over medium heat and saute onions, celery, and leek until onions brown lightly. Add the mushrooms to the saucepan and saute lightly for about a minute. Add the potatoes and chicken stock and heat to a boil.

2 Lower heat and keep soup on a fast simmer for about 25-30 minutes—until potatoes are tender. Remove from fire and strain through a coarse sieve. Put solid parts strained from soup into a food processor and puree, using ¼ cup of the soup to help things along if necessary. Return puree to soup.

3 In a skillet, boil cream and milk together and reduce by half. Stir into soup and return to a boil. Adjust seasonings with salt and pepper.

Serves eight to ten.

Suggested wine: Pinot Bianco Dell'Alto Adige

Zuppa di Lenticchie

Lentil Soup

It is almost impossible to make a bad soup with lentils. These little beans seem to have been made for the purpose. And the soup gets better the second day.

1 lb. lentils
4 slices pancetta
½ cup olive oil
½ cup chopped onions
1 rib celery, with leaves, chopped coarsely
½ carrot, chopped coarsely
2 Tbs. chopped garlic
½ tsp. crushed red pepper
1 cup dry red wine
½ cup canned, chopped Italian plum tomatoes
1 gallon beef stock
½ tsp. salt
Pinch white pepper
4 sprigs parsley, finely chopped
6 sprigs fresh oregano
1 large bay leaf
Extra virgin olive oil
Chopped Italian parsley
Grated Parmesan cheese

1 Wash the lentils well and drain.

2 In a skillet, fry the pancetta until lightly browned. Add the olive oil and heat it to almost smoking temperature. Saute onions, celery, carrot, garlic and crushed red pepper until the onions start to brown at the edges.

3 Add the red wine and bring it to a boil. Add lentils, tomatoes and beef stock, and return to a boil. Add the salt, pepper, parsley, oregano, bay leaf and celery leaves. Cover and bring to a boil.

4 Lower heat to a fast simmer for 45 minutes, or until lentils are tender. Remove from the heat.

5 Pour about a teaspoon of extra virgin olive oil, the chopped parsley, and grated Parmesan cheese at the table.

Serves eight to ten.

Suggested wine: Corvo Bianco

Crema di Pomodori

Tomato Bisque

We make our tomato bisque with two unusual touches. First, we use beef stock rather than chicken stock, to give it a fuller flavor. Second, we add rice to the soup pot and puree it along with the rest of the ingredients. Sometimes, to add special elegance, we top the soup cup with puff pastry and bake it in the oven. The aroma of the soup explodes out the top as soon as the eater punches through the baked top.

½ cup olive oil
1 cup chopped onion
2 ribs celery, coarsely chopped
½ leek, well washed and coarsely chopped
1 cup carrot, peeled and sliced
1 Tbs. chopped garlic
2 lbs. fresh ripe tomatoes
4 Tbs. tomato paste
¼ tsp. crushed red pepper
1 cup dry white wine
1 cup dry vermouth
½ gallon beef stock
½ cup fresh basil, chopped
1½ tsp. salt
¼ tsp. white pepper
1 cup uncooked rice (Uncle Ben's)
1 cup whipping cream
8 leaves fresh basil, cut into thin strips

Preheat oven to 400 degrees.
1 Cut the tomatoes in half, cut out the stem cores, and squeeze out the seeds. Reserve two tomatoes; chop the rest coarsely.
2 In a large saucepan, heat the olive oil over low heat. Saute the onion, celery, leek, carrot and garlic until moist and tender. Stir in the tomato paste and the crushed red pepper.
3 Add the white wine and vermouth and bring to a boil. Reduce liquid by half. Add the beef stock, one-half gallon of water and chopped tomatoes. Return to a boil, then lower heat and simmer for 50 minutes.
4 Add the uncooked rice to the pot. Cook for another 30 minutes. Put the contents of the pot into a food processor or blender and puree (yes, even with the rice in it). You can do this in batches if neccessary. Strain the result through a sieve. Discard the solids, of which there may be quite a bit.
5 Return the soup back to the saucepan over medium heat. Stir in whipping cream, salt, pepper and basil. Bring to a boil.
6 Meanwhile, peel the reserved tomatoes, and slice them into thin half-moons;

add to the pot. When the tomato slices are warm, remove from the heat. *Serves six to eight.*

An extra touch of elegance To serve this soup "en croute," put the soup into crocks. Cut circles of puff pastry dough big enough to overlap the crock rims by about a half-inch all around. Lightly dampen one side of the dough and press it down and around the rims, like the cap of a soft-drink bottle. Brush the tops of the dough with beaten egg. Put the crocks into a preheated 400-degree oven and bake until the pastry is golden brown—about 15 minutes.

Suggested wine: Marinasco

Crema di Porri con Arugula

Arugula Vichyssoise

The hot summer months call for cold soups. Everybody makes the standard leek-and-potato vichyssoise, so I wanted to do something different. The briary taste of arugula—perhaps the best Italian salad green—seemed just right.

12 large leaves arugula
⅓ cup extra virgin olive oil
3 cups fresh leeks, white part only, chopped coarsely
1 medium onion, chopped
3 potatoes, peeled and cubed
1 gallon chicken stock
3 oz. boiled ham
4 sprigs fresh thyme leaves
1 cup whipping cream
2 cups half-and-half cream
1 tsp. peppered salt

1 Cut stems off arugula and reserve leaves. Heat the olive oil in a saute pan. Saute the the arugula stems, leeks and onions until translucent. Add the potatoes and cook until the outsides become opaque white.

2 Add the chicken stock, ham and thyme. Bring to a boil. Keep on low simmer for one hour and 15 minutes.

3 Allow the soup to cool somewhat, then puree everything in batches in a food processor. Strain.

4 Whisk in whipping cream, half-and-half and salt and pepper to taste.

5 Ladle into soup plates and float coarsely chopped arugula leaves on top. *Serves eight to 12.*

Suggested wine: Cortese

Crema di Langoustine

Crawfish Bisque

This is one of the great New Orleans soups—but I've never found a restaurant that prepares it the way we do. By using some Italian soup-making techniques, I have been able to eliminate the need for the traditional Creole roux. If there could be any complaint about this soup, it's that too much crawfish flavor is present. This is not for people who like bland flavors.

2 lbs. boiled crawfish
¼ cup olive oil
¼ cup brandy
2 ribs celery
1 med. onion, cut up
1 medium carrot, peeled and sliced
1 cup chopped red and green bell pepper
1 Tbs. chopped garlic
1 cup coarsely chopped leeks, well washed, green and white parts
2 cups dry white wine
3 Tbs. tomato paste
½ cup all-purpose flour

Sacchetto: Put these dry seasonings into a small cheesecloth bag:
1 Tbs. black peppercorns
1 tsp. thyme
1 tsp. marjoram
1 tsp. dried dill (or 1 Tbs. fresh dill stems)
4 bay leaves

1 cup whipping cream
¼ tsp. cayenne
Salt and white pepper to taste

1 Peel the crawfish, keeping everything. Reserve the tail meat for later in the recipe. Put all the shells into a large sieve and rinse with cold water.

2 Heat the olive oil in a stockpot and put the crawfish shells in it. Stir the crawfish shells briskly over high heat to toast them. Use a heavy spoon to crush the shells a bit.

3 Pour the brandy over the shells and carefully flame it. All of these extra steps release more flavor from the shells than if we had just started boiling them.

4 After the flames die out, scoop the crawfish shells out of the stockpot and reserve.

5 Lower the heat to medium and, in the same oil in the stockpot (add a little more if necessary), saute celery, onion, carrot, bell pepper, garlic and leeks until vegetables become moist—about four minutes.

6 Stir in tomato paste and white wine. Stir well and reduce liquid by half.

7 Sprinkle in the flour and stir well to form a thick, pasty conglomerate in the pot. Add one gallon of cold water and the crawfish shells. Stir well and bring to a boil. When the first bubbles appear, add the sacchetto. Boil for one hour and remove from the heat. Remove the sacchetto.

8 Strain the solid parts out of the soup. Process this to a rough puree in a food processor, then stir it back into the soup. Return to a boil.

9 When bubbles appear, strain the soup through a sieve to remove hard particles. Simmer the soup back to a boil for 10 minutes (or longer if you want a thicker soup.)

10 Heat the cream to a boil in a skillet and whisk it into the soup. Adjust seasonings with salt, pepper and cayenne. Add the reserved crawfish tail meat. Heat through and serve.

Serves six to eight.

Suggested wine: Trebbiano D'Abbruzzo

Crema di Cozze

Mussel Soup

Mussels make a spectacularly delicate, delicious cream soup. This soup is ordinarily served hot. But it can be chilled and still be delicious—as many of our early customers found out. Cold mussel soup was on the very first menu at Andrea's.

½ cup olive oil
½ cup white part of a leek, coarsely chopped
⅓ cup chopped onions
1 Tbs. chopped garlic
1 rib celery, cut up
24 mussels, cleaned and debearded
1 cup dry white wine
1 medium potato, cut up
½ gal. fish stock
1 generous pinch saffron threads (about 20, if you're counting)
2 bay leaves
1 sprig fresh thyme leaves
1 cup whipping cream

1 Heat olive oil in a saucepan over medium heat. Saute the leek, onion, garlic, and celery until moist and tender.

2 Wash and check mussels well; there should be no open shells. (See notes about mussels in **Primi Piatti** chapter.) Add mussels to the saucepan, along with the wine. Cover the pot to let the mussels steam. After three minutes, take the mussels out and wash them in warm salted water.

3 Add the potato, the fish stock, and ½ gallon water to the saucepan and bring to a boil.

4 Select 12 of the best-looking mussels. Leave these in their shells. Take the rest out of the shells and add to the soup. Add the saffron, bay leaves and thyme, and bring the pot to a boil. Reduce heat and simmer 50 minutes.

5 Strain out the solids. Remove the bay leaves and puree the remainder with about two cups of the soup in a food processor or blender. Return the puree to the soup and continue to simmer.

6 Boil the whipping cream in a separate saucepan and reduce it by half. Whisk the cream into the soup and cook for another five minutes.

7 Place three reserved mussels on half-shells in soup plates. Ladle the hot soup over the mussels. Top with a little chopped parsley.

Serves four.

Suggested wine: Tocai

"Gumbo" di Frutti di Mare

Seafood Gumbo

Gumbo is one of the two or three most distinctive dishes in the New Orleans cuisine. There are as many different styles of gumbo as there are cooks who make it; in fact, part of the fun of eating or making gumbo is exploring the myriad taste possibilities it presents. We cook gumbo several different ways at Andrea's, but this one has become a staple of our Friday lunch menu. It's a basic Creole seafood gumbo, touched with some ideas from a soup from my native country called "zuppa di pesce."

The starting point for a good gumbo is, I believe, a good crab stock. Around New Orleans we have lots of blue crabs most of the year. Grocery stores stock something called "gumbo crabs"—not very fat, but good for making the stock.

1½ lbs. crab shells, legs, and claws, pulled apart
¼ tsp. dried thyme
3 bay leaves
2 cups olive oil
2 cups all-purpose flour
½ cup chopped onions
1 Tbs. chopped garlic
¼ leek, chopped
1 medium green bell pepper, chopped
2 ribs celery, chopped
1 tsp. crushed red pepper
1 lb. fresh okra
4 Italian plum tomatoes, broken up with the fingers
1 cup uncooked rice
¼ cup claw crabmeat
1 cup lump crabmeat, well-picked to remove shells

12 oz. small chopped shrimp
16-24 oysters, depending on size; cut large ones in half
¼ tsp. cayenne
1½ tsp. salt
1 tsp. white pepper
1 tsp. black pepper
1 tsp. Tabasco
1 Tbs. Worcestershire

1 In a covered saucepan, boil a gallon of cold water with the crab shells for 30 minutes, until you get a good crab flavor in the stock. Add the thyme and bay leaves, and continue to boil for another few minutes.

2 Meanwhile, make a roux. In a stockpot or large saucepan, heat the olive oil to medium hot (not as hot as you'd make it for sauteeing onions), and sprinkle the flour in. With a wooden spoon, stir it constantly while cooking until it has the color of a walnut. The constant stirring of the roux is essential to keep it from burning. If roux burns, it's a lost cause — throw it away, clean the pot, and start over.

3 When the roux is the right color, stir in the onions, garlic, leeks, green peppers, celery and crushed red pepper and saute in the roux until everything is tender. If the crab stock is not ready yet, take the roux off the heat until it is. Then add the crab stock, shells and all, to the roux and return to medium heat. Whisk all ingredients well and return to a boil.

4 Cut off the stem ends of the okra, then slice the rest into discs about ¼-inch thick. Once the gumbo has been boiling for 20 minutes, add the okra and the tomatoes.

5 Bring 1 quart of cold water to a boil and add the rice. Boil for 15 minutes, until cooked but still firm. Wash rice with cold water to stop cooking, and set aside.

6 After the gumbo has boiled another 20 minutes, add the crabmeat, shrimp, and oysters. Boil for another three minutes, then add the cayenne, salt, black and white peppers, Tabasco and Worcestershire. Adjust seasonings to taste.

7 Put about two Tbs. cooked rice on each soup plate, and ladle gumbo over it. *Serves 12.*

Suggested wine: Tocai

Crema di Grancevole

Crab Bisque

It's amazing how much flavor can be extracted from something that looks as trashy and unpromising as crab shells. This recipe makes a very full-flavored bisque, full of good lump crabmeat.

1 cup vegetable oil
1½ lbs. crab shells, legs, and claws, cut up into small pieces
⅓ cup brandy
¼ cup tomato paste
1 med. onion, cut up
1 large carrot, cut up
2 ribs celery, cut up
1 Tbs. chopped garlic
1 tsp. crushed red pepper
2 cups dry white wine
2 cups all-purpose flour
3 bay leaves
¼ tsp. dried thyme
1 Tbs. salt
¼ tsp. white pepper
¼ tsp. cayenne
1 Tbs. Worcestershire
1 cup whipping cream
1 cup lump crabmeat

1 Heat the vegetable oil very hot in a large saucepan. Add the crabs (they will sizzle loudly) and stir until the crab shells turn red.

2 Add the brandy and carefully flame. When flames die out, stir in the tomato paste.

3 Add the onions, carrots, celery and garlic and continue to cook over high heat, stirring often. When vegetables are tender, add the crushed red pepper and white wine. Lower the heat and bring the pot to a slow boil. Add the flour and stir well.

4 When flour is lightly browned, stir in 1½ gallons of cold water. Add bay leaves, thyme, salt and pepper and return to a boil. After one hour add cayenne and Worcestershire. Return to a boil for another 30 minutes.

5 Strain the soup. Put the solid parts into a food processor and run into a rough puree. Add this back into the pot of soup. Strain the soup again through a fine sieve. Return to a boil.

6 Heat the whipping cream to a boil, whisking frequently. Whisk the cream into the soup. Place 1 Tbs. of lump crabmeat onto each soup plate, and ladle the soup over it.

Serves eight.

Suggested wine: Inzolia

Zuppa di Ostriche

Oyster Chowder

As I have opined elsewhere in this book, the oysters we find around New Orleans are the world's best. When you make a soup with them, keep it delicate. Don't try to overpower them with odd tastes. And remember that oysters are best when cooked very lightly—just until the edges curl.

½ cup extra virgin olive oil
1 large onion, coarsely chopped
1 Tbs. chopped garlic
1 medium carrot, coarsely chopped
2 ribs celery with leaves, coarsely chopped
1 cup dry white wine
¼ cup all-purpose flour
1 quart oyster water
1 gallon fish stock
2 sprigs fresh thyme
1 sprig fresh oregano leaves, chopped
2 Tbs. salt
½ tsp. white pepper
3 canned Italian plum tomatoes, chopped, with enough juice to fill a cup
½ tsp. crushed red pepper
1 medium potato, peeled
36-60 oysters (depending on size—a generous quart)
2 cups whipping cream

1 In a skillet, heat the olive oil over medium heat. Saute the onions and garlic until blond. Add the carrots and celery and saute until the vegetables become moist. Add the wine and flour and bring to a light boil while stirring.

2 Add the oyster water, fish stock, thyme, oregano, tomatoes, salt and pepper, and return to a boil. Cut the potatoes into approximately French-fry size and add to the soup.

3 Keep the soup on a rapid boil, skimming now and then. After 50 minutes, add the oysters. Cook 10 minutes more, then stir in the whipping cream and serve with a sprinkle of chopped Italian parsley.

Serves 12.

Suggested wine: Lacrima Christi

Zuppa di Tartaruga

Turtle Soup

First of all, let me reassure those environmentalists reading this book that no endangered species are used to make our turtle soup. We recommend the "cowan" or alligator snapping turtle, which is still abundant in Louisiana marshes. It is also now raised on farms. This is a Creole-inspired turtle soup that is more like a stew than the traditional European clear turtle soup.

2 lbs. turtle meat (1 lb., 10 oz. if using boneless)
½ cup extra virgin olive oil
1 medium onion, cut up
1 medium carrot, cut up
2 ribs celery, cut up
3 cloves garlic, lightly crushed
¼ cup tomato paste
½ cup all-purpose flour
1 cup dry white wine
3 sprigs chopped Italian parsley
3 sprigs fresh thyme leaves
10 fresh sage leaves, chopped
2 bay leaves
1½ Tbs. salt
1 tsp. white pepper
8 cloves
⅓ cup flour
¼ cup vegetable oil
2 hard-boiled eggs
1 Tbs. Worcestershire
½ tsp. Tabasco

1 Bring 1 gallon of water to a boil with the turtle meat. Skim the pot of the scum that will float to the surface.

2 In a large saucepan, heat the olive oil over medium heat. Saute the onion, carrot, celery and garlic until blond. Remove the vegetables from the saucepan; leave as much olive oil behind as possible. Add tomato paste and flour. Whisk briskly over medium-high heat until you have a crumbly, somewhat dry mixture.

3 Add the wine and use it to turn the flour mixture into a smooth paste. Add ½ gallon cold water and whisk in well. Bring to a boil.

4 Return the vegetables to the saucepan. Add the parsley, thyme, sage, and bay.

5 After the turtle meat has boiled for 30 minutes, remove it and set aside. Pour the turtle stock into the pot with the vegetables, along with one gallon of plain water. Add salt and pepper, and return to a boil.

6 After the soup has boiled for 1½ hours, strain it and puree the vegetables in a food processor. Return the stock and the pureed vegetables to a boil. Add cloves. Reduce to a simmer.

7 Chop the turtle meat.

8 Make a medium-brown roux with the flour and vegetable oil. (See **Gumbo** recipe for tips on how to make a roux.) Add roux carefully to the soup and whisk in, along with chopped turtle meat. Add Worcestershire and Tabasco. Check seasonings and adjust to taste. Continue to simmer until texture is the way you like it.

9 Chop hard-boiled eggs. Put 1 Tbs. of crumbled egg in soup plates, and pour soup over. Serve soup with 1 tsp. dry sherry.

Tip From Sous-Chef Pete: Add the meat (no skin!) from one lemon, chopped coarsely, to the pot after the vegetables are pureed.
Serves 12-14.

Suggested wine: Taurasi

Zuppa di Pesche

Peach Soup

Here's another cold soup with tastes of a completely different kind. Although the sweetness of the peaches is obvious, this is really a savory soup that will fit in fine at the soup course.

⅓ cup extra virgin olive oil
1 medium onion, chopped
½ leek, white part only, chopped
½ medium carrot, chopped
¼ cup dry white wine
¼ cup dry vermouth
1 gallon chicken stock
1 tsp. salt
¼ tsp. cinnamon
Pinch nutmeg
1 Tbs. honey
2 lbs. fresh peaches, pitted, skinned, and cubed

1 Heat the olive oil in a saute pan. Saute the the onion, leek, and carrots until light brown around the edges. Add the wine and vermouth and bring to a boil.

2 Add the chicken stock, salt, cinnamon, and nutmeg and bring to a boil. Add the peaches. Lower heat to a slow boil and cook for one hour and 15 minutes. Dissolve in the honey.

3 Let cool to lukewarm, and puree the soup in a food processor. Strain the soup into a large bowl and refrigerate. Serve soup chilled, garnished with thin peach slices.
Serves eight.

Suggested wine: Bellini Spumante

Ristretto di Manzo

Consomme

It is the nature of European-trained chefs to believe that knowing how to make a consomme—a clear, intense, beefy soup—is one of the most important skills to have. Forget the fact that nobody in America likes consomme very much. It's elegant, and that's that.

2 lbs. ground inside round, chilled
1 medium carrot, chopped
2 ribs celery, chopped
1 medium onion, chopped
⅓ cup egg white
1 gallon beef stock
5 eggshells
1 Tbs. salt
¼ tsp. white pepper

1 Combine the beef, carrot, celery, onion and egg white with your hands in a large saucepan. Add the beef stock and ½ gallon cold water, and stir the contents well.

2 Put the saucepan on medium heat and gently bring toward a boil—but lower the heat if you see any bubbles break the surface. Stir the pot every two minutes until the beef floating on top becomes firm.

3 Crumble the eggshells onto the surface of the pot. Keep the heat steady, but allow the pot to come to a gentle simmer now. With a spatula, push down the cap of beef gently until it's just below the surface of the liquid. (It will float back to the top.) Repeat this process every 10 minutes. You will notice that the broth is now dark brown but almost transparent.

4 Simmer for two hours, then take the pot off the stove. Carefully skim the fat from the top of the pot.

5 Strain the soup by ladling it a little at a time through double cheesecloth in a sieve.

Makes 5 quarts (I know this is a lot, but the recipe doesn't come out as well if you make less, and you can freeze the soup for future use.)

RISTRETTO DI MANZO AL PORTO: Add 1 Tbs. port wine to 2 cups consomme, and include about 1 Tbs. each of matchstick-size strips of celery, leek, and carrots.

RISTRETTO DI MANZO AL TIO PEPE: Add 1 Tbs. dry sherry to 2 cups consomme.

RISTRETTO DI MANZO PRIMAVERA: Add 1 Tbs. each of leeks, carrots and celery, cut into matchsticks, plus 1 tsp. truffle strips.

Suggested wine: Amarone

Pasta

Pasta is one of the world's greatest foods. It is very healthful, being low in fats and high in complex carbohydrates. It is delicious. And, best of all, it is endlessly adaptable. You can make pasta in any imaginable shape and serve it with almost any food.

We are extremely proud of our pasta offerings at Andrea's. We encourage all our guests to have a pasta course at some point in their meals. (The proper point is as a course right before the entree). And whenever we do outside catering or culinary displays, we like to make a pasta station a featured part of the offerings.

We make all our own pasta at Andrea's from scratch, every single day. Not only does this allow us to control the quality of the ingredients that go into the pasta, but it gives us the flexibility to produce exactly the kind of pasta we want for a particular dish.

There is nothing wrong with buying ready-made pastas, as long as you buy a high-quality brand made with 100 percent durum semolina. Pasta is so inexpensive to begin with that it makes no sense to try to save a few pennies. I would recommend the dried pastas imported from Italy over the domestic dried product. Specific brands I like include *Fratelli Cecco, Fara San Martino,* and *Del Verde.*

But there's something even better. . . homemade pasta.

Making Your Own Pasta

I highly recommend that you invest in a small pasta machine for your kitchen and make your own fresh pasta. It is no more difficult than making any other kind of dough, and it gives superior results.

Although there are many complicated, (usually electric) pasta machines on the market, the best gadget for making pasta is hand-operated and very simple. A good pasta maker will be made of stainless steel. It is not cheap, but it pays off in long life and better pasta. It consists of a set of gear-driven rollers, about six inches long. By varying the space between the rollers, you control the thickness of the pasta.

Regardless of what shape you will ultimately make your pasta into, here is the formula for making the dough:

2 cups semolina flour
2 cups all-purpose flour
2 eggs, well beaten
1 Tbs. extra virgin olive oil
½ tsp. salt

1 Mix the two flours together and make a mound on top of a clean surface. Make a well in the center of the mound.

2 In a large bowl, beat the eggs and mix in the olive oil, salt, and 1 cup of cold water. Pour this into the flour well.

3 With your hands, mix the flours and liquids together and knead until you have a ball of dough. Add up to another half-cup of water to help things along, as necessary. (The amount depends on the temperature and humidity of your kitchen.)

4 Work the dough by rolling it away from you on the counter while simultaneously tearing it in half. Then pull it back together while rolling it back towards you, always keeping some pressure on the dough with the balls of your hands. Keep rolling and tearing (this is good exercise for your upper arms) for five minutes, until the texture is uniform and smooth. Dust the counter with flour now and then to keep the dough from sticking.

5 Make the dough into the shape of a bread loaf and dust with white flour. Cover with a dry cloth and allow the pasta dough ball to rest for 15 minutes.

6 Cut off a piece of dough about the size of your fist—about six ounces by weight. (This is approximately enough for two servings of most basic pasta dishes.) Flatten it into a disk. Dust it lightly with flour.

7 Set the dial on the pasta machine at 1—the thickest setting. Run the disk of pasta dough through. Dust it with flour, fold it over end to end, and run it through again. Change the setting to 3, and repeat the above procedure. Set the machine on 5, and go through the procedure yet again. By now, you'll have a long strip of pasta. Catch the end of it with your free hand and pull it away as it exits the machine, so it doesn't pile up.) Change the setting to 6—the thinnest setting— and run through just once more (don't fold it over this time).

You now have a basic flat pasta sheet. It can be used as is for making ravioli or lasagne. Or you can use the attachments to the machine to cut it into (from thinnest to thickest) angel hair, spaghetti, linguine, or fettuccine.

Makes about 1½ pounds of fresh pasta.

Spinach Pasta

We like to serve multicolored pastas in some of our dishes at Andrea's. The classic is paglia e fieno ("straw and hay"), in which both green and white pastas are used. The green pasta is made with spinach, which is incorporated into the pasta as it's being made. Spinach pasta comes out best if the initial mixing of the dough is done with a powerful electric mixer (KitchenAid or equivalent) with a dough hook. That's how these instructions are given. If you want to do it by hand, mix the spinach puree into the egg-and-water mixture, and make sure the spinach is well distributed in the flour.

2 lbs. fresh spinach, picked of stems and well washed (see **Basics***)*
4 eggs
1 tsp. salt
1 Tbs. extra virgin olive oil
3 cups semolina flour
3 cups all-purpose flour

1 Bring a pot of water to a boil. Plunge the spinach into it for five minutes. Strain the spinach out in a colander, and immediately wash it with cold water to stop the cooking.

2 When cool, puree the spinach in a blender or food processor.

3 Blend the eggs, 1 cup cold water, salt, and extra virgin olive oil in a bowl and set aside. Put the flours and the spinach puree into the bowl of a heavy-duty mixer with a paddle attachment. With the mixer on low speed, gradually add the egg mixture. If the dough lumps up around the paddle, stop mixing and scrape it off. Add up to another ½ cup of cold water as necessary to keep the dough moist.

4 When a uniform dough has formed, make it into a ball and put it onto a well-floured countertop. Work it, and roll it out according to the instructions in the previous recipe.

Makes about 2½ pounds fresh spinach pasta.

How To Cook Pasta

Cooking pasta is extremely easy. The few principles to keep in mind are elementary and not especially critical in terms of either quantities or timing.

As a general rule, use two gallons of water for every pound of dry pasta you're cooking. For pasta varieties for which we give cup measurements (such as corkscrew pasta), we recommend a gallon of water per three cups of pasta. It is better to have too much water than not enough. What you want is for the pasta to move around freely in the pot just through the action of the rising bubbles.

Boil the water before adding the pasta. When the water boils, add 1 Tbs. vegetable oil and 1 Tbs. salt to two gallons of water. Then add the pasta. If it's spaghetti or other long pasta, stir the pot with a kitchen fork (never a spoon!) to keep it from sticking together. You only need to do this once, when all the pasta has softened.

I strongly recommend that you cook your pasta "al dente." This is an Italian expression which means that the pasta offers some resistance to the teeth when you chew it. When using dried pasta, it is cooked al dente when the last little hair's breadth of crispness at the center is still there but is about to disappear.

You will find that the pasta will have much better flavor and will hold sauces much better if it is cooked al dente. Al dente pasta is also easier to eat, as it doesn't break when you wind it around the fork. (By the way, cutting pasta at the table is bad form.)

How long pasta takes to reach the al dente state depends on the pasta. Fresh, thin pasta cooks much faster than dried, thick pasta. The range is one minute or less for fresh angel hair to six or eight minutes for dried rigatoni. The best bet is to pull out a piece when you think it's almost ready and test it with your teeth. After your pasta is cooked, drain it well and keep it warm until it's ready to be sauced.

In most of the recipes in this book, the instructions call for tossing the pasta in the sauce. Just dump the pasta into the sauce skillet and stir it around with a kitchen fork until uniformly coated. Or just agitate the pan to slosh the sauce over the pasta.

The most famous pasta dishes are those made with tomato-based sauces, which can be found in the "Sauces" chapter.

Cappelli d'Angelo Andrea

Angel Hair Pasta with Smoked Salmon

Absolutely without a doubt the favorite pasta dish at Andrea's, this delicate combination was created for a dinner for the International Wine and Food Society. The year was 1981, I was the executive chef of the Royal Orleans Hotel, and the crowd went wild. This dish can be prepared tableside; the part where you flame the sauce is especially dramatic.

2 Tbs. butter
½ cup chopped onion
1½ tsp. chopped garlic
3 oz. smoked salmon, sliced into strips
½ cup 100-proof vodka
½ cup dry white wine
1 cup fish stock
2 cups whipping cream
Salt and white pepper to taste
1 lb. fresh angel hair pasta (cappellini)
2 tsp. black caviar (we use American sturgeon or beluga malossol)

1 In a skillet over medium heat, heat the butter until it bubbles. In it saute the onions and garlic until they turn translucent. Add salmon and saute until the color changes to a pale orange.

2 Pour in the vodka and carefully flame it. When flames die out, remove pan contents and keep warm.

3 Without cleaning the pan, add the wine and fish stock and bring it to a boil. Add the cream and reduce the sauce over medium-low heat by about half. Add salmon mixture and return to a simmer. Taste sauce, then add salt and pepper to taste. (You may not need any more salt. Smoked salmon sometimes carries a lot of it, enough to affect the salt content of the whole dish.

4 Meanwhile, cook the pasta al dente. Remember that angel hair cooks very quickly—a minute or two is enough. Drain the pasta well, but save 1 cup of the water.

5 Put pasta into skillet of sauce with 2 Tbs. of the water pasta was cooked in. Toss briefly over low heat to coat pasta well with sauce.

6 Serve the pasta with lots of sauce and ½ teaspoon caviar.

Serves four entrees or eight appetizers.

Suggested wine: Pinot Grigio

Spaghetti Aglio Olio

Spaghetti with Garlic and Olive Oil

This dish is known around New Orleans as "spaghetti bordelaise," although the people from Bordeaux would probably wonder why it was named after them. One of the simplest of pasta dishes, this is also one of the best. The trick is to keep from overcooking the garlic; the more you cook garlic, the tamer its taste gets.

4 Tbs. extra virgin olive oil
1 Tbs. chopped garlic
1 Tbs. chopped onions
¼ tsp. crushed red pepper
2 Tbs. chopped fresh Italian parsley
¼ tsp. salt
Pinch white pepper
8 oz. spaghetti or linguine, cooked al dente

1 In a skillet, heat the olive oil over medium heat. Saute the onions and garlic until translucent.

2 Add the crushed red pepper, parsley, salt, and pepper. Cook for about a minute more, then add ½ cup of the water in which the pasta was boiled. Whisk the skillet to blend the sauce thoroughly.

3 Lower the heat and add the cooked pasta to the skillet and toss with the sauce until the sauce is well distributed. Serve with grated Parmesan cheese.

Serves four.

Fettuccine Alfredo

Noodles with Cream and Egg

The sauce created at Alfredo's of Rome is so famous that many restaurateurs — most of them in America — have built reputations on their ability to make it. The funny thing to me is that most of them do it wrong, and you wind up tasting little more than cream and cheese. This recipe is, I believe, closer to what Alfredo had in mind.

1 Tbs. butter
¼ cup chopped onion
1½ tsp. chopped garlic
½ cup dry white wine
1 cup whipping cream
1 cup half-and-half
Pinch nutmeg
½ tsp. salt
Pinch white pepper
1 egg yolk
8 oz. fettuccine

1 In a skillet over medium heat, heat the butter until it bubbles. In it saute the onions and garlic until they turn translucent. Add wine and bring to a light boil until reduced by about half. Add whipping cream and half-and-half. Reduce down to about two-thirds original volume.

2 Strain the sauce through a sieve. Return to the skillet over medium heat and simmer. Add nutmeg, salt and pepper. Whisk in the egg yolk thoroughly.

3 Cook the fettuccine al dente. Drain it well, then toss it in the skillet to coat with the sauce.

4 Serve with freshly cracked black pepper and grated Parmesan cheese at the table.

Serves two.

Suggested wine: Frascati Superiore

Fettuccine con Broccoli

Fettuccine with Broccoli

A very simple, colorful, and light dish.

1 large head of broccoli
½ tsp. salt
½ cup extra virgin olive oil
2 Tbs. chopped onion
1 tsp. chopped garlic
½ tsp. crushed red pepper
¼ cup dry white wine
6 oz. (precooked weight) fettuccine, cooked al dente
1 Tbs. extra virgin olive oil

1 Heat one gallon of water with the salt to a boil. While waiting, cut off broccoli stems (you might want to save them for making soup). Cut the florets into pieces about an inch wide.

2 When the water is boiling, cook the broccoli for about five minutes—until tender, but still firm. Reserve a cup of the water. Strain out the broccoli and flood it with cold water to stop the cooking.

3 In a large skillet, heat the olive oil and saute the onions, garlic, and crushed red pepper until blond. Lower the heat and add the reserved broccoli water and the wine. Heat this to a light boil.

4 Add the broccoli and cooked fettuccine to the skillet. Toss ingredients to mix well. Pour the extra virgin olive oil over the top and serve hot.

Serves two entrees or four appetizers.

Suggested wine: Frascati Superiore

Fettuccine Piselli e Prosciutto

Fettuccine with Peas and Prosciutto

The contrasting shapes and colors of peas and fettuccine make this an interesting-looking dish. When made properly (which is not difficult), the sauce will hold the peas to the pasta so that you can eat it without a lot of random rolling around of peas.

2 Tbs. olive oil
1 Tbs. chopped onions
1 tsp. chopped garlic
½ cup dry white wine
3 oz. prosciutto, sliced thin, cut into julienne strips
½ cup green peas
1 cup whipping cream
½ tsp. salt
¼ tsp. white pepper
1 Tbs. butter, softened
1 tsp. chopped Italian parsley
2 Tbs. grated Parmesan cheese

1 Heat the olive oil in a large skillet until very hot. Saute the onions until they brown lightly around the edges. Add the garlic and saute for one minute.

2 Add the prosciutto and peas to the pan and heat through. Add the wine and bring to a bubble.

3 Add the heavy cream and bring to a light boil. Simmer until reduced by about a third — 10 minutes or so.

4 Add the cooked, drained fettuccine to the skillet and toss it with the sauce. Chip in the butter, parsley and Parmesan cheese and mix in.

Serves two.

Suggested wine: Frascati Superiore

Paglia e Fieno

White and Green Pasta with Beef and Sun-Dried Tomatoes

The Italian name means "straw and hay," and the way we prepare it at Andrea's is unique. The flavor is intense; this is a dish which will not only satisfy your appetite, but will also leave no doubt that you have eaten something.

2 Tbs. extra virgin olive oil
2 Tbs. chopped onions
1 Tbs. chopped garlic
½ tsp. crushed red pepper
10 oz. beef tenderloin tips, cubed
8 medium mushrooms, sliced
1 cup dry red wine (preferably something good, like Barolo)
2 cups tomato basil sauce (see **Sauces***)*
6 sun-dried tomatoes, cut into julienne strips
1 Tbs. chopped fresh basil
1 Tbs. chopped fresh oregano
1 cup whipping cream
½ tsp. salt
Pinch white pepper
2 cups each white and spinach fettuccine, cooked al dente

1 In a skillet, heat the olive oil over medium heat. Saute the onions and garlic until blond.

2 Add the crushed red pepper and the tenderloin tips, and saute until the beef is browned lightly on the outside. Remove the beef from the skillet and reserve.

3 Add the mushrooms and the wine to the pan and bring it to a boil. Reduce the volume of liquid by one-third, then lower the flame and add the tomato basil sauce and the sun-dried tomatoes. Simmer the sauce for 10 minutes.

4 Whisk in the whipping cream, basil, oregano, salt and pepper. Return the beef to the pan, raise the heat to medium, and cook for about 10 minutes more.

5 Add the cooked pasta to the pan and toss with the sauce. Serve with a generous amount of sauce plus grated Parmesan cheese.

Serves four.

Suggested wine: Vino Nobile di Montepulciano

Rigatoni ai Quattro Formaggi

Pasta Tubes with Four Cheeses

This has become one of our most popular pasta dishes—a step up in sophistication, perhaps, from fettuccine Alfredo. Rigatoni seems to be the perfect shape for the dish, although it works well with any kind of pasta. The sauce employs four of the best Italian cheeses. Gorgonzola is a blue cheese. Bel Paese and Fontina are both soft, mild cow's milk cheeses. And Grana Padano is one of the greatest of the hard Parmesan cheeses.

1 pint whipping cream
1 pint half-and-half cream
4 oz. Gorgonzola cheese
2 oz. Bel Paese cheese
2 oz. Fontina cheese
½ cup grated Grana Padano
2 cups rigatoni pasta

1 In a large stainless steel or copper skillet, pour in both creams and bring to a light boil. Reduce them by about half; this will take a bit over an hour.

2 Melt Gorgonzola, Bel Paese, and Fontina in a double boiler, or a bowl placed over a saucepan of boiling water. It can also be done very satisfactorily in the microwave oven; use low power and watch it carefully. Stir the melted cheeses into the reduced cream. Add grated Grana Padano and stir in well.

3 Cook pasta al dente. Drain well, then add pasta to the sauce skillet. Toss until all the pasta is coated with sauce. Serve with a lot of sauce and freshly-ground black pepper at the table.

Serves four entrees or eight appetizers.

Suggested wine: Groppello

Tortellini al Formaggio

Pasta Dumplings Stuffed with Cheese

Tortellini are like small ravioli, except that they're round. They lend themselves to simple sauces, and make excellent appetizers.

6 oz. Fontina cheese
3 oz. Gorgonzola
•1/8 tsp. nutmeg
½ cup grated Parmesan cheese
2 Tbs. butter
1 Tbs. fresh sage, chopped

1 Break the Fontina and Gorgonzola into chunks and blend it into a lumpy paste in a blender or food processor. (If the cheese is cold, the blending will go much faster if you heat the cheese in a microwave oven for 15 seconds.) Add the nutmeg and 1 Tbs. of the grated Parmesan and blend well.

2 Roll out pasta (we like to make tortellini with spinach pasta) to the number five setting on your pasta machine, or use fresh pasta sheets.

3 With a round cookie cutter or a jar lid about two inches in diameter, cut out discs of pasta. Brush one side with a little beaten egg yolk. Put a scant ¼ tsp. of the cheese stuffing in the center and fold the pasta disc over.

4 You now have *mezzaluni*—half-moons. Seal the edges with your fingers, pushing the cheese filling into the center. Wrap the half-moons around the tip of your index finger and press the two corners together to make a circle. Fold the curved tops of the half-moons out and over themselves—sort of as if you were folding down the tops of socks. You now have official tortellini.

5 Cook the tortellini al dente in boiling water—about four minutes. Toss the cooked tortellini in a skillet with the sauce of your choice—tomato basil sauce, Alfredo sauce, or sage butter sauce. (See **Sauces**.) Sprinkle grated Parmesan cheese on top at the table.

Serves four entrees or eight appetizers.

Suggested wine: Trebbiano di Romagna

Rigatoni all'Amatriciana

Pasta Tubes with Mushrooms, Tomato, and Bacon

This is a basic, but surprisingly delicious, tomato-and-mushroom sauce ladled over the tube-shaped, ridged pasta called rigatoni. When we tested this recipe, it was the first of many that day; it sat around for about four hours before we warmed it up and ate it. We all agreed that this improved the flavor of the sauce.

2 Tbs. olive oil
3 Tbs. chopped onion
1 Tbs. chopped garlic
4 slices pancetta (or bacon), coarsely chopped
1 cup dry white wine
4 cups canned Italian plum tomatoes, with lots of juice
¼ cup chopped fresh basil
½ tsp. salt
Pinch white pepper
4 cups rigatoni pasta
8 medium fresh mushrooms, sliced
1½ Tbs. butter, softened

1 In a skillet over medium heat, heat the olive oil until very hot. In it saute the onions and garlic until they turn blond. Add chopped pancetta and saute until lightly browned. Add wine and bring to a boil; reduce heat to medium-low and simmer for about ten minutes.

2 Meanwhile, puree tomatoes through a food mill (this will also remove the seeds). Add the tomato puree to the skillet and bring to a boil for about a minute. Add basil and lower heat to medium. Add salt and pepper and simmer, stirring occasionally, for about 20 minutes.

3 Cook pasta al dente. Drain well.

4 Add mushrooms and butter to sauce. Continue to simmer for about two minutes, tossing to coat the mushrooms with the sauce. Toss pasta with sauce in the skillet.

Note The mushrooms and other solid parts of the sauce will remain in skillet as you serve, conveniently allowing you to place this on top of each serving. Serve with grated Parmesan cheese.

Serves four.

Suggested wine: Casteller Rosato

Rigatoni con Melanzane Caruso

Rigatoni with Eggplant Caruso

This dish is at its best when the eggplants are ripe and firm, without any hint of greenness or bitterness. It is delectable prepared as below, but becomes outrageously wonderful (and filling) with shredded mozzarella melted over the pasta in the oven.

1 cup olive oil
4 cloves fresh garlic, peeled and crushed
1 medium eggplant, cut into large chunks
4 cups canned Italian plum tomatoes
1 cup juice from tomatoes
½ cup chopped fresh basil leaves
2 sprigs chopped fresh oregano leaves
1 tsp. salt
¼ tsp. white pepper
3 cups rigatoni, cooked al dente
1 Tbs. extra virgin olive oil

1 Heat olive oil to almost smoking in a saute pan. Saute the garlic cloves until light brown at the edges. Saute the eggplant in two batches until medium-dark brown on the outside—about five minutes over medium heat. Remove and drain on paper towels.

2 To the olive oil remaining in the pan, add the tomatoes and juice. Bring to a boil, then add basil and oregano. Reduce heat and simmer the sauce until it's reduced by half—about five minutes.

3 Stir the eggplant into the sauce, then remove from heat.

4 After cooking the rigatoni al dente and draining it, pour 1 Tbs. extra virgin olive oil over it and toss to distribute the oil. Pour about half the sauce over the pasta in the pot, toss together, then serve in bowls. Top with the rest of the sauce and grated Parmesan cheese.

Serves four.

Suggested wine: Gattinara

Penne alla Toscanini

Pasta Tubes with Italian Sausage and Tomato Sauce

This is named for the famous conductor Arturo Toscanini, who I hope liked Italian sausage.

2 cups chopped Italian sausage
2 tsp. olive oil
1 Tbs. chopped onions
1 tsp. chopped garlic
2 tsp. tomato paste
⅓ cup dry red wine
1½ cups canned Italian plum tomatoes, chopped
1½ cups juice from tomatoes
¼ cup ricotta
2 Tbs. grated Parmesan cheese
8 leaves fresh basil, chopped
1 tsp. salt
¼ tsp. black pepper
2 cups penne pasta, cooked al dente
2 tsp. chopped Italian parsley

1 In a skillet, heat the olive oil over high heat and saute the sausage.

2 When the sausage is lightly browned, lower the heat to medium and stir in onions and garlic and saute until blond.

3 Add the tomato paste and red wine. Cook for three minutes, until nearly dry, then add the tomatoes and juice. Reduce sauce by about one-third. Add salt and pepper to taste.

4 Pour half the sauce into a large skillet with the cooked pasta. Stir in ricotta, Parmesan, and basil and heat through. Serve the pasta with the remaining sauce, chopped Italian parsley, and more grated Parmesan cheese.

Serves two.

Suggested wine: Pinot Nero del Trentino

Linguine Bolognese

Linguine with Meat Sauce

The great meat sauces of Italy are made in the area of Bologna, where every family says that its meat sauce is the best. An authentic Bolognese meat sauce is so different from the standard American meat sauce for spaghetti that I hesitate to even mention them in the same sentence. Here is what the spaghetti with meat sauce you've been subjecting yourself to all your life in cafeterias was really trying to be.

1 lb., 6 oz. beef tenderloin tips and scraps (or inside or bottom round), trimmed of fat
⅓ cup extra virgin olive oil
1 rib celery, chopped
½ medium onion, chopped
1 medium carrot, chopped
½ Tbs. chopped garlic
¼ tsp. chopped fresh rosemary
1 Tbs. tomato paste
1 cup dry red wine
1 Tbs. all-purpose flour
1 quart beef stock
3 bay leaves
½ Tbs. salt
⅓ tsp. white pepper
4 canned Italian plum tomatoes, chopped, with plenty of juice
½ tsp. fresh sage, chopped
1 lb. linguine, fettuccine, mostaccioli, or other pasta

1 Chop the beef into small morsels; you may also use a meat grinder, but keep the meat coarse.

2 Heat the olive oil in a saute pan. Saute the the ground beef, stirring constantly, until uniformly browned.

3 Stir in the chopped vegetables and continue cooking until vegetables are tender and mixture is dry. Stir occasionally.

4 Stir in the chopped garlic, rosemary, and the tomato paste. Cook for a minute or two, then pour in the red wine and bring to a boil. Sprinkle in the flour and stir well. Add the beef stock, bay leaves, and peppered salt and bring to a boil.

5 Stir in the tomatoes and juice and return to a boil. Lower the heat to a simmer. Add the sage, and simmer the pot for an hour and 15 minutes.

6 Cook the pasta al dente and drain. Put the pasta into bowls and serve the sauce on top. Sprinkle grated Parmesan cheese over all.
Serves eight.

Suggested wine: Dolcetto D'Alba

86

Rigatoni o Spaghetti Carbonara

Spaghetti with Bacon, Eggs, and Cream

The dish was created—or so it is said—by the charcoal-makers and coal miners of the Alpine provinces of Northern Italy. The heat of the pasta cooks the eggs in the sauce, so make sure the pasta is good and hot.

½ cup extra virgin olive oil
4 slices pancetta, chopped
2 slices prosciutto, chopped
⅓ cup chopped onions
2 leaves fresh sage, chopped
½ tsp. fresh rosemary leaves
¼ tsp. dried marjoram
Pinch nutmeg
¼ tsp. black pepper
½ cup dry white wine
2 eggs
1 cup whipping cream
½ cup grated Parmesan cheese
1 lb. spaghetti or rigatoni, cooked al dente

1 In a skillet, saute pancetta, prosciutto, and onions in hot olive oil until onions turn blond. Add sage, rosemary, marjoram, nutmeg and pepper. Add wine and bring to a light simmer. Remove from heat.

2 In a mixing bowl with a wire whisk, beat eggs well. Whisk cream and grated cheese into the eggs until the mixture is smooth.

3 Add hot pasta to skillet, and stir in to distribute solid parts of sauce well. Pour mixture of eggs, cheese, and cream on top and stir in to blend sauce with pasta.

Serves four.

Suggested wine: Frascati Superiore

Gnocchi Regina

Potato Pasta Dumplings

Gnocchi (pronounced "nyoke-ee") are small pasta-like dumplings, usually made from potatoes. It is important that the potatoes be Idahoes, since they are exceptionally low in moisture and starchy. If you have to substitute, make sure the potatoes are firm but have absolutely no green tint inside.

This is one of my mother's favorite dishes, so I named it after her.

3 lbs. white Idaho potatoes
¼ cup butter
2 egg yolks
13 oz. all-purpose flour
¼ tsp. nutmeg

1 Scrub potatoes in cold water. Boil for between an hour and an hour and a half, depending on the size of the potatoes. Here's how to tell when the potatoes are cooked: Push the blade of a knife through the center of the potato while it's still in the pot. Pull the knife up. If the knife slides out, the potato is done. If it picks the potato up out of the water, it's not done.

2 When cooked, remove potatoes from the water. While still hot, peel and slice the potatoes, and run them through a food mill to mash smooth, with no lumps. (I find that this cannot be done properly in a food processor or blender. In the restaurant, we usually put the potatoes through a meat grinder with a "ricer" attachment.)

3 Melt the butter in a deep skillet or saucepan over low heat. Add the mashed potatoes and stir vigorously to mix. This will create a very stiff mixture, almost like bread dough. Stir egg yolks, one at a time, into the potato mixture. Do this quickly, before yolks have a chance to cook from the heat of the potatoes, and keep stirring. When eggs are incorporated completely into potatoes, remove from stove.

4 Scoop the potato "dough" on top of a clean, smooth surface dusted with flour. Add flour, about a half-cup at a time, and knead it into the potatoes, using hands and a plastic scraper. Sprinkle a little extra flour over the potato-dough and counter if necessary to prevent sticking.

5 Cut off about one-fifth of the dough ball, and roll it out to a long, thin (about a half-inch in diameter) "snake." With a flour-dusted knife, cut off pieces of the "snake" about a half-inch long.

6 With your thumb, roll each piece of dough along the tines of a table fork. As you do this, press down a little so the dough curls in on itself a little. This will result in a nugget with a large indentation on one side and ridges across the other—the classic gnocchi shape. This is very time-consuming, but it's a therapeutic, calming activity for one, or a nice conversational backdrop for two. Put the gnocchi on a floured pan in one well-spaced layer.

7 This recipe makes about 300 gnocchi—enough for six large entrees or 12 appetizers. But you can preserve a portion for later use. Allow the gnocchi to dry for about two hours on the pan, then put them into plastic bags and freeze. When you're ready to use the frozen gnocchi, put them right into the boiling water—do not defrost first.

8 Cook the gnocchi exactly as you would pasta. Boil them for about four minutes (longer, of course, if frozen). Drain them and toss them in a skillet with tomato sauce, pesto sauce, or (my own favorite) sage butter sauce (see **Sauces**).

Suggested wine: Capri Bianco

Gnocchi alla Romana

Semolina Dumplings with Two Cheeses

Not all gnocchi is made with potatoes. This version is made with the same semolina flour used to make pasta. These gnocchi are made into large dumplings.

2 cups milk
1 cup semolina flour
½ tsp. salt
1 Tbs. extra virgin olive oil
¼ tsp. white pepper
Pinch nutmeg
½ cup crumbled Gorgonzola cheese
½ cup grated Parmesan cheese

Preheat oven to 450 degrees.

1 In a saucepan, bring the milk and 2 cups of water to a boil. Stir in the olive oil, salt and pepper.

2 Sprinkle the semolina into the saucepan while stirring constantly with a wooden spoon. When all the semolina is in the saucepan, add the nutmeg and lower the heat to medium low.

3 Continue stirring the mixture for 15 to 20 minutes, until the mixture is formed into a uniform dough and breaks away from the side of the saucepan.

4 On a clean countertop spread with wax paper, spread the gnocchi dough down in an even layer about ¼ inch thick. Allow the dough to cool to room temperature.

5 Cut out two-inch rounds of the dough with a cookie cutter. Coat sheet pans lightly with olive oil. Place all the gnocchi—including the odd pieces between the round ones you cut out—onto the pans.

6 Crumble the Gorgonzola cheese over the gnocchi and top with grated Parmesan. Put the gnocchi into a preheated 450-degree oven and bake for 20-30 minutes, until the cheese is incorporated into the gnocchi.

7 Serve the round pieces on top of the odd-shaped pieces of gnocchi. This is delicious as is; it can also be served with a small amount of tomato basil sauce.
Serves six.

Suggested wine: Capri Rosso

Spaetzle

Austro-Italian Noodle Dumplings

As you move from Northern Italy into Austria and then Germany, you find that the people still eat a lot of pasta—but the form of the pasta changes. The typical pasta of Austria is spaetzle (pronounced "shpeht-zleh"). They are short, lumpy strings of pasta dough which are typically served without any more of a sauce than perhaps butter. Everyone, however, pushes them over into whatever sauce may be with the other foods on the plate.

I like spaetzle with any kind of game dish. The trick to making these delightful little pasta dumplings irresistable is to cook them until they brown a little in the last step.

Although some cooks make spaetzle with just a knife and a cutting board, I use a special gadget made specifically for this purpose. It looks like a cheese grater with a cup on rails attached to it. It is not expensive, and can be bought at a good gourmet shop. (Ask for a spaetzle maker.)

1 lb. flour
4 eggs
¼ tsp. nutmeg
¼ tsp. salt
½ cup milk
¼ cup vegetable oil
2 Tbs. butter
Salt

1 Put the flour into a mixer bowl. With your hand, make a well in the center of the flour and add the eggs, nutmeg, salt, ½ cup water and milk. Mix batter on medium speed until thoroughly blended, at which time batter will pull away from bowl. Add a little more water if necessary.

2 Boil two quarts of water. Add the vegetable oil and ½ tsp. salt. Set the spaetzle-maker on top of the pot, and pour the batter into its cup. Slide the cup back and forth over the grater to produce the characteristic irregularly-shaped noodles, which will fall into the boiling water and float on top. Boil the noodles for about two minutes. You are not fully cooking them at this point, just setting their shape.

3 With a skimmer, remove the spaetzle from the boiling water and douse them in a bowl of ice water. After noodles are completely cooled, drain them well.

4 In a skillet, heat the butter and add the spaetzle. Toss spaetzle occasionally and cook until most of it is lightly browned.
Serves 12.

Suggested wine: Traminer

Ravioli

Ravioli are pasta pillows stuffed with anything you want. At Andrea's, the most popular version is Ravioli Roberto — a cheese-stuffed ravioli. We also regularly make a spinach ravioli, and, when we can get them, a porcini mushroom ravioli. All of these are made from fresh pasta, using the same technique.

There is a special ravioli mold or form that makes ravioli-making easy. You can buy it at any good gourmet shop. It consists of a small metal rack with holes, and a plastic mold to push the pasta down through the holes to make space for the stuffing.

Here are the steps in making ravioli from scratch:

1 Use the basic pasta recipe at the beginning of this chapter to make pasta sheets about twice as long as your ravioli form.

2 Place one side of the pasta sheet over the form. Use the plastic mold to make depressions in the pasta sheet.

3 Brush the pasta on the form with beaten egg.

4 Spoon in about a teaspoon of the ravioli stuffing of your choice.

5 Fold the other half of the pasta sheet on top of the stuffing. With a rolling pin, run over the top of the pasta hard to seal and then cut out the individual ravioli. Finish the job with a knife.

6 Check each raviola to make sure the stuffing is sealed in all the way around.

7 Cook the ravioli the same way you'd cook any other pasta — in a pot of boiling water with a little oil and salt. Cook a few at a time to keep them from sticking together or damaging one another. It generally takes about four to six minutes of cooking in boiling water to cook ravioli al dente.

The quantities given in the basic pasta recipe are enough to make 60 to 75 ravioli.

Ravioli ai Funghi Porcini

Pasta Stuffed with Porcini Mushrooms

Porcini are meaty, naturally smoky mushrooms highly prized by both chefs and eaters throughout Italy. Porcini are similar to the French cepes mushrooms (in fact, some authorities say they're the same thing). They're big mushrooms—you can slice and grill them, almost like small steaks. Porcini are in season in late spring and early summer; they can be found in the better supermarket produce sections and gourmet markets.

A few years ago I made up a batch of homemade ravioli stuffed with fresh porcini for Sidney Lassen, one of our best customers and a good friend. Mr. Lassen's reaction was so strongly favorable that I decided to make the dish a regular feature at Andrea's during porcini season.

3 oz. porcini mushrooms
4 oz. fresh spinach, well washed and coarse stems removed
1 dried shallot, medium size
½ tsp. chopped garlic
1 oz. butter
1 Tbs. Cognac
3 slices sun-dried tomato
3 leaves fresh sage, chopped
½ tsp. crushed red pepper
1 tsp. chopped Italian parsley
Salt and pepper to taste
1 egg yolk
Pinch nutmeg
1 Tbs. grated Parmesan cheese

Sauce:
2 oz. butter
1 Tbs. dry chopped shallots
1 tsp. chopped garlic
3 oz. porcini mushrooms
2 oz. Cognac
1 qt. whipping cream
½ cup demi-glace
1 tsp. fresh rosemary leaves
Salt and pepper
1 egg yolk
1 Tbs. milk

1 Wash porcini well, and slice thin. Blanch spinach in boiling water for about 15 seconds. Immerse immediately in cold water to cool, then drain and chop.

2 In a skillet, saute shallots in butter over medium heat until blond. Add garlic and porcini and saute until mushrooms are heated through.

3 Carefully pour on Cognac and flame. When flames die out, add sun-dried tomatoes, spinach, sage, crushed red pepper, parsley, salt and pepper. Mix well. Set aside and let cool.

4 When the stuffing is lukewarm, add egg yolk, nutmeg and Parmesan cheese. Mix well. Chop very fine, and stuff inside pasta sheets (see instructions for **Cheese Ravioli**).

5 Begin the sauce. In a skillet over medium heat, heat the butter until it bubbles. Saute the shallots and garlic until they turn blond. Add mushrooms and saute until limp. Add Cognac and let alcohol evaporate.

6 Add whipping cream and demi-glace; bring to a boil. Add rosemary and a pinch of salt and pepper. Reduce over low heat to half the original amount.

7 Cook ravioli in boiling water just before serving, and nap with warm sauce. Garnish with fresh rosemary.

Makes four appetizers.

Suggested wine: Arneis

Ravioli al Formaggio Roberto

Cheese Ravioli Roberto

This is a blend of several cheeses and herbs. It is delicious not only in ravioli but in a few other dishes. In fact, other recipes in this book will refer back to this formula. This is the favorite dish of my partner and cousin, Roberto De Angelis.

2 cups grated mozzarella
1 cup ricotta
½ cup grated Parmesan cheese
2 Tbs. chopped fresh basil
1 tsp. chopped fresh sage
1 Tbs. chopped fresh oregano
1 Tbs. chopped Italian parsley
¼ tsp. nutmeg
1 egg yolk
Pasta dough from basic ravioli recipe, above
Tomato basil sauce (see **Sauces***)*

Combine all stuffing ingredients in a food processor. Process into a puree. With a pastry bag, pipe about 1 tsp. of stuffing into ravioli. Cook as above and serve with tomato-basil sauce and extra grated Parmesan cheese.

Makes more than enough stuffing for 60 ravioli.

Suggested wine: Capri Bianco

Ravioli con Langoustine Andrea

Crawfish Ravioli Andrea

Crawfish are in season from around Thanksgiving till early summer in the New Orleans area, and we use them in every dish we can while they're around. This dish has been a big hit, particularly at banquets and receptions. It is a lengthy process but it brings forth every last echo of flavor from the crawfish.

2 lbs. fresh crawfish (whole)
1 lb. crawfish tail meat
½ cup olive oil
½ carrot, cut up
1 rib celery, cut up
1 medium onion, cut up
¼ tsp, crushed red pepper
½ cup brandy
1½ tsp. chopped garlic
2 Tbs. tomato paste
1 cup dry white wine
⅓ cup all-purpose flour
½ gallon fish stock

Sacchetto: Put these seasonings into a cheesecloth bag:
1 Tbs. black peppercorns
2 sprigs fresh thyme
4 leaves fresh basil
4 sprigs fresh dill
3 parsley stems
2 bay leaves

2 cups heavy cream

Stuffing:
¼ cup olive oil
½ Tbs. chopped garlic
½ green bell pepper, chopped
½ red bell pepper, chopped
½ yellow bell pepper, chopped
1 rib celery, chopped
⅓ cup chopped onion
¼ cup brandy
Pinch cayenne
1 tsp. paprika
1 tsp. Worcestershire
5 basil leaves, chopped
1 sprig thyme leaves, chopped

94

5 sprigs chopped Italian parsley
5 sprigs dill, large stems removed
2 tsp. salt
½ tsp. white pepper
¼ cup bread crumbs
2 egg yolks

1 Boil the crawfish with crab boil, following the instructions on the side of the box or bottle. After they have cooled enough to handle, peel the crawfish; separate tail meat and shells, but keep it all.

2 In a large saucepan, heat the olive oil over high heat. Saute carrots, celery and onions until onions are lightly browned at the edges. Add crushed red pepper and crawfish shells. Cook, stirring every 30 seconds or so, for 4-5 minutes.

3 Add brandy and carefully flame it. Blend in tomato paste and garlic. Add white wine and let the liquid in the saucepan reduce by half.

4 Add the flour and blend in well. Add fish stock plus one quart of water. Mix everything with a wire whisk, scraping the bottom of the saucepan. Return to a boil and add the sachetto. Lower the heat to medium-low. Simmer for two and a half hours, until reduced by about two-thirds.

5 Remove the sacchetto. Strain the solid parts out of the stock. Put all of this — shells and everything — into a food processor and chop it very fine. Return this mixture to the stock, stir well, and strain through a fine sieve.

6 Heat the cream in a saucepan and reduce to half its original volume. Pour the strained crawfish stock into the saucepan and whisk to blend. This is your completed sauce; keep it warm.

7 Begin the stuffing by heating the olive oil in a large skillet. Saute bell peppers, celery, onions and garlic until lightly browned. Add the crawfish tails you peeled earlier and cook over high heat for five minutes, until crawfish are heated through.

8 Add brandy and flame it. Reduce the heat to low and stir in white wine, cayenne, paprika, Worcestershire, salt and pepper. Cook until all liquid has been absorbed or evaporated.

9 Remove contents of skillet to a cool pan (it won't have to go back on the stove.) Stir in the basil, sage, thyme, dill and parsley, and allow mixture to cool.

10 When cool, add the bread crumbs, eggs, and Parmesan cheese to the crawfish mixture. Load everything into a food processor. Process into a rough mixture — you want to have some fairly good-sized pieces of crawfish in there.

11 Spoon one generous teaspoon of the stuffing into each raviola, then cook them, following the technique as for cheese ravioli.

12 Drain the ravioli well and put 16 of them into a skillet over medium heat. Ladle one cup of the sauce over it. Bring the sauce to a light boil. Immediately remove from heat and serve. Repeat until all ravioli are sauced.

Makes 60 ravioli—about eight entrees or 16 appetizers.

Suggested wine: Sauvignon, Emiliana Romagna region

Ravioli con Grancevole Veneziana

Crabmeat Ravioli

In contrast with the robust, spicy flavors of the crawfish ravioli, our crabmeat ravioli is mild and understated. But it gets at least as many rave reviews.

1 Tbs. butter
1 Tbs. extra virgin olive oil
3 Tbs. chopped onions
1 Tbs. chopped garlic
1 lb. lump crabmeat
2 leaves fresh sage, chopped
½ tsp. dried marjoram
3 sprigs Italian parsley, chopped
1 tsp. salt
¼ tsp. white pepper
Pinch cayenne
Pinch nutmeg
2 Tbs. brandy
¼ cup dry white wine
1 tsp. Worcestershire
¼ cup bread crumbs
¼ cup Parmesan cheese
2 egg yolks

Sauce:
2 tsp. chopped garlic
2 Tbs butter
¼ cup dry white wine
1 quart whipping cream
1 quart fish stock
¼ cup Parmesan cheese
1 tsp. salt
¼ tsp. white pepper

1 Heat the butter and olive oil in a skillet over medium heat and saute the onions and garlic until translucent. Add the crabmeat and heat through—about one minute. Add the sage, parsley, marjoram, salt, pepper, cayenne and nutmeg.

2 Add the brandy and flame it carefully. Add the white wine and Worcestershire and bring to a boil. When all liquid is absorbed or evaporated, remove contents of skillet to a cool pan.

3 While waiting for the crabmeat stuffing to cool, make the sauce. Melt butter in a saucepan and saute garlic for about a minute. Add white wine and cream to skillet and bring cream to a boil. After two minutes, add the fish stock and return to a boil. Reduce by half, then whisk in Parmesan cheese, salt and pepper.

4 When the crabmeat mixture is cool, add the bread crumbs, eggs, and Parmesan cheese. Process the mixture in a food processor into a rough mixture — with some noticeable pieces of crabmeat remaining.

5 Stuff the ravioli with a generous teaspoon of crabmeat stuffing, and then cook as for instructions for cheese ravioli.

6 Drain the ravioli well and put 16 of them into a skillet over medium heat. Ladle one cup of the sauce over it. Bring the sauce to a light boil. Immediately remove from heat and serve. Repeat until all ravioli are sauced.

Makes 60 ravioli—about eight entrees or 16 appetizers.

Suggested wine: Chardonnay, Friuli region

Cannelloni Andrea

Pasta Tubes with Meat Stuffing

Cannelloni are big tubes of pasta rolled around a great variety of stuffings. It is one of the most popular dishes in the Italian restaurants of America, serving as appetizer, pasta course, or entree. We make cannelloni two different ways at Andrea's. Both start with thin sheets of freshly-made pasta. This first one is stuffed with a blend of meat, cheese, and herbs, served with tomato basil sauce.

2 Tbs. olive oil
3 oz. ground lean beef
3 oz. ground baby white veal
2 Tbs. chopped onion
1 tsp. chopped garlic
1 Tbs. chopped carrot
1 Tbs. chopped celery
1 Tbs. tomato paste
¼ cup dry red wine
12 sheets fresh pasta, 4 inches square
2 oz. mozzarella cheese
1 oz. ricotta cheese
1 oz. Parmesan cheese
1 egg
Pinch nutmeg
Pinch chopped rosemary
Pinch sage
Pinch salt
Pinch white pepper
12 oz. tomato basil sauce, strained (see **Sauces***)*

Preheat the oven to 350 degrees.

1 Heat the olive oil in a skillet and in it cook the ground meat, stirring well until it is lightly browned throughout.

2 Add the onions, garlic, carrots and celery and cook over medium-low heat until the vegetables are moist.

3 Stir in the tomato paste and the wine. Bring the mixture to a boil and reduce the liquid by about half. Remove the skillet from the heat and allow the mixture to cool.

4 Meanwhile, cook the pasta al dente. Drain the sheets well and spread them out on a sheet of waxed paper.

5 When the stuffing is lukewarm, stir in the cheeses and herbs. Then stir in the egg. The best way to do this is with your fingers. Don't use a food processor, as it will pulverize the meat too much.

6 When the mixture is uniform in texture, put it into a pastry bag with a broad tip and pipe about two ounces along one short edge of the pasta sheets. Roll up the sheets carefully to form tubes. Place the tubes, close but not touching, into a baking pan coated lightly with olive oil. Put two Tbs. of water into the pan.

7 Cover the pan with aluminum foil and bake in a preheated 350-degree oven for 15 minutes.

8 Allow the cannelloni to cool for five minutes. Remove with a spatula and serve two per person. Nap with 4 oz. tomato basil sauce, parsley and grated Parmesan cheese.

Serves six.

Suggested wine: Greco di Tufo

Cannelloni ai Frutti di Mare

Seafood Cannelloni

This may be the best new dish we created for this cookbook. The Louisiana seafoods lend themselves very well to being stuffed inside big tubes of pasta, and the rich sauce with crabmeat finishes it elegantly. This dish takes a little work, but it's worth it. One simple white sauce—a bechamel—is the starting point for both the filling and the sauce on top. The seafood gets a little poaching and then is mixed with the white sauce to make the stuffing—without using any bread crumbs.

¼ cup extra virgin olive oil
¼ cup chopped onion
1 carrot, slivered
1 rib chopped celery
1 tsp. chopped garlic
6 oz. large shrimp (about 12), peeled and deveined
12 oz. of fillets of any firm, light-meat fish, cut into chunks
1½ cups oysters (12-24, depending on size)
2 sprigs fresh oregano leaves
2 sprigs fresh thyme leaves
1 green onion, chopped
½ tsp. dried marjoram
1 Tbs. chopped Italian parsley

Cream sauce:
1 Tbs. butter
¼ cup all-purpose flour
1 cup milk
¼ cup dry vermouth
1 cup dry white wine
1 cup fish stock
1 cup whipping cream
½ tsp. Worcestershire
½ tsp. salt
Pinch white pepper
4 drops Tabasco

Seafood sauce:
¼ tsp. salt
Pinch white pepper
½ tsp. Worcestershire
1 cup jumbo lump crabmeat
1 egg yolk

12-15 pasta sheets, about 4 inches by 6 inches, cooked until flexible

1 Heat the olive oil in a large saute pan over medium heat. Saute the onions, carrots, and celery until the onions turn blond. Add the garlic and saute for a few seconds, then add all the the seafoods. Simmer over low heat. The seafoods will throw off a good deal of liquid. Add the thyme, oregano, green onions, marjoram and parsley. Watch the oysters; when they start visibly shrinking, take the skillet off the heat.

2 Meanwhile, in a separate skillet, melt the butter and add the flour. Whisk together over medium heat to make a blond roux. Whisk in the milk and stir until thickened—about two minutes—to get a bechamel sauce.

3 Put ¼ cup of the bechamel into a small saucepan with the vermouth and wine. Add the fish stock and the whipping cream, and bring to a simmer. Add ½ tsp. Worcestershire and ½ tsp. peppered salt, along with Tabasco.

4 Begin the seafood sauce by blending the liquid from the stuffing skillet into the remainder of the bechamel sauce. Add salt, pepper, and Worcestershire, and reduce over a low fire.

5 Chop the seafoods coarsely, and add half the crabmeat. Blend seafoods into the seafood sauce. Adjust seasonings with salt and pepper. Stir in the egg yolk.

6 Put the reserved half of the crabmeat into the cream sauce. Simmer without stirring until the sauce is reduced by two-thirds. (That will take long enough that you can finish the rest of the steps.)

7 With a pastry bag with a broad tip, extrude about two Tbs. of the seafood mixture along one short edge of the pasta sheets. Roll up the sheets carefully.

(**Note:** We do not extend the stuffing with bread crumbs at Andrea's. But you may find it easier to stuff it into the pasta if you add up to a cup of plain bread crumbs.)

8 Place the cannelloni into a 12-by-9-by-2 inch baking pan. Pour ½ cup of water over it. Put the pan into a 450-degree preheated oven for 10 minutes.

9 Place two cannelloni on each plate and spoon ¼ cup of the crabmeat cream sauce over them.

Serves six.

Suggested wine: Gavi

Lasagna "Nello"

Lasagna with Meat and Cheese

Lasagna, easily one of the most popular pasta dishes in the United States, is not just one dish. The name "lasagna" refers, in fact, not to a specific dish, but to the broad sheets of pasta used to make it and the layering process for which the dish is celebrated.

At Andrea's, we build our lasagna with either regular or spinach pasta sheets that we make ourselves. The basic pasta recipe at the beginning of this chapter makes the perfect amount and kind of pasta for this recipe. We bake lasagna in pans 18 by 12 inches. If you don't have a pan this big, or would prefer to use two smaller pans, or want to prepare the recipe for six instead of 12, divide all the ingredients in half. But don't try to break down the recipe any further than that, because some ingredients will go out of balance.

Meat stuffing:
1 lb. ground inside round or chuck
1½ Tbs. chopped garlic
¼ cup chopped onions
1 Tbs. chopped fresh oregano
2 Tbs. chopped Italian parsley
1 Tbs. chopped fresh basil
1 tsp. salt
¼ tsp. white pepper
¼ cup grated Parmesan cheese
¼ cup bread crumbs

8 sheets pasta dough, 6 inches by 18 inches
1 Tbs. olive oil
2 quarts tomato basil sauce (see **Sauces***)*
1 lb. spinach, well washed and coarse stems removed
7 cups shredded mozzarella
3 cups ricotta cheese
3 cups grated Parmesan cheese

Preheat oven to 400 degrees.
1 Combine ground meat, garlic, onions, oregano, parsley, basil, peppered salt, Parmesan cheese and bread crumbs in a mixer or food processor. Scoop out irregular one-teaspoon meatballs and place them, well apart from one another, on a baking sheet. Bake the meatballs for five minutes at 400 degrees. Remove and reserve.
2 Cook the pasta sheets, four at a time, in two gallons of boiling water with 1 Tbs. salt and 1 Tbs. oil until al dente—about four minutes. Take the pasta out and wash it with cold water. Set aside to drain.
3 Poach spinach for two minutes in boiling water, then chop very fine in a food processor.

4 Coat the bottom of the baking pan (or pans) with the olive oil, then cover it with a layer of pasta—two sheets lengthwise across the pan. Pour two cups of tomato basil sauce over the pasta and spread it out.

5 Intersperse about a third of the meatballs, a cup of ricotta, two cups of mozzarella, and ¼ cup of the chopped spinach for the next layer.

6 Lay down, at right angles to the sheets of pasta in the first layer, another layer of pasta. Top this with another layer of sauce, meatballs, cheeses and spinach, as before.

7 Repeat step 6. Then another layer of pasta, topped with 2 cups of sauce and the remaining mozzarella and Parmesan cheeses.

8 Place the entire pan inside another pan of the same size filled about one-third full with water. Put the entire double pan inside a preheated 450-degree oven and bake for 30 minutes. Lower the heat to 350 degrees and continue baking for another ten minutes.

9 After taking it out the oven, allow the lasagna to cool for 15 minutes before attempting to serve it. Slice it into eight to twelve pieces, and serve with 4 oz. of tomato basil sauce.

Serves eight to twelve.

Lasagna di Legume all'Ortolano

Vegetable Lasagna

This is a completely meatless lasagna designed not only for our vegetarian guests, but also those who want to eat something that tastes good.

2 lbs. fresh spinach, well washed and coarse stems removed
¼ cup olive oil
1 lb. zucchini
1 medium eggplant
24 medium mushrooms
3 medium carrots
1 lb. green beans
1 lb. fresh asparagus
1 leek, well washed
1 Tbs. olive oil
1 medium onion, sliced
2 red bell peppers
2 green bell peppers
8 sheets pasta dough, 6 inches by 18 inches
1½ quarts Italian plum tomato basil sauce
1 cup sun-dried tomatoes, julienne sliced
1 cup grated fresh Parmesan cheese

1 Wash all the vegetables well. You will need to cook most of them, and each

102

one needs to be cooked a different way. Here goes:

2 Spinach: poach for two minutes in boiling water, trying all the while not to break the leaves. When cooked, plunge it into cold water to stop the cooking.

3 Zucchini, eggplant, and mushrooms: Slice lengthwise to the thickness of two stacked quarters. Heat the olive oil in a skillet and saute for two minutes on each side. Drain and keep warm.

4 Carrots and green beans: Slice carrots diagonally to the thickness of two quarters. Poach in boiling water for five minutes, then wash with cold water.

5 Asparagus: Peel woody skin and poach for six minutes, until slightly soft but still firm. Chop into ¼-inch segments.

6 Leek: Slice in half from top to bottom. Discard the outer tough leaves and poach the inner sections two minutes. Slice about two inches long.

7 Onion: Slice about two quarters' thickness and saute in 1 Tbs. olive oil until light brown.

8 Bell peppers: Roast over open fire or under broiler until skin is blackened and blistered all over. Peel skin off. Remove stem, seeds, and membranes. Slice about a half inch wide, two inches long.

Preheat the oven to 450 degrees.

9 Cook the pasta sheets as for the basic lasagna. Wash with cold water and drain.

10 In a pan 18 by 12 inches (or two 9 by 12 inches), spread 1 Tbs. of olive oil and cover the bottom with slightly overlapping sheets of pasta. Pour on two cups of the basil tomato sauce.

11 Then stack up the layers, as follows: Eggplant. Red bell pepper. Pasta (arranging the sheets at right angles to the first pasta layer). Two cups tomato basil sauce. Spinach (lay leaves flat). Carrots. Zucchini. Pasta (at right angles to the previous layer). Sun-dried tomatoes. Mushrooms. Leeks. Two cups tomato basil sauce. One cup grated Parmesan cheese. Pasta. Asparagus. Green bell pepper. Green beans. Two cups tomato basil sauce. One cup Parmesan cheese.

12 Put the lasagna pan inside a bigger pan with enough water to come halfway up the sides of the lasagna pan. Bake at 450 degrees for 45 minutes.

13 Take the lasagna out and allow to cool on the top of the stove for 15-30 minutes. Make two slices the long way and three to five slices across. Serve with about 4 oz. tomato basil sauce.

Serves eight to 12.

Suggested wine: Sangiovese

Lasagna ai Frutti di Mare "Battistella"

Seafood Lasagna

We were so pleased by the results of our experiments with seafood cannelloni that I thought I'd try to make a seafood lasagna. This has a major contradiction: you can hardly make lasagna without cheese, yet no self-respecting Italian chef would ever put cheese and seafood together. We'll let you make up your mind about that and print the recipe by the rules.

The dish is named after Preston Battistella, one of the South's leading purveyors of fresh seafood. He helped us immeasurably when we opened Andrea's, and his gourmet credentials are unimpeachable.

1 cup dry white wine
2 sprigs Italian parsley
2 bay leaves
6 black peppercorns
½ carrot, sliced
½ onion, cut up
1 Tbs. salt
2 lbs. fillets of trout, salmon, and red snapper
1 lb. shrimp, peeled and deveined, 21-25 count per pound
1 quart fresh oysters
10 oz. fresh scallops

Sauce:
½ cup olive oil
1 cup chopped onions
⅓ cup chopped garlic
½ cup dry white wine
½ cup flour
1 gallon fish stock
1 cup loosely-packed fresh chopped dill
1 Tbs. chopped fresh rosemary leaves
2 Tbs. chopped fresh sage
1 quart half-and-half cream
1 qt. whipping cream
¼ tsp. Worcestershire
2 dashes Tabasco

8 sheets pasta dough, 6 inches by 18 inches
1 Tbs. olive oil
1 cup sun-dried tomatoes, julienne sliced
12 large fresh mushrooms
¼ cup extra virgin olive oil

1 Bring one gallon of water with the white wine added to a boil in a large saucepan. Add the parsley, bay leaves, peppercorns, carrot, onion, and salt. Let the pot boil for 15 minutes.

2 Poach each seafood separately. Place the seafood in a large sieve and lower it into the water. When the water returns to a vigourous boil, take the seafood out and set it aside. Continue to do this until all seafood has been poached.

3 Break the trout, salmon, and snapper into small pieces. Slice the scallops in half or fourths, depending on the size. Cut the shrimp into fourths. Do not chop the oysters. Strain the boiling liquid (which now qualifies as a fish stock) and set aside.

4 In a large saucepan, heat the olive oil and saute the onions and garlic until lightly browned. Add the wine and bring to a boil. Stir in flour well.

5 Add the fish stock to the saucepan and bring to a boil. Let this simmer over medium-low heat for 45 minutes, until it thickens somewhat.

6 Strain the sauce through a fine sieve into another saucepan. Reserve one quart of this sauce. Put the seafoods into the saucepan along with the dill, rosemary, and sage, and bring it to a boil. Remove the saucepan from the heat and set aside.

7 Put the reserved quart of fish stock into another saucepan and add the half-and-half and the whipping cream. Bring this to a boil and then lower to a simmer. Let this simmer for 30 minutes, until thickened. Season with Worcestershire, Tabasco, and salt and pepper to taste. That's the sauce.

Preheat the oven to 450 degrees.

8 Cook the pasta sheets in two gallons of boiling water with 1 Tbs. salt and 1 Tbs. oil until al dente—about four minutes. Take the pasta out and wash it with cold water. Set aside to drain.

9 Slice the mushrooms and saute them for two minutes in a skillet with the extra virgin olive oil and set aside.

10 Coat the bottom of the pan with the olive oil, then cover it with a layer of pasta—two sheets lengthwise across the pan.

11 Use about one-fourth of the seafood mixture to put down a layer of seafood on top of the bottom pasta layer.

12 Cover the seafood with a second layer of pasta. This time, place the sheets at right angles to the first layer. This will help the lasagna hold together after it's cut. Top the pasta with the sun-dried tomatoes and the sauteed mushrooms.

13 Put down another layer of seafood, followed by another layer of pasta (reversing the direction of the pasta again), and so forth, until you have five layers of seafood, with seafood on the top. Top with one cup of grated Parmesan cheese, if you like.

14 Put the lasagna pan inside a bigger pan with enough water to come halfway up the sides of the lasagna pan. Bake at 450 degrees for 45 minutes.

15 Take the lasagna out and allow to cool on the top of the stove for 15-30 minutes. Make two slices the long way and three to five slices across. Serve with about 4 oz. of sauce.

Serves eight to twelve.

Suggested wine: Tocai

Rotolo di Pasta Tricolore

Pasta Pinwheels with Cheese and Herbs

This dish, which I thought of one day while making crepes, was first served at Andrea's in April, 1989, at a dinner for the New Orleans Chapter of the Chaine des Rotisseurs, one of the city's premier gourmet societies. As a result of this dish and a few others, their bailli, Carol Lise Rosen, declared their dinner at Andrea's to be the best the society had ever had.

6 oz. fresh spinach, well washed and coarse stems removed

Herbed Cheese Stuffing:
8 oz. mozzarella cheese
2 oz. goat cheese
1½ oz. mascarpone
¾ cup grated Parmesan cheese
1 cup ricotta cheese
½ Tbs. oregano, chopped
½ Tbs. chopped fresh basil leaves
½ tsp. sage, chopped
Pinch nutmeg

1 sheet fresh pasta dough, about 18 inches by 8 inches
5 oz. ham, sliced very thin
½ roasted red bell pepper, cut into thick strips
10 fresh basil leaves, sliced
8 sprigs chopped Italian parsley

1 Clean and poach the spinach, leaving it firm enough that the leaves can be stretched out.

2 Blend all the cheese stuffing ingredients into a thick paste in a food processor.

3 Dust a work area well with flour. With a rolling pin, roll out the pasta to about the thickness of two pennies. Cut off and reserve two pieces about three by five inches. Put a large sheet of cheesecloth under the pasta.

4 Make a one-leaf-thick layer of spinach atop the pasta, leaving about ½ inch free along the long sides.

5 With a rubber spatula, spread the cheese mixture on top of the spinach.

6 The ham makes the next layer. Make a one-inch-wide stripe down the middle of the pasta with the basil and parsley, topped by the bell pepper.

7 Using the cheesecloth to maintain uniform pressure, roll up the pasta sheet — starting from one of the long sides — to make a long tube about three inches in diameter. Brush all the edges of the pasta with water.

8 Roll out the two reserved pieces of pasta a little thinner than they already are. Brush them with water on one side. Fold them over the open ends of the pasta roll.

9 Roll the entire pasta roll up inside the cheesecloth, and twist the two ends

106

of the cheesecloth to hold the roll tightly. Tie both ends. (The effect will be like a giant wrapped taffy.)

10 With string, tie loops around the roll spaced about four inches apart. They should pinch the pasta roll a little.

11 Bring a large pan of water (about a gallon) to a boil with 1 Tbs. of oil and 1 Tbs. salt. Carefully lower the rotolo di pasta into the water and cook for 35 minutes on a low simmer.

12 Remove the rotolo from the water and place on two thicknesses of towels to drain. Allow to rest for 10 minutes. Then cut off the string and the cheesecloth, and carefully unroll onto a serving plate.

13 With a serrated knife, slice the rotolo about a half-inch thick. Serve with the sauce for pasta Alfredo, or with strained tomato-basil sauce.

Serves twelve.

Timballo di Pasta

Pasta Dome

This dish is a fantasy I had one day that turned out much better than I thought it would. The best description of it is art deco lasagna. No question about it: this is a show-off dish, and it takes a lot of time to prepare. But its appearance is very striking, and its contrasting layers of flavors are very satisfying. Your guests will wonder how you did it.

1 lb. ziti (ridged pasta tubes, about ½ inch in diameter), at least 10 inches long, but the longer the better
1 lb. fresh spinach, well washed and coarse stems removed
1 small eggplant, sliced lengthwise ¼ inch thick
Flour
1 egg, beaten
Seasoned bread crumbs
¼ cup olive oil
4 red bell peppers, roasted, seeded, and sliced
6 slices cooked ham, thinly sliced

Cheese stuffing:
½ cup grated mozzarella
¼ cup ricotta
2 Tbs. grated Parmesan cheese
2 leaves chopped fresh basil
Pinch dried sage
¼ tsp. chopped fresh oregano
2 sprigs chopped Italian parsley
Pinch nutmeg

Meat stuffing:
12 oz. ground inside round or chuck
1 Tbs. chopped garlic
3 Tbs. chopped onions
2 tsp. chopped fresh oregano
4 sprigs chopped Italian parsley
3 leaves chopped fresh basil
1 tsp. salt
¼ tsp. white pepper
3 Tbs. grated Parmesan cheese
3 Tbs. bread crumbs

¼ cup olive oil
1 qt. tomato basil sauce (see **Sauces***)*

1 Cook the pasta al dente—about six minutes for fresh pasta, ten minutes for dried. Wash ziti with cold water. Drain well.

2 Drain spinach and stretch out the leaves.

3 Slice the eggplant lengthwise about ¼ inch thick. Dust lightly with flour, pass through the beaten egg. Coat lightly with bread crumbs and shake off the excess. In a large skillet, heat the olive oil and saute the eggplant until light brown. Drain and reserve.

4 Assemble the timballo in a rounded metal bowl, about nine inches in diameter and four inches deep, lightly wiped with olive oil. Make a clockwise spiral with the longest piece of ziti you can find at the bottom of the bowl. Continue the spiral with more ziti, going around and around with the pasta and working up the sides of the bowl. Stop the spiral about ½ inch from the top of the bowl. If you do this carefully, it will not all come tumbling down.

5 Spread spinach leaves on top of the pasta, completely covering the inside of the spiral.

6 Create another pasta spiral like the first on on top of the spinach.

7 Place strips of roasted red bell pepper on top of the second layer of pasta. Cover that with the eggplant, placed in the bowl vertically. Let some of the eggplant overlap the top of the pasta "wall."

8 Spiral up another layer of pasta. (This one will be much smaller than the first or second spirals, so take heart.)

9 Cover the pasta with the ham slices, allowing them to overlap the top as you did with the eggplant. Combine all the ingredients for the cheese stuffing in a food processor or mixer, and spread it on top of the ham.

10 Another pasta spiral.

11 Combine all the ingredients for the meat stuffing, and use this to fill the hole in the middle of the timballo.

12 Fold the overlapping eggplant and ham over the top of the timballo. Make one more spiral of ziti. (This one will be flat.) Pour ¼ cup of olive oil over the top.

13 *Preheat the oven to 400 degrees.* Find a pot big enough to hold the bowl. Fill it with enough water to completely surround the sides of the bowl up to an inch of the top. Bring the water to a boil. Put the entire pot with the bowl in it into the 400-degree oven and bake for one hour and fifteen minutes.

14 Remove the bowl from the pot and place it on the counter to cool and set for 15 minutes. Cover the bowl with a serving plate and invert it. Tap the side of the bowl all the way around to loosen the timballo. Remove the bowl by twisiting it slowly counter-clockwise while lifting it. Some of the outside spiral may come loose anyway, but this instability is just on the outside; just replace the loose ziti.

15 Slice the timballo carefully with a serrated knife, cutting all the way across rather than trying to cut wedges. Serve with basil tomato sauce and grated Parmesan cheese.

Serves eight.

Suggested wine: Pignatello

Risotto and Polenta

Rice As Pasta

A simple way to describe risotto would be to call it rice in the guise of pasta, but that wouldn't quite capture it. "Italian jambalaya" also suggests risotto, but that's not quite it either. The best way to understand risotto, I guess, is to make some, taste it, and figure out where it fits into your culinary picture. It is a very important part of our menu at Andrea's.

Some people are surprised that rice is a classic Italian dish. Rice has been raised in Italy for at least five hundred years. That's long enough for some distinctive Italian varieties of rice to emerge. The best of these is *riso Arborio*. Arborio rice has a distinctive appearance: the grains are quite large and bulge somewhat in the center, like little footballs. While you can make risotto with Uncle Ben's, I think it is worth your while to find Arborio rice. It is available in Italian, specialty, and gourmet grocery stores.

Every Italian cook has his way of cooking risotto, and he will try to make you believe that his method was handed down from heaven and cannot be fooled with. I, too, will try to convince you of this. I have never seen the exact method I use in any other book. I can assure you that it makes great risotto. As a bonus, it doesn't require the constant attention that some "authentic" recipes tell you is essential. A critical point is when the rice is added. The butter must be very hot, to give a quick toasting to the outside of the rice. This will keep the grains from turning to mush later.

Basic Risotto

Here is the recipe for a basic risotto. It is the starting point for all the other risotto recipes that follow.

2 qts. chicken stock
4 oz. butter
1 Tbs. chopped onion
½ Tbs. chopped garlic
1 lb. Arborio rice
1 cup dry white wine
½ tsp. salt
Pinch white pepper

1 Bring the chicken stock to a boil in a large saucepan.

2 Heat the butter in a second saucepan (minimum five-quart capacity) over medium heat. When it begins bubbling, add the onions and garlic and saute until blond.

3 Increase the heat to high and add the rice. Stir well with a kitchen fork (never stir rice with a spoon!) to coat all the rice with the hot butter. When you see the first hint of browning, stir in the wine and lower the heat.

4 Pour in the boiling chicken stock and add the salt and pepper. When the saucepan returns to a boil, put it into a preheated 450-degree oven for 15 to 20 minutes. The rice should have absorbed all but some small wells of unabsorbed, bubbling liquid when you remove it from the oven.

5 Remove the risotto from the saucepan immediately. Spread it out in a large skillet, a pizza pan, or a sheet pan, and allow it to cool. Do not let it cool in the saucepan, as it will continue to cook from its own heat.

Serves six to eight.

Suggested wine: Cortese

Risotto Milanese

Since Milan is the center of Italian rice cultivation, Milan has always been the city most identified with risotto. Here is a polished-up version of the Basic Risotto.

1 Tbs. butter
½ tsp. saffron
¼ cups dry white wine
1 cup chicken stock
1 cup Basic Risotto (see above)
¼ cup grated Parmesan cheese
2 sprigs chopped fresh Italian parsley

1 Heat butter to bubbling and add the saffron. Add the white wine and bring to a boil; add chicken stock, and return to a boil.

2 Add risotto and simmer for three minutes, until risotto is thick but still very saucy. Remove from the heat, add cheese and parsley, and serve.
Makes one entree or four side dishes.

Risotto Champagne

Champagne Risotto

This risotto has a silvery, elegant taste, and will accompany any entree, no matter how magnificent.

½ cup Domaine Chandon sparkling wine
Generous pinch saffron threads
¼ cup dry vermouth
⅓ cup chicken stock
1 cup Basic Risotto (see above)
1 Tbs. grated Parmesan cheese
½ tsp. softened butter
1 Tbs. roasted pine nuts (see **Basics***)*

1 Combine the sparkling wine, saffron, and vermouth in a skillet and bring to a boil. Add the chicken stock and return to a boil.

2 Add the prepared risotto and stir in. Cook over low heat until the risotto absorbs the liquid.

3 Remove skillet from the heat. Stir in butter and Parmesan cheese. Top each serving with pine nuts.
Serves four side dishes.

Suggested wine: Prosecco di Conegliano

Risotto con Pollo

Chicken Risotto

This is classic, simple, satisfying risotto. Its taste stays interesting no matter how much of it you eat.

1 Tbs. extra virgin olive oil
1 chicken breast, boneless and skinless, cubed
1 tsp. chopped onions
¼ tsp. chopped garlic
2 sprigs Italian parsley, chopped
1 tsp. fresh rosemary leaves, chopped
1 pinch crushed red pepper
¼ cup dry white wine
½ cup chicken stock
1 cup Basic Risotto (see above)
1 Tbs. Parmesan cheese
¼ tsp. salt
Pinch white pepper

1 Heat the olive oil over high flame and saute the chicken breast until it turns white. Add the onions, garlic, parsley, rosemary, and crushed red pepper, and saute until onions are blond.

2 Add white wine and bring to a boil. Add chicken stock and return to a boil. Add the risotto and heat through. Remove from the heat.

3 Stir in the butter, Parmesan cheese, salt and pepper.
Serves one entree.

Suggested wine: Sassella

Cioppino

Barbecued Shrimp

Giant Shrimp Tommaso

Red Snapper Basilico

Pompano with Pesto Cream Sauce

Timballo di Pasto

Seafood Lasagna

Risotto with Squid and Squid Ink

Risotto Verde

Green Risotto

This is the favorite risotto of my co-author, Tom Fitzmorris. He says he remembers enjoying risotto very much like this during a trip to Friuli. It involves green vegetables and lots of herbs.

1 Tbs. butter
½ Tbs. chopped onions
½ tsp. chopped garlic
¼ cup dry white wine
8 leaves of spinach, cut into strips
4 medium asparagus, two-inch tips only
⅓ zucchini, quartered and sliced
1 cup Basic Risotto (see above)
½ cup chicken stock
2 sprigs fresh parsley
Pinch crushed red pepper
8-10 leaves fresh rosemary,
2 fresh sage leaves, chopped
1 sprig fresh oregano leaves, chopped
2 fresh basil leaves, chopped
½ tsp. salt
Pinch white pepper
½ cup chicken stock
1 tsp. butter
2 Tbs. Parmesan cheese

1 Heat the butter to bubbling in the skillet and saute the onions and garlic until blond.

2 Stir in the rest of the ingredients in the order listed. The entire cooking time, over medium heat, should be about three minutes. The risotto should still be very saucy when served, and the asparagus will be firm enough to use as a garnish.

Serves one entree or four side dishes.

Suggested wine: Vespaiolo

Risotto Pescatore

Seafood Risotto

This is an outstanding taste, using a variety of seafoods. It easily makes a satisfying meal in itself.

1 Tbs. extra virgin olive oil
1 Tbs. chopped onions
1 tsp. chopped garlic
½ tsp. crushed red pepper
4 fresh mussels in shells, washed well
4 clams in shells, washed well
¼ cup dry white wine
1 cup chopped canned Italian plum tomatoes, with juice
½ cup fish stock
2 medium squid, cleaned and sliced (see Basics)
2 oysters
2 shrimp, peeled and deveined
1 oz. trout fillet
2 sea scallops
2 sprigs Italian parsley
1 sprig fresh oregano leaves
1 cup Basic Risotto (see above)
½ tsp. salt
Pinch white pepper

1 In a skillet, heat the olive oil over medium heat. Saute the onions, garlic and crushed red pepper until blond.

2 Add mussels and clams and cook, agitating the pan. As they open, remove them to a bowl of warm, salted water. Clean out the sand inside the shells. Drain the water and set shellfish aside.

3 Add wine, tomatoes and fish stock to the skillet and bring to a boil. Add other seafoods, parsley and oregano, and return to a boil.

4 When all the seafoods are cooked, stir in the risotto. Return the mussels and clams to the pan and warm through with the sauce. Add salt and pepper to taste.

Makes one entree.

Suggested wine: Vermentino

Risotto ai Funghi del Boschi

Wild Mushroom Risotto

The more different wild, woodsy mushrooms you can get to prepare this, the better. We first created it when, by some miracle, we had morels, chanterelles, and porcini all fresh in the kitchen on the same day. Other mushrooms that would be good are oyster mushrooms, pleurottes, Crimini, or shiitake.

1 Tbs. extra virgin olive oil
1 Tbs. chopped onions
½ tsp. chopped garlic
1 oz. porcini mushrooms
1 oz. morel mushrooms
1 oz. chanterelle mushrooms
1 Tbs. Cognac
¼ cup dry white wine
½ cup chicken stock
1 cup Basic Risotto (see above)
1 tsp. softened butter
1 Tbs. grated Parmesan cheese
½ tsp. salt
Pinch white pepper
2 sprigs fresh chopped Italian parsley

1 Heat the olive oil over medium flame and saute the onions and garlic until onions are blond. Add the mushrooms and saute for one minute, until softened slightly.

2 Add the Cognac and carefully flame it.

3 When the flames die down, add white wine and bring to a boil. Add chicken stock and return to a boil. Add the risotto and heat through. Remove from the heat.

3 Stir in the butter, Parmesan cheese, salt and pepper. Serve with chopped Italian parsley at the table.

Serves one entree or four side dishes.

Suggested wine: Vespaiolo

Risotto con Inchiustro di Seppie

Squid Ink Risotto

I was overjoyed to find a source of cuttlefish ink one spring, and created a number of dishes using it. This one can also be made with squid ink, which you can get from fresh squid or, now and then, in bottles. The ink gives a fascinating flavor and a jet-black color to whatever it's cooked with. Be careful not to get any of it on your clothes! It won't come out!

Note that this recipe is cooked all the way from raw rice, not with prepared risotto as in the other recipes.

¼ cup extra virgin olive oil
1 Tbs. chopped onions
1 tsp. chopped garlic
⅓ cup dry white wine
1 tsp. squid ink
1 cup fish stock
1 cup uncooked Arborio rice

¼ cup extra virgin olive oil
2 tsp. chopped garlic
1 lb. calamari, cleaned and sliced (see **Basics***)*
¼ cup dry white wine
¼ cup fish stock
1 Tbs. chopped Italian parsley
1 tsp. salt
¼ tsp. white pepper

1 Heat olive oil in a saute pan over medium heat. Saute onions and garlic until lightly browned.

2 Add the white wine and the squid ink and bring to a boil. Add the fish stock and return to a boil over medium-low heat.

3 Add the rice and simmer over low heat (or in a preheated 400-degree oven) until most of the liquid is absorbed (but rice is still very wet).

4 To make the sauce, heat the olive oil in a saute pan over medium heat. Saute garlic until lightly browned.

5 Add the calamari and toss until covered with oil and garlic. Add wine, fish stock, parsley, salt and pepper, and cook lightly until reduced by about one-fourth.

6 Divide the risotto on plates. Pour the sauce with the calamari right down the middle of the rice pile, keeping the white calamari in the center as a striking contrast to the black risotto.

Serves four.

Suggested wine: Cortese di Gavi

Polenta

Depending upon how you look at it, polenta is either Italian grits or Italian cornbread. Particularly in the northern part of the country, it is served as a side dish the way potatoes are served in America—which is to say, with almost anything. This recipe makes polenta with approximately the consistency of mashed potatoes.

Polenta was my favorite dish when I was a child. My mother used to make a big pot of it with broccoli and sausages. It's a great dish in the wintertime.

1 Tbs. butter
1 cup cornmeal
1 tsp. salt

1 In a shallow saucepan, bring 3 cups of water to a boil. Add butter and allow to melt. Stir in well. Add salt. Lower heat to medium low.

2 Sprinkle in cornmeal slowly, stirring briskly as you add it so lumps do not form. After all cornmeal is added, continue to stir for about 7-10 minutes, or until polenta begins to noticeably separate from the pan. Spoon onto the plate and serve as a side dish with the entree.
Serves six.

Suggested wine: Collio Goriziano

Polenta Fritta

Fried Polenta

This version of polenta is like a very dense, undercooked cornbread. It is delicious with sausages—particularly the cotechino—or even by itself.

Polenta from recipe above
1 Tbs. butter
1 Tbs. olive oil
½ cup grated Parmesan cheese

Preheat the oven to 450 degrees.
1 Cook the polenta as above, but cook and stir it until it is relatively dry and solid. Mold it into a small shallow bowl and pack it down. Turn the the dish upside down onto a cutting board. Slice it into six slices, like a pie.

2 Heat the butter and olive oil in a skillet over medium-high heat. Saute all the polenta slices until just barely brown on one side. Turn and lightly brown the other side.

3 Sprinkle Parmesan cheese atop the polenta, and put the skillet in a 450 degree oven for about two or three minutes, until cheese gets crusty.
Serves six.

Salse

Salsa di Pomodoro

Tomato Sauces

While Italy has the New World to thank for the tomato, over the centuries Italian farmers—particularly those around San Marsano—have raised the red fruit-vegetable to its highest form. It's little wonder that tomato sauces are an extremely important part of any Italian kitchen.

Tomato sauces show an incredible range of variety. Not only do you find regional variations, but even within a given area there are many ways to skin a tomato and make sauce out of it. In my kitchen, the tomato sauces are stylistically from the northern provinces of Italy. We make quite a few of them, each designed to match the food with which it will be paired.

Tomato Basil Sauce

This is our most popular tomato-based sauce. It finds its way into a great variety of dishes at Andrea's.

¼ cup olive oil
¼ cup chopped onion
2 tsp. chopped garlic
½ cup red wine
4 cups canned Italian plum tomatoes
4 cups juice from tomatoes
1 tsp. salt
¼ tsp. white pepper
4 sprigs chopped fresh oregano leaves
16 chopped fresh basil leaves
8 chopped sprigs Italian parsley
2 bay leaves

1 In a saucepan over medium heat, heat the olive oil until very hot. In it saute the onions and garlic until they turn blond. Add wine and bring to a boil.

2 Immediately add tomatoes, squeezing them between your fingers to break them up as you add them. Add tomato juice. Lower heat and simmer sauce.

3 After 30 minutes, add water (a cup or less) if necessary to give sauce the right consistency. You want the sauce thin enough to be able to easily coat pasta, yet not so thin that it runs off the pasta. Add salt, pepper, oregano, basil, parsley and bay leaves. Simmer sauce another 15-20 minutes. Adjust seasonings.

Makes about two quarts of sauce, enough for about 16 pasta entrees.

Suggested wine: Capri Rosso

Salsa di Filletto di Pomodoro

Fillet of Tomato Sauce

The name of this sauce captures its essence: the heart of the tomato. The taste of the tomato is allowed to display its elemental tastes with only very slight enhancements from the other ingredients. It is cooked quickly, and is especially delicious with angel hair or other thin pasta, or with gnocchi.

6 very ripe cherry tomatoes or 3 fresh Italian plum tomatoes
4 canned Italian plum tomatoes
2 Tbs. extra virgin olive oil
2 garlic cloves, lightly crushed to break skin
1 cup juice from canned tomatoes
½ tsp. salt
Pinch white pepper
6 leaves fresh basil, chopped

1 Cut off ends of cherry or plum tomatoes and peel. Squeeze the seeds out with your fingers. Chop all tomatoes into small pieces.

2 Heat olive oil over high flame, and then saute garlic cloves until they begin to brown around the edges. Add tomatoes, tomato juice, salt and pepper, and let the mixture come to a boil. Reduce the heat to medium low and simmer gently for 12 minutes.

3 Stir in the basil. Simmer two or three minutes more, and serve over pasta of your choice.

Makes about two cups—enough for four pasta entrees.

Suggested wine: Lagrein Rosato

Salsa Arrabbiata

"Angry Sauce"

This is a spicy variation on the filletto di pomodoro sauce. The extra zing comes from crushed red peppers. Some of our guests ask us to use a very heavy hand with this ingredient. "Arrabbiata" means angrily or furiously. This is a sauce to prepare when you're rabidly hungry. The classic pasta to serve this with is penne. For some reason, it is also equally good with either sauteed fish or a grilled beefsteak.

2 Tbs. extra virgin olive oil
2 garlic cloves, lightly crushed to break skin
1 tsp. crushed red pepper flakes
¼ cup dry white wine
2 cups chopped Italian plum tomatoes
1 cup juice from canned tomatoes
½ tsp. salt
Pinch white pepper
6 leaves fresh basil, chopped
2 sprigs Italian parsley, chopped

1 Heat olive oil very hot in a skillet and saute garlic cloves until they begin to brown around the edges. Add crushed red pepper and wine and bring to a boil.

2 Add tomatoes, tomato juice, salt and pepper. Return to a boil, then lower heat and simmer for about 30 minutes, stirring now and then. Add water if necessary to get the desired thickness.

3 Stir in basil and parsley and adjust seasonings. Toss with cooked pasta in the skillet and serve.

Makes about two cups—enough for four pasta entrees.

Salsa per Pesce al Pomodoro

Tomato Sauce for Pasta with Seafood

When you're serving seafood with pasta, or a fish with a tomato sauce, this is an exceptionally good one. It is quite similar to the arrabbiata sauce, but there are some substitutions to match the seafood flavors. And remember: in authentic Italian cooking, cheese is never served with seafood.

2 Tbs. extra virgin olive oil
2 garlic cloves, lightly crushed to break skin
1 tsp. crushed red pepper flakes
¼ cup dry white wine
2 cups chopped Italian plum tomatoes
2 cups fish stock
½ tsp. salt
Pinch white pepper
2 leaves fresh basil, chopped
3 sprigs fresh oregano leaves, chopped
2 sprigs Italian parsley, chopped

1 Heat olive oil very hot in a skillet and saute garlic cloves until they begin to brown around the edges. Add crushed red pepper and wine and bring to a boil.

2 Add tomatoes, fish stock, salt and pepper. Return to a boil, then lower heat and simmer, stirring now and then, until reduced in volume by about half.

3 Stir in basil, oregano and parsley and adjust seasonings. Toss with cooked pasta in the skillet and serve.

Makes about two cups—enough for four pasta entrees.

Suggested wine: Lacrima Christi

Salsa Puttanesca

Tomato Sauce with Olives, Capers, and Anchovies

The name is slightly naughty; it's the sauce in the style of the, shall we say, ladies of the night. Regardless of that connection, this is a spectacular sauce for pasta, especially big pasta like penne or rotelli.

1 Tbs. extra virgin olive oil
4 anchovies, chopped
1 Tbs. chopped onions
1 tsp. chopped garlic
6 black olives, crushed
1/8 tsp. crushed red pepper
1 cup canned Italian plum tomatoes, chopped
1 cup juice from canned Italian plum tomatoes
¼ cup dry white wine
1 tsp. chopped Italian parsley
1 tsp. chopped fresh oregano leaves
1 Tbs. tiny capers

1 Heat olive oil in a saute pan until very hot. Saute anchovies, onions, and garlic until the onions are blond.

2 Add all other ingredients in order while maintaining medium heat. Bring to a simmer and reduce by about a third.

3 Add salt and pepper to taste. Toss with cooked pasta and serve with chopped Italian parsley and grated Parmesan cheese.

Makes about two cups—enough for four pasta entrees.

Suggested wine: Taurasi

Salsa Dragoncello

Tarragon Sauce

Fresh tarragon has a distinctive flavor—like that of anise, but with a "greener" aspect. In a sauce like this one, it enhances the flavor of any kind of fresh fish—especially pompano, salmon, grouper, or redfish—broiled, sauteed, or poached.

1 Tbs. butter
¼ cup chopped onion
½ tsp. chopped garlic
5 sprigs fresh tarragon
½ cup dry white wine
½ cup vermouth
2 cups fish stock
1 cup whipping cream
1 cup half-and-half
½ tsp. salt
Pinch white pepper

1 Heat the butter in a skillet and saute the onions and garlic until blond. Add stems only from tarragon, wine, vermouth and fish stock. Bring to a boil and reduce by half.

2 In a separate skillet, bring whipping cream and half-and-half to a simmer and reduce by half.

3 Meanwhile, chop the tarragon leaves. Stir chopped tarragon into reduced cream. Add salt and pepper to taste.

4 Strain the contents of the first skillet into the cream skillet and stir in. Continue to simmer for about five minutes, until sauce thickens.

Makes two cups of sauce—enough for six to eight servings.

Suggested wine: Verduzzo

Salsa alla Salvia

Sage Sauce

This is a delightful taste that goes extremely well with tortellini or gnocchi. The sauce happens lightning fast, so be sure your reflexes are quick. By the way, if you can't get fresh sage, forget the recipe—it won't work with dried sage, which is too bitter.

3 Tbs. butter
3 leaves fresh sage, chopped

1 Heat the butter in a skillet over high heat. When it starts bubbling, add the sage. When the butter starts to brown—which it will just seconds after it bubbles—the sauce is finished. Toss in the tortellini or gnocchi and coat with the sauce, or pour directly over whatever else you might be moved to pair this with.
Serves two.
Note: Don't prepare more than the above quantity of sauce at a time. If you need more, make it in batches.

Salsa al Minuto

White Wine Herb Sauce "In a Minute"

This sauce will surprise you. Although it will seem unfinished and too simple at the end of the procedure, it will prove to be a spectacularly good touch for grilled fish, shrimp, veal, or thin paillards of beef.

1 cup olive oil
¼ cup chopped onion
1 tsp. crushed red pepper
2 Tbs. chopped garlic
1 cup dry white wine
½ cup lemon juice
1 tsp. salt
¼ tsp. white pepper
⅓ cup chopped Italian parsley
1 Tbs. softened butter

1 Heat olive oil in a skillet over medium-high heat. Add onion, garlic, and pepper and saute about a minute—until onions are clear.
2 Add wine, lemon juice, parsley, salt and pepper and bring just to a boil. Take the sauce off the heat and whisk in the butter. Although at this point the sauce may seem runny and unfinished, it is now perfect—take my word for it.
Makes about two cups, enough for eight entrees.

Salsa al Barolo

Barolo Red Wine Sauce

Barolo is one of the greatest of Italian wines. Ordinarily, the quality of the wine you use in cooking is unimportant, as long as the wine is decent. But in this case the wine contribites so much of the sauce's flavor that it has to be first-class. This is a robust sauce that enhances the flavor of a filet mignon or a veal chop. As always, it is especially good if you use the skillet you just cooked the steak or chop in for the making of your sauce.

2 Tbs. butter
¼ cup onions
½ tsp. chopped garlic
1 sprig fresh rosemary leaves, chopped
1 sprig fresh thyme leaves, chopped
2 cups Barolo wine
2 cups demi-glace
½ tsp. salt
Pinch pepper
1½ tsp. softened butter

1 In bubbling butter in a skillet, saute onions, garlic, and herbs until onions turn blond. Add wine and reduce half its original volume.

2 Add demi-glace and simmer until the sauce has been reduced by half again.

3 Strain sauce through a sieve. Add salt and pepper to taste. Whisk the softened butter into the sauce.

Makes enough for six entrees.

Salsa Pesto

Pesto Sauce

Pesto sauce—green and aromatic—is a rich, herbal concoction which has seemingly endless uses. Once you make it, you will find yourself putting it not only in pasta (the classic pesto employment), but also in soups, on top of chicken, with fish, and lots of other things. We make a pesto butter sauce—not really traditional, but most delicious.

2 cups fresh basil leaves, loosely packed
¼ cup chopped onions
2 Tbs. chopped garlic
2 sticks (½ lb.) butter, softened
1 cup olive oil
½ cup grated Parmesan cheese
¼ cup toasted pine nuts (see **Basics***)*
1 tsp. salt
¼ tsp. white pepper

1 Pick through basil and remove large stems and bad leaves. Chop basil fine in a food processor. Add onions and garlic to the processor bowl and puree. Set aside in a large bowl.

2 Put one stick of butter into the processor and give it a whirl. Add half the olive oil, followed by another stick of butter, followed by the other half of the olive oil, blending well as you go until you have a thick liquid.

3 Pour butter-oil mixture into the bowl with the basil puree. Add Parmesan cheese, salt and pepper. Stir well until completely blended.

Note: When making pasta with pesto, put hot cooked pasta into a skillet over medium heat. Spoon four tablespoons of pesto sauce over the pasta and, with a kitchen fork, toss and blend with the pasta. The sauce will break if you put it into the skillet first—always stir the sauce into the pasta rather than vice-versa.

Makes three cups—enough for 12 servings.

Salsa Piccata

Lemon Butter Sauce

"Piccata" refers not to a sauce but to the thin slices of veal in the original version of the dish. The sauce accompanied the veal so often that it became known as "piccata sauce," and then we started getting dishes like chicken piccata, made with the same sauce. It is a slightly tart, translucent, elegant, and simple sauce that shows off the quality of whatever it's applied to. So if you put it on veal, make it baby white.

2 cups dry white wine
½ cup lemon juice
1 tsp. salt
¼ tsp. white pepper
¼ tsp. Tabasco
4 sprigs Italian parsley
½ lb. butter, softened

1 In a large skillet, bring wine to a boil and reduce for three minutes, to evaporate about one-third of the liquid.

2 Add lemon juice, salt, pepper, Tabasco and parsley, then lower fire. When pan contents return to a boil, remove skillet from heat.

3 Whisk in the softened butter until incorporated. Do not do this over heat; the sauce will break.

Makes enough sauce for six to eight portions of veal or chicken cutlets.

Salsa al Pepe Verde

Green Peppercorn Sauce

This is a relatively light cream sauce that has the pungency of the green peppercorns—which are not as hot as black peppercorns. It goes very well with a surprisingly wide range of dishes, from steak to chicken to salmon to duck.

Per person:
1 Tbs. butter
1 Tbs. chopped onion
½ tsp. chopped garlic
⅓ cup dry white wine
⅓ cup demi-glace
2 Tbs. green peppercorns
½ cup whipping cream
⅓ tsp. salt
Pinch white pepper

1 In a skillet over medium heat (preferably the one you just finished using to cook the steak, fish, or whatever, with the excess oil poured out), heat the butter and saute the onions and garlic until translucent.

2 Add the wine and demi-glace and bring to a boil.

3 Add the peppercorns, whipping cream, salt and pepper and simmer for two minutes.

4 Spoon 2 Tbs. of the sauce on the plate and place the main item of the dish on top of it.

Serves one.

Salsa di Crema e Limone

Lemon Cream Sauce

Lemon and cream make a fine, mellow sauce, particularly for fish. The problem is that lemon juice makes cream curdle. We get around that by using a special technique.

½ cup lemon juice
½ cup dry white wine
½ tsp. Worcestershire
3 cups whipping cream
1 tsp. salt
¼ tsp. white pepper

1 Combine the lemon juice, dry white wine, and Worcestershire in a skillet and reduce by half over medium-low heat, then remove from heat.
2 At the same time, reduce the cream over medium heat in a second skillet. When cream is reduced, add salt and pepper.
3 Briskly whisk the lemon juice-wine mixture, a little at a time, into the cream. Not the other way around!
Makes 2½ cups—enough for eight fish entrees.

Maionese

Mayonnaise

When you first make your own mayonnaise, you have crossed the threshold separating you from those who let mere convenience stand in the way of their gustatory standards. Freshly-made mayonnaise is much better than the best in jars. And it's not as difficult as it seems. Two tips: always use the freshest eggs you can find, and start off with just a little oil added at a time.

4 egg yolks
1½ tsp. Cremona mustard, Dijon mustard, or prepared yellow mustard
1 Tbs. white vinegar
3 cups vegetable oil
½ tsp. Worcestershire sauce
4-6 drops Tabasco
1 tsp. lemon juice
½ tsp. salt
Pinch white pepper

1 With a wire whisk attachment to an electric mixer, or by hand, whisk the yolks, mustard, and vinegar until well blended.
2 Slowly drip in the oil while continuing to whisk. At a certain point, the sauce

will suddenly thicken noticeably; from then on, you can add the oil a little faster.

3 When all the oil is whisked into the mayonnaise, add the Worcestershire, Tabasco, lemon juice, salt and pepper. Continue to mix until mayonnaise begins to form peaks, at which time it's finished.

Makes about a quart of mayonnaise.

Salsa Olandese

Hollandaise Sauce

I don't believe there are two cooks who make hollandaise the same way, although all agree on the major ingredients: egg yolks and butter. I personally like a thinner sauce than the very fluffy, sticky hollandaise many mass-production kitchens make. The only reason you would make a hollandaise so thick is so it will hold for a long time. In our kitchen, we make hollandaise all night in small batches.

1 lb. butter
2 Tbs. white wine
1 Tbs. white vinegar
2 sprigs Italian parsley
4 egg yolks
Juice of one lemon
Dash Tabasco
Dash Worcestershire

Bring a large saucepan of water to a simmer.

1 In a large skillet over very low fire, melt the butter but don't allow it to become hot enough to bubble. Skim off the foam. Keep the butter melted and clear.

2 At the same time, in a small skillet, combine the wine, parsley, and vinegar and bring to a boil. Reduce by half, then pour into a metal bowl.

3 Add the egg yolks to the bowl and place the bowl atop the saucepan of simmering water (you can also use a double boiler). Whisk briskly until yolks become creamy and thick.

4 Pour the warm butter into the egg yolks in a slow stream, whisking constantly. When all butter is incorporated, add the lemon juice, Tabasco and Worcestershire. Continue whisking until sauce has attained the thickness you like.

Makes about 1½ cups.

Frutti di Mare

Fish And Shellfish Entrees

If you asked me which part of our menu makes me most proud, it would have to be our seafood entrees. New Orleans is blessed with such an abundance of seafood that I always have many species of fin fish and shellfish to work with. And New Orleans diners are so enthusiastic and knowledgeable about seafood that when I get a compliment I know I've really accomplished something.

No matter what kind of seafood I cook and no matter how I cook it, one rule is always the same. It is the most important piece of advice I can give you about fish. *Buy only fresh fish!* At Andrea's, we buy only whole fish that were swimming the day before. I check the eyes to make sure they're clear (a fish that's been around too long will have cloudy pupils). And I pull back the gill slits to make sure the gills are still moist and red. (I am happiest when I see that they are still moving a little bit.)

As for crustaceans and shellfish, I insist on crabs, crawfish, and shrimp that are still live and moving. Clams, mussels, and oysters must have tightly-shut shells. Squid must be firm and limpid. Scallops have to be bulging and have a pink cast.

And nothing, absolutely nothing, should smell "fishy."

If you are very scrupulous about freshness, you have an enormous head start on cooking spectacular seafood entrees. Then all you need are a few basic techniques.

How We Cook Fish at Andrea's

We use every method imaginable for cooking our seafood, from grilling to deep-frying to poaching. But the approach we use most often goes something like this:

1 Marinate briefly.

2 Coat lightly with flour, salt, and pepper.

3 Saute in a little olive oil.

4 Turn and bake until done.

This results in a tender, moist interior with a good flavor, and a thin, light exterior crust with just enough seasoning to enhance the fish's natural flavors.

For fish that normally cooked in fillet form (trout, redfish, red snapper, amberjack, pompano, drum, and others) I recommend using fillets of about six to eight ounces. Large fish usually cut into steaks (tuna, swordfish, and sometimes salmon) come out better if they're about eight to ten ounces.

The marinade is simple and brings out the flavors of the fish.

ANDREA'S FISH MARINADE:

1 Tbs. extra virgin olive oil
1 Tbs. dry white wine
1 tsp. lemon juice
½ tsp. Worcestershire sauce
Dash Tabasco

PREPARING FISH FOR THE PAN:

1 Mix the marinade ingredients in a platter big enough to contain the fish you're cooking.

2 Wash the fish under cold water and pat dry. Place the fillets or steaks in the marinade, one minute on a side, and drain.

3 Sprinkle pinches of salt, white pepper, and flour on both sides. Fish is now prepared for cooking.

BASIC FISH COOKING METHOD:

1 Heat olive oil in a skillet over medium-high heat (with other ingredients that vary from recipe to recipe).

2 Put the fish in)skin side down, if it has a skin) for about a minute, until very lightly browned.

3 Turn the fish over and immediately put the skillet into a preheated 400-degree oven. Leave the average piece of fish in there for five to ten minutes, depending on the fish and the thickness.

Important! The biggest mistake you can make is overcooking the fish. If it starts to fall apart, it has cooked too long. When the fish is opaque and has just begun to flake, it's done or nearly done.

Pesce Rosso Arlecchino

Harlequin Redfish

This delectable dish is best made with that favorite New Orleans swimmer, redfish. (Drum, red snapper, or sea trout also turn out well.) The multi-colored bell pepper strips in it give it the look of a carnival clown's costume — hence the name. It is inspired by the cooking of the Tuscany region.

4 redfish fillets, 6 to 8 oz.
Fish marinade (see beginning of chapter)
4 Tbs. extra virgin olive oil
½ onion, sliced
1 cup mixed red, green, and yellow bell pepper, thinly sliced
1 tsp. minced garlic
Pinch crushed red pepper
½ cup dry white wine
1 cup fish stock
1 Tbs. lemon juice
Leaves from 2 sprigs of fresh oregano
½ tsp. Worcestershire
1 ripe tomato, peeled and seeded, coarsely chopped
½ tsp. salt

Preheat oven to 400 degrees.

1 Wash the fish under cold water and pat dry. Marinate the fish for a minute or two on each side in the marinade. Sprinkle the fillets lightly with salt, pepper, and flour.

2 Heat 2 Tbs. of the olive oil in a hot skillet. Saute the fish for about one minute, then turn. Put the skillet into a preheated 400-degree oven and bake for about five minutes. Do not allow the fish to dry out or crack. Remove the fish to serving plates and keep it warm.

3 To the same skillet add 2 Tbs. olive oil over medium heat. Saute onions, bell peppers, garlic and crushed red pepper until onions turn translucent.

4 Add wine and bring to a boil. Add fish stock, lemon juice, oregano, Worcestershire, tomato and salt. Return to a boil and cook until peppers have just lost their crispness, but are still al dente. Drape peppers and onions across fish and pour liquid part of sauce around fish. Garnish with fresh oregano.
Serves four.

Suggested wine: Pinot Grigio Oltredo Pavese

Dentice in Umido

Red Snapper Simmered with Wine and Tomatoes

Red snapper is rightly one of the most celebrated denizens of the Gulf waters, but for some reason it is not frequently served around New Orleans. I buy it whenever I can get it fresh. This dish is finished in a rather wet sauce. Its steaming effect makes the fillet extremely moist but not mushy.

2 Tbs. extra virgin olive oil
2 garlic cloves, lightly crushed to break skin
1 tsp. crushed red pepper flakes
4 red snapper fillets, 4-6 oz. each
1 cup dry white wine
1 cup canned Italian plum tomatoes, chopped
2 cups fish stock
½ tsp. salt
Pinch white pepper
3 sprigs fresh oregano leaves

Preheat the oven to 400 degrees.
1 Heat olive oil in a skillet over high heat. Saute garlic cloves until they begin to brown around the edges. Add crushed red pepper.
2 Put two fish fillets at a time into the hot skillet, and saute 30 seconds on each side. Remove from pan and keep warm.
3 Add the wine, tomatoes, fish stock, salt, pepper and oregano to the skillet and bring to a boil over high heat. Lower the heat to medium and simmer the sauce for five minutes.
4 Put the fish back in the skillet and put the skillet into the oven for about five minutes, until fish is cooked. Nap with the sauce and serve with a sprig of fresh oregano.
Serves four.

Suggested wine: Tocai Collio

Dentice al Basilico

Red Snapper with Basil

No fish entree is as popular at Andrea's as the fish of the day al basilico. The sauce is light but complex, with all sorts of understated herbal flavors enhancing the taste of fresh fish. My favorite match to the basilico sauce is red snapper, but it works with almost any fish.

4 red snapper fillets, 8-10 oz. each
Fish marinade (see beginning of chapter)
¼ cup vegetable oil
3 Tbs. extra virgin olive oil
3 Tbs. chopped onion
2 tsp. chopped garlic
½ cup fresh tomatoes, peeled, seeds removed, and cut into small cubes
⅔ cup dry white wine
½ cup fish stock
1 Tbs. small capers
1 tsp. lemon juice
¼ tsp. Worcestershire sauce
¼ cup sliced fresh mushrooms
4 Tbs. fresh basil leaves, chopped
1 Tbs. Italian parsley, chopped

1 Wash the fish under cold water and pat dry. Marinate the fish for a minute or two on each side in the marinade. Sprinkle the fillets lightly with salt, pepper, and flour.

2 Heat the vegetable oil in a large saute pan over medium heat. Put two fillets of snapper at a time into the pan and saute three to five minutes per side, until the exterior of the fish is crusty. Remove the fish and keep warm.

3 Pour out the oil, but don't clean the pan. Add and heat the extra virgin olive oil over medium heat. Saute the onion and garlic until lightly browned around the edges.

4 Stir in the tomato, heat it through, and then add the white wine. Bring to a boil, then add the fish stock, capers, lemon juice and Worcestershire. Return to a boil and reduce by about half over low heat.

5 Add mushrooms and heat through. Add basil and parsley. Adjust salt and pepper to taste. Nap the hot sauce over the fish.
Serves four.

Suggested wine: Pomino Benefizio

Tonno alla Fiorentina

Grilled Fresh Tuna with Spinach

Fresh tuna, in case you haven't had the pleasure of its company at your table, has a fine taste and meaty texture that has nothing in common with the canned tuna you've eaten all your life. It goes very well with the fresh spinach that they love in the city of Florence.

½ cup extra virgin olive oil
1 Tbs. chopped onions
½ Tbs. chopped garlic
½ tsp. crushed red pepper
1 tsp. salt
¼ tsp. pepper
1 lb. fresh spinach, washed well, stems removed (see **Basics***)*
4 sprigs chopped Italian parsley
4 steaks of fresh tuna, 8-10 oz. each

Sauce:
⅓ cup extra virgin olive oil
1 Tbs. onion
1 tsp. chopped garlic
¼ tsp. crushed red pepper
¼ cup lemon juice
¼ cup white wine
4 sprigs chopped Italian parsley

1 Heat 4 Tbs. of the olive oil over medium heat and saute the onion, garlic and crushed red pepper until onions are translucent. Add spinach along with one cup water, salt and pepper. Saute until spinach wilts uniformly—about two minutes. (You now have a very good side dish of spinach, although that's not what we're using it for in this recipe.)

2 Blend 4 Tbs. olive oil with chopped parsley. Run tuna steaks through oil. Grill in preheated broiler, on top of a hot barbecue grill, or in a very hot skillet for only about a minute, then turn over and cook another 30 seconds. Careful! Overcooked tuna is like rubber. It should have a slight blush of pink at the center when done.

3 For sauce, heat the olive oil in a skillet. Saute onions, garlic, and crushed red pepper until onions begin to brown around the edges. Add lemon juice, wine and parsley and bring to a very fast boil. When that happens the sauce is finished; remove it from the fire immediately.

4 To serve, spread out the spinach on the plate first. Top it with the tuna steak, and then nap the tuna with 2 Tbs. of sauce.
Serves four.

Suggested wine: Vermentino from Liguria

Luccio Caruso

Puppy Drum Caruso

Drum is a Gulf fish related to the redfish. It is at its best when small—four pounds or less. I like to prepare it with the eggplant-chunky Caruso sauce. Make sure the eggplant are ripe—if you see any greenness, the eggplant may be bitter.

4 puppy drum (or trout or red snapper) fillets, 8-10 oz. each
Fish marinade (see beginning of chapter)
¼ cup olive oil

Sauce:
¼ cup extra virgin olive oil
¼ tsp. crushed red pepper
1 clove fresh garlic, peeled and crushed
⅓ medium eggplant, cut into small cubes
1 cup canned Italian plum tomatoes
⅓ cup juice from tomatoes
½ cup fish stock
6 chopped fresh basil leaves
1 sprig chopped fresh oregano leaves
¼ tsp. salt
Pinch white pepper

1 Wash the fish under cold water and pat dry. Marinate the fish for a minute or two on each side in the marinade. Sprinkle the fillets lightly with salt, pepper, and flour.

2 Heat the ¼ cup olove oil in a large saute pan over medium heat. Put two fillets of drum at a time into the pan and saute three to five minutes per side, until the exterior of the fish is crusty. Remove the fish and keep warm.

3 Pour out the oil, but don't clean the pan. Add and heat the extra virgin olive oil over medium heat. Saute crushed red pepper and garlic until lightly browned around the edges.

4 Add the eggplant and saute until medium-dark brown on the outside—about five minutes over medium heat. Remove and drain on paper towels.

5 To the olive oil remaining in the pan, add the tomatoes, juice and fish stock. Bring to a boil, then add basil and oregano. Reduce heat and simmer the sauce until reduced by half—about five minutes.

6 Stir the eggplant into the sauce, then remove from heat. Divide sauce among four plates, and place a puppy drum fillet atop each.
Serves four.

Suggested wine: Chardonnay from Friuli

Sardine Origanate

Giant Sardines with Oregano

A good, creative cook siezes every opportunity. One day I was offered some fresh, beautiful sardines. These are nothing like the sardines you get in tin cans, but eight-inch fish with a fairly strong but delicious taste. I grabbed them and turned them into a delicious lunch for the Italians on our staff (plus Tom, whom I have named an honorary Italian). If you ever run into these, try them. It will be like a trip to Portofino.

12 fresh large sardines
2 Tbs. extra virgin olive oil
2 large cloves garlic, peeled
2 cups chopped Italian plum tomatoes, with juice
½ cup fish stock
¼ cup chopped fresh oregano
½ tsp. salt
2 pinches white pepper
¼ tsp. crushed red pepper

1 Cut a slit in the bottom of each fish and remove the entrails and the backbones with all other bones. Cut off the heads of the sardines if you want (in Italy we would leave them on). Spread the fish apart (butterfly them) and remove any remaining small bones. Wash the fillets well under cold water, pat dry, and sprinkle with salt and pepper.

2 Heat the olive oil in a skillet over medium heat. Saute the fish skin side up for 45 seconds. Remove from skillet and keep warm.

3 Slice the garlic thin and cook it to light brown edges in the same skillet and oil. Add tomatoes, fish stock, oregano, salt, pepper and crushed red pepper and bring to a boil. Reduce liquid to one-third its original volume.

4 Carefully return the fish to the skillet, this time skin side down. Gently agitate the pan to slosh the sauce over the fish. Let it simmer for one minute, then serve two fish per person with lots of the sauce.

Serves six.

Suggested wine: Chardonnay Del Trentino

Trota Reale

Speckled Trout With Crabmeat

The favorite fish in first-class restaurants in New Orleans is and always has been speckled trout. This is a much larger fish than the rainbow trout served in the rest of America, and comes from brackish waters. It is a member of the bass family. It lends itself well to the saute pan. Orleanians love it topped with lump crabmeat in a light butter sauce.

Per person:
1 speckled trout fillet, 8-10 oz.
¼ cup vegetable oil
Fish marinade (see beginning of chapter)
1 tsp. butter
⅓ cup jumbo lump crabmeat
½ cup lemon cream sauce (see **Sauces***)*

Preheat the oven to 400 degrees.
1 Wash the fish under cold water and pat dry. Marinate the fish for a minute or two on each side in the marinade. Sprinkle the fillets lightly with salt, pepper and flour.
2 Heat the oil in a skillet very hot. Saute the fish until lightly browned on one side. Turn the fish and put the skillet into a 400-degree oven for six minutes.
3 Melt the butter in the skillet and add the crabmeat. Saute by agitating the pan (to avoid breaking up the lumps) for about two minutes. Add the lemon cream sauce and combine with the crabmeat, mixing by shaking the pan rather than stirring. When heated through, nap the sauce over the trout fillet.
Serves one.

Suggested wine: Cortese

Sogliola di Dover alla Mugnaia

Dover Sole Meuniere

The Dover sole is the queen of the seas. I think it is important for any restaurant that takes seafood seriously, no matter where in the world it is, to prepare this dish well. We fly in sole fresh from England for a fairly good-sized contingent of customers who appreciate the fish and are willing to pay the price for it. We get it in whole and fillet it ourselves. With the subtlety of flavor that the sole possesses, it would be folly to cover it with thick, overpowering sauces. We send our sole out merely moistened with a classic French meuniere sauce.

In New Orleans, we have access to superb Gulf flounders, which some local gourmets (Tom among them) say is every bit as good as a sole. It is similar in many ways, and you can prepare it exactly as below.

1 whole Dover sole, about 1 lb.
Fish marinade (see beginning of chapter)
1 Tbs. olive oil
1½ Tbs. butter
1 tsp. lemon juice
¼ cup dry white wine
3 drops Tabasco
3 drops Worcestershire sauce
¼ tsp. salt
Pinch white pepper

1 If you have the good fortune to get a whole Dover sole, here's how to get it ready for cooking. Start with the dark side of the sole up. Hold the tail and, with a sharp knife at a 45-degree angle to the table, edge pointed to the head, scrape off a tab of skin right where the tail meets the body. Make the tab big enough to grasp. Then pull the skin off. This is easier than you might think, but do it carefully. Repeat on the other side. With kitchen shears, trim off the tail and the fins. Cut the fins just above the small bones visible inside the fish. Cut off the head. Spread the bottom of the fish and remove all the dark-colored entrails.

Preheat the oven to 450 degrees.

2 Mix the marinade in a shallow platter and marinate the fish for 30 seconds on each side. Dust the fish lightly with salt, pepper, and flour.

3 Heat the olive oil in a skillet over medium heat. Saute the fish for about a minute on one side, until lightly browned in spots. Turn the fish and put the entire skillet in the preheated 450-degree oven. After four minutes, turn the fish over and cook another four minutes.

4 Remove the fish from the oven and place it on a cutting board. With a very sharp knife, cut down the lateral line in the center of the fish to the bone (but not through the fish). Insert the tip of the knife into the slit and work it under the upper part of the fillet. Carefully separate it and fold it back, scraping away any of the small bones which may stick to the fish at the edges. Do the same for the opposite fillet.

5 Pull the backbone with all the ribs out. With a knife, scrape away the small bones around the margin and any dark, unattractive areas. Reassemble the fillets into the original fish shape and place on a hot platter.

6 Heat the skillet over medium heat and bring the butter to bubbling. Quickly add the lemon juice, white wine, Tabasco, Worcestershire, salt and pepper. When bubbles reappear, pour the sauce over the fish in the platter and serve immediately.
Serves two.

Suggested wine: Gavi di Gavi

Trota Mugnaia

Trout with Brown Butter

This is almost certainly the most popular fish dish in New Orleans — and simplicity itself.

1 speckled trout fillet, 8-10 oz.
Fish marinade (see beginning of chapter)
¼ cup vegetable oil
2 Tbs. butter
1 Tbs. lemon juice
1 Tbs. dry white wine
3 drops Tabasco
3 drops Worcestershire
Pinch salt

1 Prepare the trout as for **Trota Reale** above, and put it on the serving plate.

2 The sauce happens so quickly that it's finished by the time all the ingredients are in the pan. Heat a skillet fairly hot over medium heat. Drop in the butter, which will immediately begin to bubble, and swirl it around the pan until it's completely melted. Add all the other ingredients and pour the sauce over the sauteed trout.
Serves one.

Suggested wine: Capri Bianco

Pampano al Pomodoro ed Erbe Aromatiche

Pompano with Tomato and Herb Sauce

It is the opinion of most seafood connoisseurs that there is no better Gulf fish than the pompano. This handsome, meaty, silver fish makes long migrations along the coast from Florida to Mexico and back every year, and when the school passes in front of New Orleans we eat very well. The flesh of a pompano has a great, smooth texture and a refined, slightly oily flavor. This fish is excellent when prepared as for Dover sole. Our most unusual pompano dish is this one, created especially for this book.

4 pompano fillets, 8-10 oz. each
Fish marinade (see beginning of chapter)
¼ cup extra virgin olive oil
1 Tbs. chopped onions
1 tsp. chopped garlic
4 slices sun-dried tomatoes
4 anchovies, crushedt
1 cup fresh tomato, peeled and seedless, chopped
1 Tbs. capers
½ cup dry vermouth
½ cup dry white wine
⅔ cup fish stock
1 Tbs. chopped Italian parsley
10 leaves chopped fresh basil
1 sprig chopped fresh oregano leaves
•1/8 tsp. Tabasco
¼ tsp. Worcestershire
1 tsp. salt
Pinch white pepper
2 Tbs. butter

Preheat the oven to 450 degrees.

1 Blend the fish marinade in a large, shallow platter. Marinate the fish for about a minute on each side, then drain excess marinade. Sprinkle salt, pepper and flour lightly on the fish.

2 In a skillet, heat 2 Tbs. of the olive oil over medium heat. Saute the pompano on one side for one minute, until fish is lightly browned in spots. Turn the fish and place the entire skillet into a preheated 450-degree oven for six minutes.

3 Remove the fish from the skillet and add the rest of the olive oil. Over medium heat, saute the onions and garlic until blond. Add the sun-dried tomatoes, anchovies, tomatoes, and capers. Cook until tomatoes soften.

4 Add the vermouth and wine and bring to a boil. Add fish stock and return to a boil. Reduce by about one-third. Add parsley, basil, oregano, Tabasco and

142

Worcestershire. Add salt and pepper to taste.

5 Remove the skillet from the heat and whisk in the butter. Divide the sauce on serving plates and place the pompano on top. Garnish with oregano.
Serves four.

Suggested wine: Lacrima Christi Bianco Secco.

Pampano al Pesto

Pompano with Pesto Cream Sauce

There is hardly a fish creation at Andrea's that gets people as excited as this one does. When pompano isn't available fresh, our regulars get upset—until we tell them that there are other fish with which this great, light green sauce can be served.

4 fillets pompano, 8 to 10 oz. each
Fish marinade (see beginning of chapter)
½ cup dry vermouth
½ cup white wine
1 cup fish stock
1 cup whipping cream
½ cup pesto sauce (see **Sauces***)*
Dash Worcestershire sauce
4 drops Tabasco
Salt and pepper to taste

1 Blend the fish marinade in a large, shallow platter. Marinate the fish for about a minute on each side, then drain excess marinade. Sprinkle salt, pepper and flour lightly on the fish.

2 In a skillet, heat 2 Tbs. of the olive oil over medium heat. Saute the pompano on one side for one minute, until fish is lightly browned in spots. Turn the fish and place the entire skillet into a preheated 450-degree oven for six minutes.

3 Remove the fish from the skillet and keep it warm. In the same skillet, bring the vermouth and wine to a boil, reduce the heat, then simmer for three minutes.

4 Add fish stock and reduce to half the original volume.

5 Stir in the cream and return to a boil. Reduce by about a third, then remove from the heat. Whisk in the pesto, Worcestershire, Tabasco, salt and pepper.

6 Spoon the sauce onto plates and place the pompano on top. Garnish with fresh basil.
Serves four.

Suggested wine: Vermentino

Dentice Americana

Red Snapper Indian Style

The result is somewhat similar to the recently-popular Cajun "blackening" method, but the technique is different. Because of the very high heat with which the fish is cooked, you'll need two special things for this recipe: a good exhaust hood over your oven (or tolerance of your smoke alarm going off), and fish fillets at least ¾ inch thick in the center.

2 fillets of fresh red snapper, 10 oz. each
½ cup olive oil
4 drops Tabasco
¼ tsp. Worcestershire
¼ tsp. crushed red pepper
1 tsp. fresh oregano, chopped
½ tsp. paprika
¼ tsp. cayenne
½ tsp. fresh basil, chopped
¼ tsp. fresh savory, chopped (optional)
½ tsp. salt
Pinch white pepper

Sauce:
⅓ cup dry white wine
Juice of 1 medium lemon
¼ cup fish stock
1 Tbs. butter
¼ tsp. salt
Pinch white pepper
¼ tsp. Tabasco

Preheat the oven to 400 degrees.
1 Place a large iron skillet over the highest possible fire and heat it up, dry.
2 In a large, shallow platter, blend olive oil, Tabasco, Worcestershire, crushed red pepper, oregano, paprika, cayenne, basil, savory, salt and pepper. Marinate the red snapper fillets about 30 seconds on each side.
3 When the skillet is very hot, put the fillets in skin side up and let them cook for two minutes. Turn the fish and put the entire skillet into the preheated 400-degree oven for eight minutes.
4 Remove the skillet from the oven. Remove the fish and keep warm. In the same skillet, add the white wine, lemon juice, fish stock and butter. Bring to bubbling and remove from the stove. Stir in salt, pepper and Tabasco to taste and spoon sauce over fish.
Serves four.

Suggested wine: Lagrein Rose Dell'Alto Adige

Pescespada alla Padovana

Swordfish Padova

Swordfish are huge and their fillets are usually cut into steaks. The fish has a medium-dark color and a pronounced, but not exactly oily, taste. I would call it a robust taste. Seafood adventurers will find it an exciting change of pace.

4 swordfish steaks, 8 oz. each
Fish marinade (see beginning of chapter)
Salt and pepper
3 Tbs. extra virgin olive oil
1 Tbs. chopped onions
2 tsp. chopped garlic
½ cup dry white wine
¼ cup dry vermouth
½ cup fish stock
½ tsp. fresh thyme leaves
5 leaves chopped fresh basil
5 sun-dried tomatoes, sliced julienne
1 tsp. salt
¼ tsp. white pepper

1 Blend the fish marinade in a large, shallow platter. Marinate the fish for about a minute on each side, then drain excess marinade. Sprinkle salt, pepper and flour lightly on the fish.

2 Heat 1 Tbs. of olive oil in a skillet over medium heat. Cook the swordfish steaks in the skillet for just 45 seconds on each side—until very lightly browned in spots. Remove from the skillet and keep fish warm.

3 To the same skillet over medium heat, add the rest of the olive oil and saute the onions and garlic until lightly browned. Add wine, vermouth, fish stock, thyme, sun-dried tomatoes, basil, salt and pepper. Bring to a rapid simmer, then return the swordfish to the skillet. Cook until the sauce permeates the fish—just about 30 seconds—and serve.

Note: Swordfish, like tuna, should not be cooked until it's gray all the way through. It should not be tough at all.

Serves four.

Suggested wine: Greco di Tufo

Gamberi Tommaso

Stuffed Giant Shrimp

In the summer of 1988, we began receiving some enormous fresh-water shrimp from various exotic ports of call. They are about four to six to the pound, and although they look like large versions of the white or brown shrimp that come from the Gulf around New Orleans, they are better cooked as if they were lobsters. We sauteed, stuffed, and baked them to come up with this unforgettable dish.

Stuffing:
¼ *cup extra virgin olive oil*
3 slices pancetta (bacon), chopped
1 tsp. chopped onions
½ *tsp. chopped garlic*
½ *red bell pepper, chopped*
½ *green bell pepper, chopped*
½ *tsp. crushed red pepper*
½ *tsp. salt*
1/8 tsp. white pepper
¼ *cup dry white wine*
1 Tbs. chopped Italian parsley
2 sprigs celery leaves, chopped
¼ *cup bread crumbs*
¼ *cup grated Parmesan cheese*
½ *tsp. fresh oregano*

6 giant fresh-water shrimp
Salt and pepper
3 Tbs. brandy
¼ *cup extra virgin olive oil*
1 Tbs. chopped onions
1 tsp. chopped garlic
½ *tsp. crushed red pepper*
1 lb. fresh Italian plum tomatoes, chopped coarsely
¼ *cup dry white wine*
1½ cup fish stock
1 Tbs. chopped fresh oregano
1 Tbs. chopped Italian parsley
½ *tsp. chopped fresh basil*

1 Make the stuffing first. In a skillet, heat the olive oil and pancetta over medium heat. Saute the onions and garlic until blond. Add bell peppers and crushed red pepper, and saute until peppers are tender.

2 Add wine, parsley and celery leaves and continue cooking until the liquid is almost entirely absorbed.

3 Remove the skillet from the heat and stir the bread crumbs, grated Parmesan

146

cheese and the oregano. Set aside.

4 Cut the shrimp in half from head to tail. Wash them well (the orange stuff is not fat but offal) and dry. Sprinkle with salt and pepper.

5 Heat the olive oil in a skillet over medium heat, and put the shrimp open side down in it. Let them cook for a minute, then pour the brandy over them and carefully flame. When the flames die down, remove the shrimp from the pan. (They cook very quickly. They should be in the skillet no longer than three minutes.)

Preheat oven to 400 degrees.

6 In the same skillet with the remaining oil, saute the onions and garlic until translucent. Add the crushed red pepper, tomatoes (no need to peel or seed them), fish stock, one cup of water, wine, oregano and parsley; bring to a simmer. Cook the sauce for a total of 10-12 minutes, until it has been reduced to a stew-like consistency.

7 Pour the sauce into a food mill, which will strain out most of the peels, seeds, etc. and turn out a smooth sauce. Return the sauce to a boil.

8 Stuff the head cavities of the shrimp with the stuffing, and place them stuffing side up in the sauce in the skillet. Put the entire skillet into a preheated 400-degree oven for six minutes, until the shrimp are heated through, the stuffing is slightly crusty, and the sauce is bubbly. Divide sauce on two plates and serve three shrimp per person on top of the sauce.

Serves two.

Suggested wine: Greco Di Tufo

Gamberi al Barbecue

Barbecue Shrimp

A classic Creole-Italian dish is completely misnamed barbecue shrimp. It's not grilled over wood, nor is the sauce thick and red. I like the idea of barbecue shrimp, but I have not much cared for the style in which it is usually served—overcooked, soft shrimp swimming in butter with not much else for flavor other than black pepper. I set out to find a better way, and here's what I offer to you. The most essential ingredient is gigantic fresh shrimp with the heads on. The fat in the heads makes the dish. I have two styles.

Gamberi al Barbecue Andrea Uno

1 Tbs. olive oil
3 cloves garlic, crushed
7 jumbo shrimp (15 count or bigger), heads on
1 tsp. chopped fresh rosemary leaves
¼ tsp. crushed red pepper
1 tsp. paprika
¼ cup dry white wine
2 leaves chopped fresh basil
½ tsp. chopped oregano
2 Tbs. shrimp stock
2 bay leaves, crushed

1 Heat olive oil very hot in a saute pan. Saute the garlic cloves until light brown at the edges.

2 Add the shrimp, rosemary, crushed red pepper and paprika, and cook the shrimp over medium-high heat until pink.

3 Add the wine and cook until absorbed by shrimp. Lower heat and add the basil, oregano, shrimp stock and bay leaves. Bring to a boil, then put the skillet into a preheated 400-degree oven for five minutes. (Or: lower heat and simmer, covered, on top of the stove for seven minutes.)

Serves one.

Gamberi al Barbecue Andrea Due

1 Tbs. olive oil
1 Tbs. chopped onions
½ Tbs. chopped garlic
7 jumbo shrimp (15 count or bigger), heads on
1 Tbs. brandy
½ tsp. tomato paste
¼ cup dry white wine
½ cup fish stock
½ chopped canned Italian plum tomatoes
Pinch cayenne
1 Tbs. chopped oregano
1 Tbs chopped fresh basil leaves
1 Tbs. chopped Italian parsley
1 tsp. chopped fresh rosemary
½ tsp. liquid crab boil
½ tsp. Worcestershire
½ tsp. salt
Pinch white pepper

Preheat oven to 400 degrees.

1 In a skillet, heat the olive oil over medium heat. Saute the onions and garlic until blond.

2 Add the shrimp and saute for ten seconds our so, agitating the pan. Add the brandy and carefully flame it. When flames die out, remove the shrimp and keep warm.

3 Add all the other ingredients and bring to a boil. Put the shrimp back in. Add a little water if necessary to moisten the sauce.

4 Put the skillet into a preheated 400-degree oven for five minutes.
Serves one.

Suggested wine: Lagrein Rosato

Gamberi Caprese

Shrimp Capri Style

Orleanians and the people of my home of Capri share a love for big fresh shrimp. Here's a way we prepare it that everyone loves.

1 Tbs. extra virgin olive oil
1 Tbs. chopped onions
½ tsp. chopped garlic
Pinch crushed red pepper
6 medium shrimp, peeled and deveined
½ Tbs. brandy
¼ cup dry white wine
½ cup fish stock
1 tsp. chopped Italian parsley
½ tsp. chopped fresh basil leaves
½ tsp. chopped fresh oregano
½ tsp. fresh rosemary leaves
1 Tbs. lemon juice
3 drops Tabasco
½ tsp. Worcestershire sauce
¼ tsp. salt
Pinch white pepper

1 Heat olive oil in a saute pan until very hot. Saute onions, garlic and crushed red pepper until lightly browned.

2 Add shrimp and saute until pink. Add brandy and carefully flame it. When flames die down, remove shrimp and keep warm.

3 Add white wine and fish stock. Bring to a boil, then add all the other ingredients. Return the shrimp to the pan and simmer for about 30 seconds on each side.

4 Take the shrimp out of the pan and arrange on a plate, then pour the sauce over them. This can be served with angel hair pasta.

Serves one.

Suggested wine: Capri Bianco

Aragosta allo Zafferano

Maine Lobster with Saffron

This is probably the most expensive dish in this catalog. It is something we do for very special customers, if you know what I mean. Besides the lobster, there are truffles and saffron, all of which are high-ticket. To add a little touch of humility to the dish, I left out the beluga caviar. Maybe you can figure out a place for it. By the way, this thing is as delicious as it is visually striking and fiscally demanding.

Per person:
5 sprigs celery leaves
2 sprigs fresh thyme
½ carrot, cut up
2 green leek leaves
1 tsp. lemon juice
1 live Maine lobster, 1½ to 2 lbs.
2 Tbs. dry vermouth
¼ cup dry white wine
¼ tsp. loose saffron threads
1 cup whipping cream
½ tsp. salt
Pinch white pepper
¼ tsp. Worcestershire
4 drop Tabasco
3 slices black truffle, cut into strips

1 Put the first five ingredients into a large pot with two gallons of water and boil. When you have a good, rolling boil, put the lobster in and return to a boil. Boil the lobster for ten minutes.

2 Meanwhile, heat vermouth and wine in a skillet over medium heat to a boil. Add saffron and ¼ cup of the water from the lobster pot.

3 In a second skillet, reduce the whipping cream by half. When the cream begins to simmer, add salt and pepper. When reduced, whisk the cream slowly into the wine-saffron skillet. Add the Worcestershire and Tabasco, and simmer until the mixture will coat a spoon.

4 After the lobster is cooked, pull it apart at the joint between the head and the tail. Either discard or retain the green tomalley (fat) and/or the orange coral (roe), according to your taste. Carefully shell the lobster, then arrange the meat on a platter in approximately the natural layout. Place the truffle strips across the lobster and pour the sauce on the platter all around. Decorate the sauce with remaining truffle strips.

Serves one.

Suggested wine: Greco di Tufo

Melanzane Farcite

Stuffed Eggplant Olympic

This is the kind of dish for which New Orleanians have a great love. Fortunately, they also have the perfect raw materials for it—especially those "buster" crabs, which are small soft-shell crabs captured on the verge of molting their old shells. The old shell is removed by hand, leaving a legless crab body with great intensity of flavor.

Sauce:
½ cup vegetable oil
¼ cup flour
1½ cups chopped green onions
¼ tsp. thyme
4 cloves garlic
Pinch cayenne
1½ lbs. small shrimp
3 cups fish stock
3 bay leaves
¼ cup Herbsaint
½ tsp. salt
Pinch white pepper

3 medium eggplants
Flour
1 beaten egg
Bread crumbs
Vegetable oil for frying
½ stick butter
¼ cup chopped green onions
1 lb. lump crabmeat
6 buster or small soft shell crabs
¼ cup olive oil

1 Start by making the sauce. In a thick 2-quart saucepan, heat the oil over medium heat and when it's hot stir in the flour. Keep stirring constantly to make a roux the color of milk chocolate. Add green onions, thyme, garlic, and cayenne, and cook until onions are limp.

2 Stir in the shrimp and the fish stock. Add the bay leaves and bring to a boil. Lower heat to a simmer and cook for 30 minutes. Add Herbsaint, remove from heat, but keep warm.

3 Peel the eggplants and slice them in half lengthwise. Hollow out a shallow depression in each half. Dust lightly with flour, then brush with the beaten egg. Coat liberally with bread crumbs.

4 Heat about two inches of oil in a heavy saucepan to 375 degrees. Deep-fry the eggplants until golden brown on the outside—about six minutes—then drain and keep warm.

152

5 In a saute pan, melt the butter and saute green onions until limp. Stir in the crabmeat gently and saute until the crabmeat is heated through. Add salt and white pepper to taste, remove from pan and keep warm.

6 Clean the crabs and dust with a little salt and pepper. Dredge the crabs through flour, and shake off excess.

7 Heat the olive oil in the saute pan. Saute crabs until golden brown.

8 To serve, place one eggplant boat on each plate. Divide crabmeat mixture and fill hollows of eggplants. Place one crab atop each. Spoon about 4 oz. sauce over each eggplant.

Serves six.

Suggested wine: Valpolicella

Scampi Fra Diavolo

Jumbo Shrimp "Brother Devil"

Not real scampi, of course. It is next to impossible to get the large Adriatic Sea crustaceans in this country. Very large shrimp, however, perform admirable duty as a stand-in in all the classic scampi dishes. This one is good and spicy, hence the name.

¼ cup olive oil
24 fresh shrimp, 10-15 count to the pound, peeled and deveined
2 Tbs. chopped onion
1 Tbs. chopped garlic
1½ tsp. crushed red pepper
2 Tbs. brandy
½ cup dry white wine
4 cups chopped Italian plum tomatoes, with juice
1 Tbs. chopped fresh oregano
8 leaves chopped fresh basil
1 tsp. salt
¼ tsp. white pepper

1 In a skillet, heat the olive oil over medium heat. Saute the onions, garlic and crushed red pepper until lightly browned.

2 Put the shrimp in the pan and saute, making sure pan contents covers them about a minute. Add brandy and carefully flame it.

3 When flames die out, add white wine and bring to a boil. When shrimp are pink and firm, remove from skillet and keep warm.

4 Add tomato to skillet and bring to a boil. Lower heat, add oregano and basil and simmer for 15 minutes, or until sauce has thickened to about the consistency of vegetable soup. Add salt and pepper to taste.

5 Return the shrimp to the pan and simmer another five minutes. Serve six shrimp per person with plenty of sauce.

Serves four.

Grancevola alle Noci

Soft Shell Crabs with Pecan Butter

From April through September, soft-shell crabs of meaty, large size are available live in the New Orleans area. When I recommend them to my guests, I say that they just came walking in the back door. That is almost literally true, since I always buy only crabs whose legs are still moving. Soft-shells make for grand, interesting eating. The pecan idea was something Tom Fitzmorris suggested while we were testing recipes for this book. We wanted to do something different, and we really liked the way this came out. The sauce is also superb with fried trout, catfish, or oysters.

2 large soft-shell crabs, very fresh
Fish marinade (see beginning of chapter)
2 Tbs. extra virgin olive oil
½ Tbs. chopped onions
½ tsp. chopped garlic
½ Tbs. chopped Italian parsley
1 Tbs. chopped celery
1 Tbs. chopped red bell pepper
½ tsp. flour
¼ cup dry white wine
½ cup fish stock
¼ tsp. salt
Pinch cayenne
4 drops Worcestershire
½ tsp. lemon juice
2 sprig fresh thyme leaves
2-inch white heart of a leek, chopped
½ tsp. chopped Italian parsley
¼ cup roasted pecans, coarsely chopped
1 Tbs. softened butter

Preheat oven to 450 degrees.

1 The soft-shell crabs must be cleaned first. With kitchen shears, trim off the front part of the crab with the eyes and mouth parts. Pull off the "tab" on the bottom, and open the crab. Clean out the "dead man's fingers"—the gills—and the funny-looking tissues near the mouth. Wash under cold water.

2 Mix the marinade in a bowl and marinate the crabs for about two minutes on each side. Dredge them lightly in flour.

3 Heat 1 Tbs. of the olive oil in a skillet over medium heat. Saute the crabs top side down for about 90 seconds. Turn them and put the skillet into a 450-degree preheated oven for five minutes (less, if crabs are small).

4 Remove the crabs from the skillet and keep them warm. Heat the other Tbs. of olive oil in the skillet over medium heat and saute the onions and garlic until lightly browned.

154

5 Add the parsley, celery, bell pepper and flour in turn, stirring the skillet frequently after adding the flour to keep it from burning.

6 When flour is lightly browned, add the wine, fish stock, salt, cayenne, Worcestershire, lemon juice, thyme, leeks, and parsley. Reduce the sauce by half over medium-low heat, then add the pecans and butter and heat through. Nap sauce over soft-shell crabs.

Serves two.

Suggested wine: Breganze Bianco

Ostriche allo Champagne

Oysters with Champagne

The oysters we have in South Louisiana are so delectable in their raw state that they can carry dishes with very delicate, subtle sauces. This is one of those. The flavor of the Champagne is distinctly present in the final dish—so it pays to use a good quality Champagne.

32 large oysters
½ leek, white part only, julienned
½ carrot, julienned
¼ cup extra virgin olive oil
2 tsp. chopped onions
1 tsp. chopped garlic
1 cup Champagne
¼ cup lemon juice
Dash Tabasco
1½ cups whipping cream
2 Tbs. butter, softened

1 Bring a pan of water to a light boil and poach the oysters for about a minute—just until the edges start to curl. Do not overcook! Oysters can turn to rubber! Remove the oysters with a slotted spoon and allow to cool.

2 In the same water, poach the leeks and carrots until they begin to turn tender. Strain out and cool.

3 Heat the olive oil in a saute pan over medium heat. Saute the onions and garlic until light brown around the edges. Add the Champagne and reduce by about one-third while stirring occasionally. Add the lemon juice and Tabasco. Whisk in the cream and the butter, then add the leeks and carrots. Agitate the pan to completely coat the vegetables.

4 Place eight oysters in a circle on each plate. Ladle the sauce in the center of each circle.

Serves four.

Suggested wine: Prosecco di Conegliano

Cappe Sante Andrea

Scallops Andrea

Scallops have a light flavor but a meaty, slightly chewy texture that I find very satisfying. Scallops are usually featured as an appetizer or as one of several seafoods in a dish. But I think they can stand on their own as an entree. Here are a pair of such.

Per person:
1 Tbs. extra virgin olive oil
1 Tbs. chopped onions
1 Tbs. chopped garlic
1 Tbs. chopped red bell pepper
2 sun-dried tomatoes, sliced
Pinch crushed red pepper
Light-green part of one leek leaf
8 oz. sea scallops (about 12)
½ Tbs. dry vermouth
1 Tbs. dry white wine
¼ cup fish stock
4 drops Worcestershire
½ tsp. lemon juice
1 sprig fresh oregano leaves
2 leaves chopped fresh basil
½ tsp. chopped Italian parsley
½ tsp salt
Pinch white pepper

1 In a skillet, heat the olive oil over medium heat. Saute the onions and garlic until blond. Add the bell peppers, sun-dried tomatoes, leek and crushed red pepper and cook until bell peppers are tender.

2 Add the scallops and saute for about a minute, turning them after 30 seconds. Remove them from the pan and keep warm.

3 Add the vermouth and white wine and bring to a boil. Add the fish stock and return to a boil. Reduce by about one-fourth. Add Worcestershire, lemon juice, oregano, basil and parsley. Add salt and pepper to taste.

4 Toss the sauce with the scallops over medium heat. When the pan is bubbling and the scallops are bulging, serve immediately.
Serves one.

Suggested wine: Rapitala Alcamo Bianco

Cappe Sante e Scampi Valentino

Broiled Shrimp and Scallops on Skewers

This is a savory, fragrant dish in which giant shrimp (not real scampi, as we admitted earlier, but a good substitute) are paired up with scallops before being broiled. This is great cooked over a barbecue pit.

12 extra-large shrimp (10-15 per pound)
12 large scallops
12 slices Canadian bacon
2 Tbs. olive oil
1 Tbs. chopped onions
1 tsp. chopped garlic
1/8 tsp. crushed red pepper
1 Tbs. chopped fresh basil leaves
1 Tbs. chopped Italian parsley
1 tsp. fresh oregano, chopped
Pinch crushed rosemary leaves
2 Tbs. brandy
⅓ cup dry white wine
1 cup whipping cream
2 dashes Worcestershire sauce
2 Tbs. butter, softened
Salt and white pepper to taste

1 On each of four skewers, put three each of the scallops, shrimp, and Canadian bacon. Fold the Canadian bacon in quarters, or fold them in half over a scallop or a shrimp. This is best cooked over an open fire on a rotisserie, but it can also be cooked under the broiler.

2 To make the sauce, heat the olive oil in a saute pan. Saute the onions and garlic until light brown around the edges. Add the crushed red pepper, basil, parsley, oregano and rosemary. Carefully add the brandy and touch a flame to it. Add the wine, bring to a boil, and reduce by half.

3 Add the cream and Worcestershire and reduce by about one-fourth. Whisk in the butter. Add salt and white pepper to taste. Strain the sauce and serve 2 Tbs. on each of four platters.

4 Place the skewers on the plate and pull them out of the seafood.
Serves four.

Suggested wine: Trebbiano

Cappe Sante Chiaroscuro

Scallops with Squid Ink

This is a unique way to blacken scallops.

Per person:
½ cup whipping cream
½ cup fish stock
1 tsp. squid ink
¼ tsp. salt
Pinch white pepper
8 oz. sea scallops (about 12)

1 Reduce the cream by half in a skillet. In a separate skillet, bring ¼ cup of the fish stock to a boil and add the squid ink.

2 Reduce the ink stock to half. Add this to the cream. Add salt and pepper to taste.

3 Add the scallops and cook them in the bubbling sauce for two to three minutes, turning once. Nap the scallops with the sauce.

Serves one.

Suggested wine: Cortese di Gavi

Cozze allo Zafferano

Mussels with Saffron Sauce

By weight, the most expensive foodstuff in the world is saffron. It's taken by hand from the stigmas of crocus flowers. Its inimitable taste is particularly well suited to seafood—shellfish best of all. Fortunately for kitchen economy, a little bit of saffron results in a great deal of flavor and yellow color. The right way to eat this is to eat the mussel right from the shell, using the shell to scoop up some sauce.

1 tsp. butter
1 tsp. chopped onions
½ tsp. chopped garlic
1 dozen mussels, well washed and debearded (See **Basics***)*
⅓ cup dry white wine
⅓ cup fish stock
⅓ cup whipping cream
Generous pinch saffron threads
Dash Worcestershire sauce
3 drops Tabasco
¼ tsp. salt
Pinch white pepper

1 Heat the butter in a skillet over medium-low heat until bubbling. Saute the onions and garlic in the butter until onions are lightly browned.

2 Add the mussels (in their shells), white wine, and fish stock. Bring to a boil and cover the pan; steam for 30 seconds, until shells open. Remove the pan from the heat. Drain the sauce out of each mussel, then drop it into a bowl of warm, salted water. Use this to clean the mussels of any sand or vestiges of beard.

3 Return the skillet without the mussels to the heat and add the cream and the saffron. Stir until the sauce becomes a bright yellow-orange.

4 Bring to a boil and add the Worcestershire, Tabasco, salt and pepper. Stir sauce well and add mussels to skillet. Slosh the sauce around in the pan to get it inside the mussel shells. Cook for another minute or so and serve in soup bowls with lots of sauce and finger towels.

Serves one entree or two appetizers.

Suggested wine: Pinot Grigio Collio

Calamari Farciti Positano

Stuffed Squid

Anything with the hollow configuration of a squid body begs to be stuffed. The stuffing can be almost anything that you would combine with seafood. This one is unusual in that it contains rice, and so perhaps can be called an inside-out jambalaya, Italian style.

2 Tbs. extra virgin olive oil
3 slices pancetta, coarsely chopped
1 Tbs. chopped onions
½ tsp. garlic
⅓ cup chopped red and green bell peppers
¼ tsp. crushed red pepper
10 medium-to-large fresh mushrooms, coarsely chopped
4 sprigs parsley, chopped
2 sprigs celery leaves, chopped
16 medium-large calamari (bodies about threee inches long)
¼ cup dry white wine
1 cup cooked rice
½ tsp. salt
Pinch white pepper
¼ cup bread crumbs
¼ cup grated Parmesan cheese
1 egg

Sauce:
¼ extra virgin olive oil
½ tsp. chopped garlic
Pinch crushed red pepper
1 cup chopped canned Italian plum tomatoes
1 cup juice from tomatoes
1 cup fish stock
3 leaves fresh basil, chopped
3 sprigs fresh parsley, chopped
Salt and white pepper to taste

1 Clean and skin the calamari. (See **Basics**.) *Leave the bodies whole, and chop the tentacle portion coarsely.*

2 In a skillet, heat the olive oil and pancetta over medium heat. Saute the onions, garlic, red and green bell peppers, and crushed red pepper until onions are lightly browned.

3 Stir in the mushrooms and cook until mushrooms become moist. Add parsley, celery leaves and chopped squid tentacles and cook for a minute while stirring lightly. Add wine and bring to a boil.

4 Stir in the rice thoroughly. Remove from heat and allow to cool.

5 When mixture is lukewarm, stir in bread crumbs, cheese, and egg, plus salt and pepper to taste. Load the mixture into a pastry bag with a large tip. Squeeze the stuffing into the bodies of the calamari. After stuffing all the calamari, fold the open ends shut and secure with toothpicks.

Preheat the oven to 400 degrees.

6 To make the sauce, heat the olive oil in a skillet over medium heat. Saute the garlic and crushed red pepper for 30 seconds, then add tomatoes, juice, and fish stock. Bring to a boil and reduce by about one-third. Add basil and salt and pepper to taste.

7 Put the stuffed calamari into the sauce. Return the sauce to a boil, then put the skillet into a 400-degree oven for 10 minutes.

8 Remove the calamari from the sauce and keep warm. Put the sauce over a medium heat and reduce for 10 minutes, until appropriately thick. Add chopped parsley and stuffed calamari. Heat through, and serve with lots of sauce.

Serves four.

Suggested wine: Lacrima Christi Rosato

Calamari in Umido

Squid Simmered in White Wine

Italians and Orleanians both love squid, and so we prepare the cephalopods several different ways. While most of our customers think of calamari as an appetizer, this and the following recipe make superb entrees.

16 fresh small calamari
¼ cup extra virgin olive oil
1 Tbs. chopped onion
½ Tbs. chopped garlic
¼ tsp. crushed red pepper
⅓ cup good-quality California Chardonnay
¼ cup fish stock
3 sprigs Italian parsley, chopped
½ tsp. salt
•1/8 tsp. white pepper

1 Clean and peel the squid if this has not already been done by the fish market. (See **Basics**.)

2 Heat the olive oil in a skillet over medium heat. Saute the onion, garlic, and crushed red pepper for 30 seconds over medium-high heat, then add the sliced calamari and all the other ingredients. Bring the skillet to a boil and simmer for about three minutes, until sauce is reduced by about one-third.

Serves two entrees or four appetizers.

Suggested wine: Bianco di Custoza

161

Cacciucco alla Livornese (Cioppino)

Seafood Stew with Saffron

The word "cioppino" became well-known in this country by way of the Italian restaurants in San Francisco, who even claim to have invented the dish. But this robust fish stew is identical to the cacciucco of Livorno and Genoa. You toss in just about every kind of seafood you have on hand when making it. The dish is a second cousin to the French bouillabaisse, in that it contains a great deal of different seafoods, usually in big chunks. Like bouillabaisse, it is also flavored with saffron. It's a little spicy and is a great treat for serious lovers of seafood. Wear a bib!

Per person:
1 Tbs. extra virgin olive oil
1 Tbs. chopped onions
1 tsp. chopped garlic
4 clams in shells, well washed
4 mussels in shells, well washed and debearded
¼ tsp. crushed red pepper
½ cup dry white wine
½ cup fish stock
2 canned Italian plum tomatoes with lots of juice
4 medium shrimp, peeled and deveined
4 medium-large oysters
4 scallops
4 calamari, cleaned and sliced
½ tsp. salt
Pinch white pepper
1 Tsp. fresh basil leaves, chopped
1 tsp. fresh oregano, chopped
1 tsp. chopped Italian parley
3 drops Tabasco
¼ tsp. Worcestershire
2 oz. trout fillet, sliced
1 portion cooked linguine

1 Heat olive oil in a saucepan pan until very hot. Saute onions and garlic until lightly browned. Add the clams, mussels, crushed red pepper and white wine. Cover and steam the shellfish until they open, then take them out of the pan and put them into a quart of warm water with 1 tsp. salt. (The mussels will open first.) Wash the sand and beards off the mussels and clams.

2 While the shellfish are soaking, add the fish stock and tomatoes to the pan and bring to a boil. Add the shrimp, oysters, scallops, and calamari and cook over medium-low heat.

3 When the pan returns to a boil, add the salt, pepper, basil, oregano, parsley, Tabasco and Worcestershire. Cook another three minutes, then add the trout,

162

clams and mussels. Cook for another three minutes, until the trout begins to flake.

4 Place the clams and mussels around the edge of a large platter. Place the linguine in the center of the plate, and pour the rest of the contents of the pan onto the pasta.

Serves one very amply.

Suggested wine: Pinot Grigio

Vitello

Veal

Italian chefs practically own the worldwide franchise for veal dishes. It would be impossible to open a first-class Italian restaurant without a substantial repertoire of great veal creations. At Andrea's, veal is rivalled only by pasta in popularity among our guests. The most-ordered entree on the whole menu is our veal chop Valdostana.

The best veal is baby white. It comes from calves which are still consuming only their mother's milk. As soon as the animal starts eating grass, the meat gets darker and changes drastically in character. It's still good, but it doesn't have the delicate flavor or tenderness of baby white veal. If you cannot locate baby white veal (it is getting easier to find in stores, although it remains very expensive), you will find that most of these recipes also work well for the darker "calf."

Vitello al Marsala

Veal with Marsala Wine Sauce

The highly distinctive ruddy-brown sauce, made from the aromatic Marsala wine of Sicily, is the perfect partner for veal—in almost any form, from cutlets to chops to even sweetbreads. Marsala comes in both sweet and dry forms. Although we usually cook with dry Marsala, the sweet kind also makes an excellent sauce with an interesting caramel background flavor.

2 tsp. butter
Sprinkles of salt, pepper and flour
4 slices baby white veal scallops

Sauce:
1 Tbs. butter
1 Tbs. chopped onions
¼ tsp. chopped garlic
5 medium-large mushrooms, sliced
¼ cup dry Florio Marsala
¼ cup dry white wine
½ cup demi-glace
¼ tsp. salt
Pinch black pepper

1 Dust veal scallops very lightly with salt, pepper and flour.

2 Heat skillet very hot. Put half the butter into it and swirl around. Saute veal for 45 seconds on each side. Remove from skillet and keep warm. Add the rest of the butter if necessary to finish sauteing all the veal.

3 Make the sauce in the same skillet to get the veal juices. Heat the butter in the skillet until it bubbles. Add onions and garlic and saute until translucent.

4 Add mushrooms and saute until mushrooms are tender. Add Marsala and white wine and bring to a boil. Reduce for two minutes, stirring occasionally.

5 Add demi-glace, return to a boil and add salt and pepper to taste. Sauce will still be rather light in consistency, and will have the distinct flavor echoes of the Marsala.

Serves four.

Suggested wine: Marsala Vergine Secco

Paillard di Vitello

Grilled Thin Slices of Veal

The word "paillard" is French, and was originally applied to a thin grilled steak. In Italy, we apply the same technique to a large, thin piece of veal. It's cooked it very quickly (we're talking seconds) over (or under) high heat. Few things are as simple or as elementally delicious. The sauce should be either absent or very simple and herbal. Keep cream and butter away!

¼ cup extra virgin olive oil
6 large slices veal leg, 4 oz. each, pounded thin
Salt and white pepper

1 Pass the veal paillard through the olive oil. Sprinkle lightly with salt and pepper.
2 You can cook this on a grill, on a griddle, in a black-iron skillet, or under a broiler—but the critical element is a great deal of heat. Put the paillard on a very hot surface and let it grill until small areas of brown form. The cooking time here is incredibly short. In our broiler, this took 15 seconds on the first side and 10 seconds on the other; on top of our flat-top stove, it was less than 20 seconds before the paillard was completely cooked.

A good sauce for this is the Abruzzese sauce in the recipe for veal birds, but leave out the sage and butter.

Serves six.

Suggested wine: Bardolino

Vitello Tanet

Panneed Veal with Romaine

I created this dish in the late Seventies at the Royal Orleans Hotel's Rib Room. It quickly became — and still is — one of the most popular dishes in that restaurant, particularly at lunchtime. I am flattered to learn that the dish, complete with the name (dish names have a way of changing when they move to different locations), has appeared on a few other New Orleans menus.

I must share credit for this dish with the man for whom it is named, attorney Ronald Tanet, one of New Orleans' foremost gourmets. He wanted a sauceless variation on veal Milanese; that day, he also wanted a lettuce and tomato salad on the side. This is what I came up with for him.

4 large slices veal leg, 4 oz. each, pounded thin
Sprinkles of salt, pepper and flour
4 eggs, beaten
3 cups plain bread crumbs
1 cup vegetable oil
1 head romaine lettuce, well washed and dried
2 medium ripe tomatoes
1 cup vinaigrette dressing (see **Salads***)*

1 Sprinkle salt and pepper over the veal. Liberally coat the veal with flour. Pass the veal through the beaten egg, then bury in bread crumbs and coat well. Shake off excess.

2 Heat oil very hot in a skillet. Very carefully slide the veal into the skillet. With a gentle shaking motion, slosh the hot oil (carefully!) over the veal. After one minute, turn over and cook another 30 seconds. During the cooking, the coating will sort of "bubble up" over the veal to create an almost souffle-like appearance.

3 Remove veal to a plate with a paper towel to absorb excess oil. Meanwhile, arrange six medium, tender leaves of romaine lettuce on a plate with four slices of tomato. Nap with two ounces of vinaigrette dressing. When veal is well drained, place atop romaine and serve good and hot.

Serves four.

Suggested wine: Merlot Collio

Uccelletti di Vitello

Veal Birds

"Birds" are what we in Italy call small rolls of veal stuffed with this or that. We had a lot of fun with the sauces for this. In short order, we had three delicious sauces, each quite different in character. (In the interest of full disclosure, we must admit that the consensus was that the Abbruzzese version was best.)

10 oz. veal leg, ground
4 oz. pork, ground
2 oz. pate de foie gras
2 Tbs. brandy
1 egg yolk
4 sprigs Italian parsley, chopped
4 leaves fresh sage
3 basil leaves, chopped
½ tsp. chopped garlic
¼ tsp. nutmeg
½ tsp. salt
½ cup whipping cream
⅓ cup pine nuts, toasted (see **Basics***)*
8 slices veal leg (scalloppine), about 2 oz. each, pounded thin
Sprinkles of salt, pepper and flour
⅓ cup vegetable oil

1 Put the veal, pork, foie gras, brandy and egg yolk into a food processor and turn it into a fine paste. Add parsley, sage, basil, garlic, nutmeg, salt and whipping cream, and puree again to get a smooth mixture. With a rubber spatula, scrape the inside of the processor cup to get herbs well incorporated.

2 Scoop out a small "hamburger" of the puree. Cook it in a hot skillet with a little butter. It is necessary to check the taste now, mainly because of great variations in the taste and fat components of the veal, pork and foie gras. Past this point, it will be impossible to do anything to correct a problem with the stuffing. If all goes well, this foie-gras-laced hamburger should be pretty good (can you imagine a chain of places selling this?)

3 Stir the roasted pine nuts into the stuffing mixture.
Preheat the oven to 400 degrees.

4 Put 2 Tbs. of stuffing atop each slice of veal. Fold up two sides of each veal slice around the stuffing, then roll up the veal into a cigar-shaped package. Wrap lightly with butcher string.

5 Dust veal packages lightly with salt, pepper and flour. Heat vegetable oil in a hot skillet and lightly brown the veal packages on both sides. Put entire skillet in a preheated 400-degree oven for ten minutes, or until rolls feel firm to the touch. Remove veal rolls, cut off string and keep warm.

6 Now make one of the sauces below. Nap two veal birds per person with it.
Serves four.

168

TURINESE AND SAN MARCO SAUCES FOR VEAL BIRDS

1 cup white wine
3 cups demi-glace
1 cup whipping cream

Pour off fat from the skillet in which the veal birds were cooked. Add white wine and bring to a boil over medium heat. When wine has reduced by about half, add demi-glace and return to a boil. Reduce by half again, and the sauce for the Turinese version is complete.

For the San Marco sauce, add the whipping cream to the sauce above and reduce another five minutes.

ABBRUZZESE SAUCE FOR VEAL BIRDS

1 cup extra virgin olive oil
½ cup chopped onions
1 Tbs. plus 1 tsp. chopped garlic
8 sprigs Italian parsley, chopped
6 leaves sage, chopped
½ tsp. crushed red pepper
1 cup white wine
¼ cup lemon juice
⅓ cup butter, softened
1 tsp. salt
Pinch white pepper

1 Heat olive oil over high heat. Add onions, garlic, parsley, sage and crushed red pepper. Saute for about 30 seconds, then add wine and bring to a boil. Add lemon juice and return to boil.

2 Just as soon as the sauce bubbles, remove it from the heat and whisk in butter. Add salt and pepper to taste. Although the sauce will seem unfinished at this point, it is now perfect to nap over veal birds and garnish with fresh sage leaves.

A perfect side dish with the Abbruzzese veal birds is sauteed spinach (see the recipe for **Tonno Fiorentina**).

Serves four.

Suggested wine: Teroldego Rotaliano

Saltimbocca Forestiera

Veal Stuffed With Sage And Prosciutto

"Saltimbocca" means "jump into the mouth," which gives you an idea of how delicious this aromatic, delicate veal dish is—at least if you prepare it this way.

½ cup dried porcini mushrooms, or 1 cup sliced regular mushrooms
8 slices veal leg, 2 oz. each
8 fresh sage leaves
8 slices prosciutto
1 Tbs. olive oil
1 Tbs. chopped onion
1 tsp. chopped garlic
¼ cup brandy
⅓ cup dry Marsala
1 cup demi-glace
1 cup veal stock

1 Soak porcini mushrooms at least a half hour—or, better still, overnight. Wash them seven or eight times to get all of their abundant dirt and sand off.

2 Pound veal slices to about twice their original area, using the smooth side of a meat mallet. It helps to place the veal between two thick sheets of plastic; food storage bags work very well. Top each slice of veal with a sage leaf and a slice of prosciutto. Press down so the three things stick together.

3 Heat the olive oil in a skillet over medium heat. Holding each veal slice so as to keep the prosciutto in place, put the veal slices prosciutto-side down in the hot oil. Saute for just 30 seconds, turn and saute the other side 30 seconds. Remove and keep warm.

4 In the same skillet, same oil, saute onion and garlic until blond.

5 Add brandy to pan and carefully flame it. Add Marsala and bring to a boil. Add mushrooms, demi-glace and veal stock and return to a boil. Lower heat and simmer for five minutes, then serve two ounces of hot sauce over saltimbocca medallions.

Serves four.

Suggested wine: Chianti Classico

Vitello Michelangelo

Veal Rolls with Prosciutto and Cheese

These are pinwheels of four things that go very well together: veal, spinach, prosciutto and mozzarella cheese. With a few more flavors, of course.

4 scallops baby white veal, 4 oz. each
12 large leaves fresh spinach, very well washed, large part of stems removed
4 slices prosciutto (about ¾ oz. each)
4 oz. mozzarella, thinly sliced
4 large fresh basil leaves
4 Tbs. dry white wine
1 Tbs. lemon juice
1 cup whipping cream
½ tsp. salt
Two pinches white pepper
⅓ cup demi-glace
1 Tbs. vegetable oil
1 Tbs. flour

Preheat the oven to 400 degrees.

1 Pound veal slices to about twice their original area, using the smooth side of a meat mallet. It helps to place the veal between two thick sheets of plastic; food storage bags work very well.

2 Into a quart of boiling water in a saucepan, put the salt and spinach. As soon as the spinach returns to a boil, remove and rinse it in cold water.

3 Spread spinach leaves over the top of veal slices. On top of that add layers of prosciutto, mozzarella and basil. Fold up a half-inch or so of veal along the long sides, then roll up the entire thing like a jelly roll. Tie loosely but securely with string. Dust with flour.

4 In a skillet, heat whipping cream to a boil. In a second skillet at the same time, warm the white wine and lemon juice together. When cream is reduced by half, slowly whisk in wine-lemon mixture and return to a boil. Add salt and pepper.

5 In the skillet where you had the wine, warm the demi-glace to a simmer.

6 In a third skillet, heat vegetable oil very hot. Brown veal rolls lightly on all sides for a total of about 30 seconds, and place entire skillet in a preheated 400-degree oven. Roast for eight minutes, until tops are lightly encrusted with brown. Remove from oven, cut string off and, with a very sharp or serrated knife, slice the rolls into half-inch thick slices.

7 To serve, coat the bottoms of the plates with the cream sauce and place the veal pinwheels on top. Spoon demi-glace across top of sauce in thin lines. With the tip of a skewer, spread demi-glace strings across white sauce for a beautiful visual effect.

Serves four.

Suggested wine: Sangiovese

Osso Buco Milanese

Braised Veal Shanks In Brown Sauce

"Osso buco" means "bone with a hole." The hole is the most interesting part of this dish, since it is filled with marrow that will cook to a delightful morsel. (Any serious fan of osso buco will go for the marrow as soon as the plate hits the table.) The bone is that of the lower part of the calf's leg; it is surrounded by some delicious meat which lends itself to a long, slow cooking in its natural juices.

8 slices veal shank, cut 1½ inches thick (12-14 oz. each)
Sprinkles of salt, pepper and flour
1 cup olive oil
1 lb. veal bones, cut one inch long
2 ribs celery, cubed
1 medium onion, cubed
1 cup chopped carrots
3 garlic cloves, lightly crushed
½ cup chopped leek
2 Tbs. tomato paste
1½ cups dry red wine
⅓ cup flour
4 leaves fresh sage
1 tsp. dry marjoram
2 sprigs Italian parsley
½ tsp. dried thyme
2 bay leaves
2 short sprigs fresh rosemary
½ tsp. salt
¼ tsp. white pepper

Brunoise: Chop these vegetables coarsely:
½ carrot
¼ onion
1 rib celery
¼ leek (white part only)

   Preheat the oven to 450 degrees.
   1 Sprinkle salt, pepper and flour over the veal shanks. Heat olive oil in a saucepan over high heat. Put veal shanks in and brown on both sides. Remove from saucepan and drain shanks.
   2 In the same saucepan, brown the veal bones in the remaining oil over high flame, stirring frequently. After meat on bones is a medium brown, add celery, onion, carrots, leeks and garlic cloves. When edges of onion start to brown, add tomato paste and red wine and continue to cook over high heat, stirring frequently.
   3 When liquid reduces by a little more than half (you will now have an appeal-

172

ing, red-brown sauce in the pan), sprinkle in flour and stir well. When flour is completely blended, add one gallon of water and stir. Add sage, marjoram, parsley, thyme, bay and rosemary.

4 When pot returns to boil, put veal shanks in and put the entire saucepan into a preheated 450-degree oven.

5 After an hour and 15 minutes, check one of the veal shanks for doneness. It is completely cooked when a kitchen fork can be inserted deep into the meat and pulled back out without resistance. When it reaches that point, remove veal shanks from sauce and reserve.

6 Put saucepan full of stock back on a hot fire and continue to reduce. After 30 minutes, skim top of pot to remove foam and fat. Strain stock through cheesecloth.

7 Return stock to a medium simmer and return veal shanks into it. Add salt and pepper to taste.

8 Using a sieve to hold them, boil the brunoise vegetables in about a quart of water for about a minute. Add the brunoise to the stock and cook another three or four minutes, until sauce is the desired thickness. It is the style in many restaurants around New Orleans to make the sauce for osso buco so thick that you can eat it with a fork. But this is not the way it is done in Italy, where the sauce is very light, yet no less flavorful. In any case, the osso buco should be served with the bone upright and lots of the sauce. Angel hair pasta is a perfect accompaniment, moistened with the sauce.

Serves eight.

Suggested wine: Barbera Oltrepo Pavese

Girello di Vitello Primavera

Roasted Veal Shank

The veal shank is the lowest part of the front leg of the veal. Although there is an enormous bone-to-meat ratio, the meat is very tender and delicious after being roasted awhile in its own juices.

2 veal shanks, about 2 lbs. each
2 tsp. salt
½ tsp. white pepper
½ cup olive oil
3 lbs. veal bones
1 large onion, cut up
1 large carrot, cut up
½ leek, cut up
3 ribs celery, cut up
1 whole garlic head, cut up, unpeeled
2 sprigs fresh rosemary
2 bay leaves
2 Tbs. tomato paste
1 cup dry white wine
1 Tbs. olive oil
½ tsp. chopped garlic

Preheat the oven to 450 degrees.

1 Sprinkle the shanks with the salt and pepper. Heat the olive oil very hot in a large saucepan and brown the shanks on the outside. Put the veal bones into the saucepan about five minutes after the shanks and brown them too.

2 When the meat has browned nicely, add one-half the quantities of onion, carrot, leek and celery, and all of the garlic, rosemary and bay leaves. Stir them into the pot and cook until moist.

3 Add the tomato paste and the dry white wine. Cook for another two minutes, then add 1 gallon of cold water. Stir the pot, cover, and bring to a boil. When that happens, uncover the pot and put it in a preheated 450-degree oven for one hour. The shanks are cooked when a kitchen fork inserted into the meat cannot pull them straight up out of the pot.

4 Put the saucepan back on the stove over medium heat and remove the shanks to a warm place. Taste the sauce and adjust the seasonings with salt and pepper. Continue to reduce sauce for another 45 minutes. Strain the sauce through a china cap or large sieve.

5 While sauce is straining, heat 1 Tbs. olive oil in a skillet and add the remainder of the onion, carrot, celery and leek, along with the ½ tsp. chopped garlic. Saute till browned at the edges. Pour in the strained stock, and bring to a boil. Cook the sauce with the vegetables over low heat for five minutes.

6 Meanwhile, make two cuts down the bones of the veal shanks, resulting in two large pieces of meat per shank. Slice the meat across the grain about ⅓ inch thick. Array slices of meat on a platter with the bones (which are full of delicious marrow for the serious connoisseur). Nap the meat with the sauce and lots of the vegetables.

Serves four.

Suggested wine: Grumello

Costoletta di Vitello Milanese

Panneed Veal Chop

This will appear to be much the same idea as Veal Tanet, but the flavor is completely different. For this dish we use thinly-sliced, bone-in veal rib chops.

4 bone-in veal rib chops
Sprinkles of salt, pepper and flour
4 eggs, beaten
3 cups plain bread crumbs
1 cup vegetable oil
⅓ cup Grana Padano cheese, grated

Preheat the oven to 400 degrees.

1 Pound the veal rib chops very thin with the smooth side of a meat mallet. Sprinkle with salt and pepper, then liberally coat the veal with flour. Pass the veal through the beaten egg, then bury in bread crumbs and coat well. Shake off excess.

2 Heat oil very hot in a skillet. Very carefully slide the veal into the skillet. With a gentle shaking motion, slosh the hot oil (carefully!) over the veal. After one minute, turn the veal over and put the entire skillet into the 400-degree oven. Turn the veal after seven minutes, and cook two minutes more.

3 Remove the veal, pour off the excess oil, then put the veal back into the skillet. Sprinkle cheese over veal and put the veal under a hot broiler for 15 seconds. Serve immediately.

Serves four.

Suggested wine: Rosso Piceno

Costoletta di Vitello Valdostana

Veal Chop Stuffed With Cheese And Ham

Almost since the day Andrea's opened, this dish has been our most popular entree. It starts with a superlative baby white veal chop, which we stuff with Fontina cheese and prosciutto, then moisten with an intense mushroom sauce.

4 oz. Fontina cheese
4 slices prosciutto
4 baby white veal chops, 10-12 oz. each including bone
Sprinkles of salt, pepper and flour
2 eggs, beaten
Salt and pepper
1 cup bread crumbs
⅓ cup olive oil
1 Tbs. flour
1 Tbs. chopped onions
1 tsp. chopped garlic
⅓ cup butter
16 medium mushrooms, sliced
1 cup dry white wine
1 cup demi-glace sauce
2 cups whipping cream

Preheat the oven to 450 degrees.
1 Cut the Fontina cheese into four slices, each about a half-inch thick, two inches long and one inch wide. Wrap each piece of cheese with prosciutto. Cut a slit in the side of each veal chop. Insert the prosciutto-wrapped cheese into the slits deep enough so it can't come out. Dust the chops with a little flour, salt and pepper.
2 Pass each veal chop through the egg to to get it good and wet. Then dredge through bread crumbs to coat thoroughly.
3 Heat oil very hot in a large skillet. Brown the breaded, stuffed veal chops, two at a time, to a medium-dark, crusty brown on both sides — about one minute. Then put entire skillet into a preheated 450-degree oven for 12-15 minutes, until top is brown and dry and cheese is beginning to flow from the pocket. Remove chops and keep warm. Repeat procedure for other two chops.
4 After cooking all chops, pour off oil and wipe out skillet lightly. Saute onions and garlic in butter till translucent. Add mushrooms and saute about 30 seconds, coating mushrooms well with butter.
5 Add white wine and allow to come to boil. Add demi-glace and whipping cream and return to a boil. Reduce liquid volume by about half.
6 Serve veal chops with four ounces of sauce each and garnish with fresh rosemary.
Serves four.

Suggested wine: Gattinara

176

Veal Tanet

Veal Chop Valdostana

Veal Michelangelo

Porcini Ravioli

Filet Mignon Andrea

Quail ''Princess Anne''

Roast Duckling with Plum Sauce

Carpaccio

Scaloppine di Vitello Maria Louisa

Veal Slices Sauteed with Crabmeat

Veal seems to lend itself to small amounts of rich, intense sauces. In New Orleans, we also like to top baby white veal with adult white crabmeat. Here goes.

Per person:
1 Tbs. extra virgin olive oil
Baby white veal scallop, about 5 oz.
Sprinkles of salt, pepper and flour
1 oz. lump crabmeat
2 oz. lemon cream sauce (see **Sauces***)*
1 Tbs. bearnaise sauce (see **Sauces***)*

1 Heat the olive oil in a saute pan over medium heat. Sprinkle the veal scallop with salt, pepper and flour very lightly. Saute the veal for one minute on each side.

2 Lower the heat and add the crabmeat to the pan. Agitate pan (do not stir) to warm evenly.

3 Spoon the lemon cream sauce onto the plate. Place the veal on top of the sauce. Top the veal with crabmeat, and cover the crabmeat with bearnaise.
Serves one.

Suggested wine: Capri Bianco

Animelle di Vitello

Sweetbreads

I love veal sweetbreads. They have a delicate flavor like that of other cuts of veal, but much purer and more intense. Unfortunately, sweetbreads have an image problem which owes to the fact that the word "sweetbreads" has two meanings. It can be used to denote the entire range of organ meats, from liver to kidney to brains to even testicles (that last one is what many people think sweetbreads really are).

The other, much more commonly-used meaning of sweetbreads is the thymus glands of a calf. These are present in the young animal only and disappear later, so they're always young and tender. This is what we mean by sweetbreads in this book.

The following procedure is the first step for any sweetbreads dish.

BASIC SWEETBREADS
1½ lbs. sweetbreads
1 large carrot, peeled and cut up
1 rib celery, washed and cut up
½ leek, inside light part only
1 sprig parsley
2 bay leaves
½ tsp. black peppercorns

1 Put all ingredients into a large saucepan with 2 quarts cold water. Bring the water to a boil. Reduce the heat to a rapid simmer and cook for 25 minutes.

2 Remove the sweetbreads with a skimmer and plunge into a bowl of cold water. After about five minutes, peel off the membrane which surrounds the sweetbreads. Be careful to get the parts of the membrane inside the many cracks and fissures of the meat.

3 Slice the sweetbreads about a quarter-inch thick. Salt and pepper the slices lightly.

You now have sweetbreads ready for preparation in the dishes that follow.

Animelle Mugnaia

Sweetbreads Meuniere

This is the simplest and most classical preparation of sweetbreads.

1 Tbs. cottonseed oil
6 oz. poached, sliced sweetbreads (see **Basic Sweetbreads,** *above)*
Sprinkles of salt, pepper and flour
1 Tbs. butter, softened
2 leaves fresh sage, chopped

178

1 Heat the oil in the skillet very hot. Coat the sweetbreads slices with flour and sprinkle with salt and pepper. Saute the sweetbreads in the hot oil until lightly browned—about two minutes.

2 Pour off the excess oil. Put the skillet back over a high flame until it begins to smoke. Add the butter and sage and agitate the pan until the butter sizzles—about 15 seconds. Pour the hot browned butter over the sweetbreads slices and serve with lemon to squeeze on top of the slices.

Serves one.

Suggested wine: Marzemino

Animelle al Marsala

Sweetbreads Marsala

The same idea as veal Marsala, but with the light, pure taste of veal sweetbreads.

Per person:
1 Tbs. cottonseed oil
6 oz. poached, sliced sweetbreads (see **Basic Sweetbreads,** *above)*
Sprinkles of salt, pepper and flour
2 Tbs. butter
1 tsp. chopped garlic
1 Tbs. chopped onion
1 Tbs. dry Marsala wine
2 Tbs. white wine
½ cup demi-glace
¼ tsp. salt
Pinch white pepper
2 Tbs. whipping cream

1 Saute sweetbreads in the cottonseed oil as for meuniere recipe above. Pour off the excess oil and add 1 Tbs. butter, onions and garlic. Saute until onions are translucent.

2 Add the Marsala and the white wine and bring to a boil. Add demi-glace, salt and pepper and return to a boil. Add cream. Reduce for about a minute. Add the rest of the butter and 1 Tbs. of water. Reduce for another minute.

3 Strain the sauce through a coarse sieve. Nap the sweetbreads slices with the sauce.

Serves one.

Suggested wine: Bardolino Superiore

Animelle alla Mostarda

Sweetbreads With Mustard Sauce

This version was preferred by Tom over all the other sweetbreads dishes we tested.

1 Tbs. cottonseed oil
6 oz. poached, sliced sweetbreads (see **Basic Sweetbreads,** *above)*
Sprinkles of salt, pepper and flour
1 Tbs. dry white wine
3 Tbs. water in which sweetbreads were boiled
2 Tbs. whipping cream
½ cup chicken stock
¼ tsp. salt
Pinch white pepper
1 Tbs. Cremona or Dijon mustard

1 Saute the sweetbreads in the same manner described above for sweetbreads meuniere.
2 Pour off the excess oil and in the same skillet bring the wine, whipping cream, sweetbreads water, chicken stock, salt, pepper and mustard to a boil. Blend well. Reduce by about half. Nap sweetbreads with sauce.
Serves one.

Suggested wine: Bardolino Superiore

Animelle al Filetto di Pomodoro

Sweetbreads in Tomato Sauce

The tender veal morsels also lend themselves to a sweet, slightly spicy tomato sauce.

6 oz. poached, sliced sweetbreads (see **Basic Sweetbreads,** *above)*
Sprinkles of salt, pepper and flour
1 Tbs. grated Parmesan cheese
1 egg
¼ cup olive oil
⅓ cup filleto di pomodoro sauce (see **Sauces***)*
3 leaves fresh basil, chopped
¼ tsp. salt
Pinch white pepper

1 Mix egg and cheese together. Dust sweetbreads with salt, pepper and flour, then pass sweetbreads through egg-and-cheese wash.

2 Heat the olive oil in a skillet to just short of smoking temperature, and saute the sweetbreads until golden brown—about three minutes per side. Remove sweetbreads and keep warm.

3 In same skillet, warm the tomato sauce, scraping the bottom of the pan. Add the basil, salt and pepper and warm through. Nap sweetbreads with the sauce.
Serves one.

Suggested wine: Dolcetto D'Asti

Animelle Impanate

Panneed Sweetbreads

Here we go again with the favorite New Orleans approach to veal. It's crusty, oozy, buttery, rich and good.

12 oz. poached, sliced sweetbreads (see **Basic Sweetbreads,** *above)*
Sprinkles of salt, pepper and flour
Two eggs, well beaten
Bread crumbs for coating
¼ cup extra virgin olive oil
¼ cup dry white wine
1½ tsp. butter
Juice of ½ lemon
¼ tsp. salt
Pinch white pepper
Grated Parmesan cheese

1 Dust the sweetbreads slices with flour, salt and pepper. Dip them in the egg, then coat with bread crumbs.

2 Heat the olive oil in a hot skillet and saute the coated sweetbreads slices until lightly browned—about 90 seconds on each side. Remove the sweetbreads and drain.

3 Pour off the excess oil. Add wine, butter, lemon juice, salt and pepper to the skillet and bring to a boil. Nap over sweetbreads. Serve with grated Parmesan cheese.
Serves two.

Suggested wine: Marzemino

Carne

Meats Other Than Veal

Italians are hearty meat-eaters; America produces the best beef and lamb in the world. Italy makes a wide array of spectacular sausages; New Orleanians love to eat sausage. The combination of all these facts makes for a lot of excitement for our menu, and for this section of our cookbook. In addition to the more familiar meats, I have included a number of recipes for some items you may never have experienced before. And perhaps by the time we're ready to produce a sequel to this volume, we will be able to obtain kid easily, and I'll have many more treats for you.

Filetto di Manzo Andrea

Filet Mignon with Shrimp and Mushrooms

This is our restaurant's premier beef dish, made with a beautiful thick cut of tenderloin, big shrimp, and a somewhat piquant, herbal sauce. If you serve this as a main course, go easy on the previous courses. The perfect side dish for this is risotto alla Milanese.

4 filet mignons, 8 oz. each
½ cup extra virgin olive oil
1 Tbs. chopped onion
½ Tbs. chopped garlic
½ cup roasted red and green bell pepper, chopped (see **Basics***)*
8 medium mushrooms, sliced
8 peeled, deveined fresh shrimp, 20-25 count
½ tsp. cracked black pepper
⅓ cup brandy
1 cup dry white wine
1 cup brown sauce
1 cup whipping cream
½ tsp. salt
Pinch white pepper

1 Slice the filets across into two medallions, but leave them hinged.

2 Heat olive oil very hot. Put steaks in two at a time and cook for two minutes on each side for medium rare. Remove steaks and keep warm.

3 In the same oil, saute all vegetables until tender, adding them to the pan in the order given above. Add shrimp and cook until pink. Add brandy and carefully ignite it. Let the flame burn out, then add wine and bring to a boil for about two minutes.

4 Remove shrimp. Reduce sauce by half. Add brown sauce, whipping cream, salt and pepper. Return to a boil and reduce by about a third.

5 Return filets (two at a time) and shrimp (four at a time) to sauce and cook till heated through—about 15 seconds. Remove to plates with about three ounces of sauce on each.

Serves four.

Suggested wine: Amarone Della Valpolicella

183

Filetto di Manzo Tartare

Filet Mignon Tartare

Steak tartare is a great favorite of gourmets, but one has to cross a threshold to enjoy it. Many people are turned off by the idea of eating raw beef—but they usually change their minds the first time they taste it. The dish (known in Europe as "beef American" for some reason, or as "beef cannibal" for the obvious reason) must be prepared to order. Part of our service of steak tartare is to prepare it right in front of the customer, who can then tell us to add a little more of this ingredient, a little less of that, etc. Please note that this recipe includes the only mention of catsup in the entire book.

5 filets of anchovy, chopped
1 egg yolk
2 Tbs. chopped onions
1 tsp. chopped garlic
2 Tbs. chopped capers
2 tsp. chopped Italian parsley
1 tsp. Dijon mustard
½ tsp. Tabasco
1 Tbs. Cognac
1 Tbs. paprika
¼ tsp. cayenne
1 tsp. Worcestershire
1 tsp. extra virgin olive oil
1 Tbs. catsup
½ tsp. salt
6 oz. filet mignon

1 Blend all the ingredients except the beef in a large wooden salad bowl.

2 Slice the filet across and, with a meat mallet, beat it down hard until all the membranes break. Slice the beef first one way then another, then chop it with fast hammer-strokes of the knife (or even two knives) on a chopping block. (Some cooks grind the beef, but this is not classic.)

3 Put the beef into the bowl and, with two forks, blend the sauce with the beef. Adjust the seasonings, and serve on a leaf of lettuce. You can use a knife and fork to form the beef into whatever form looks good to you.

Serve with a wedge of lemon and freshly-ground black pepper.

Serves one.

Suggested wine: Barbera

Bistecca Pizzaiola

Steak with Spicy Tomato Sauce

The idea is as simple as it is appealing: you make a sauce somewhat like the one you'd make for pizza, but instead of spreading it on a crust you cook a steak in it. Spicy and delectable.

4 strip sirloin steaks, 12-14 oz. each
½ cup extra virgin olive oil
4 cloves garlic, sliced very thin (not chopped)
1 Tbs. chopped onion
½ cup red wine
½ tsp. crushed red pepper
8 canned Italian plum tomatoes, plus 1 cup of juice
2 sprigs Italian parsley, chopped
2 sprigs oregano leaves, chopped
½ tsp. salt
Pinch white pepper

1 Trim excess fat from sirloin. Dust with salt and pepper, and pound with your fist to spread it out a little.

2 Heat olive oil very hot in a skillet and put the steak in to brown for about two minutes on each side. Add garlic and onion and saute with steak about a minute more. Remove steak, which will now be medium rare.

3 Add red wine, crushed red pepper, tomatoes, and tomato juice, and bring to a boil. Add parsley and oregano. Reduce heat to medium low, and simmer for five minutes.

4 Serve about four ounces of sauce over each steak.
Serves four.

Suggested wine: Barbera D'Alba

Bistecca al Pepe Nero

Steak with Peppercorns

This dish is one of the criteria by which European chefs — especially French chefs — judge themselves and others. I would not hesitate to put this version up against anybody else's in a taste test. The sauce is complex, involving cream, demi-glace, and peppers.

Per person:
1 9-to-12-oz. filet mignon
2 Tbs. black peppercorns
1 Tbs. butter
1 Tbs. chopped onion
½ tsp. chopped garlic
⅓ cup dry red wine
½ cup demi-glace
⅓ cup whipping cream
⅓ tsp. salt
Pinch white pepper

1 With something heavy (the side of a heavy cleaver works well), break the peppercorns into coarse bits. Roll the filet mignon through the peppercorns and coat the outside.

2 In a hot skillet, cook the filet to the desired degree of doneness. It takes about three minutes on each side for medium rare. Set the steak aside and keep it warm.

3 In the same skillet, heat the butter and saute the onions and garlic until lightly browned. Add the red wine and demi-glace and bring to a boil. Add whatever pepper was left over from coating the steak. Stir in the whipping cream, salt and pepper and bring to a simmer for two minutes.

4 Place the sauce on the plate, put the steak in the center, and nap a little sauce over the steak.

Serves one.

To make a green peppercorn sauce: Substitute white wine for red wine and green peppercorns for black peppercorns in the recipe above. Also, increase whipping cream to ½ cup and decrease demi-glace to ⅓ cup.

Suggested wine: Refosco Del Pedunculo Rosso

Coniglio al Forno

Roasted Rabbit

Rabbit became very popular in New Orleans in the late 1980s, which was reason for cheer at Andrea's. I had many great recipes for rabbit, which we Italians have always loved. This one uses the entire rabbit. Since it cooks for a long time, the meat—some of which tends to be on the tough side—gets nice and tender.

2 whole domestic rabbits, 3 lbs. each, cut up into eight pieces
½ cup chopped Italian parsley
Two sprigs fresh rosemary leaves
½ tsp. crushed red pepper
1 tsp. garlic, minced
¼ cup pine nuts

Sauce:
1 cup olive oil
3 cloves garlic
1 medium onion, sliced and pulled apart into rings
One sprig fresh rosemary leaves
2 cups dry white wine
1 tsp. salt
¼ tsp. white pepper
2 bay leaves
2 potatoes, peeled and cut up

Preheat oven to 400 degrees.

1 Cut pockets in the thigh sections of the rabbit legs, and stuff with a mixture of the parsley, rosemary, garlic, and pine nuts. Use toothpicks to close the pockets.

2 Heat the olive oil in a large saucepan over medium-high heat. Put all the pieces of rabbit into the skillet and cook about 20 minutes, until lightly browned around the edges. Remove rabbit from the saucepan and reserve.

3 Add onion to the saucepan and cook until lightly browned. Add rosemary and return rabbit to pan. Add white wine and one quart of water. Bring to a boil, then put the whole saucepan into a 400-degree oven.

4 After 15 minutes, stir contents of pan around to distribute sauce on rabbit pieces. Add salt, pepper and bay leaves. Continue to cook in the oven for 35 minutes more—a total of 50 minutes in the oven.

5 Add 1 quart of water, cover the pot, and return to oven. After another 20 minutes, add potatoes and stir into sauce. Keep in oven another 15 minutes, until potatoes are tender.

6 Return saucepan to stovetop and bring to a boil. Cook until all rabbit pieces are very tender.

Serves four.

Suggested wine: Brunello Di Montalcino

Girello d'Agnello alla Mantovana

Rack of Lamb Mantovana

There is no better lamb in the world than what we raise here in America. The public likes it better all the time—particularly when presented grandly, as this rack is. It should be carved tableside.

2 racks of American spring lamb, trimmed of excess fat
Salt and pepper
2 sprigs fresh rosemary
8 cloves garlic, cut in half
¼ cup vegetable oil

Sauce:
¼ cup olive oil
1 Tbs. chopped onion
½ tsp. chopped garlic
¼ tsp. crushed red pepper
¼ cup dry white wine
1 sprig fresh rosemary leaves, chopped
1 sprig fresh oregano, chopped
2 sprigs Italian parsley, chopped
⅓ cup butter

Coating for lamb:
½ cup dry white wine
2 Tbs. dry mustard
1 cup bread crumbs
Salt and pepper
½ Tbs. chopped garlic
1 sprig fresh oregano, chopped
2 sprigs Italian parsley, chopped
2 Tbs. olive oil

Preheat oven to 450 degrees.

1 Sprinkle lamb racks lightly with salt and pepper. Push a sprig of rosemary under the small flap of exterior fat which remains adjacent to the bones. With a narrow knife, cut a deep pocket in each end of the racks and push four pieces of garlic into each pocket.

2 Heat vegetable oil in a skillet and lightly brown racks, one at a time, on each side for about 30 seconds. Put the whole skillet into a preheated 450-degree oven. Roast racks 15 minutes for medium rare. Remove from skillet.

3 To begin the sauce, pour oil and fat from skillet. In it, without cleaning, heat olive oil hot and saute onions, garlic, and crushed red pepper. Add the white wine and bring to a boil. Add rosemary, oregano, parsley, salt and pepper. Remove from heat, then whisk in the butter.

188

4 Coat the racks as follows: Blend mustard into white wine and spread over lamb racks. Blend garlic, salt and pepper, oregano, parsley, and olive oil into bread crumbs. Pat this mixture all over lamb racks. Return racks to the oven for ten minutes, until crust browns. Serve with about two ounces of sauce and chopped parsley.

Serves four.

Suggested wine: Grumello

Medaglioni di Cervo Natalizzi

Medallions of Venison, Christmas Style

I originally developed this sauce for my own family's Christmas dinner, and I have served it every Christmas since. (I would be in trouble if I decided to skip it one year.) The sauce evolved over the years as I experimented with it. The sour cream, for example, took the place of whipping cream one year because I had just cooked a lot of German food for the hotel at which I was working. I thought the sour cream made a great improvement in the sauce.

Not only is this a fantastic complement to any cut of venison, it also goes very well with turkey, duck, or a veal chop. This recipe makes quite a bit of this sauce, which you can refrigerate or freeze for a future use. Just leave out the sour cream from the portion you will be saving, and add it when you're ready to serve the sauce again.

As for the venison itself, I am finding it more widely available since they started raising Axis deer commercially in Texas. In Southeast Louisiana, a lot of people hunt deer and wind up with more of it than they know what to do with. Here's what.

3 lbs. venison bones, cut up
½ cup cottonseed oil
5 oz. pork fatback
1 carrot
2 ribs celery
1 medium onion, cut up
2 cloves garlic, sliced
⅓ cup tomato paste
1 Tbs. juniper berries, broken with the side of a heavy knife
3 cups dry red wine
½ cup flour
½ tsp. thyme
½ tsp. marjoram
2 bay leaves
1 tsp. salt
¼ tsp. white pepper
½ cup currant jelly
½ cup sour cream

1 Put the bones, the oil, and the pork fat into a large stockpot. Brown over high heat for 20 minutes. Add the carrot, celery, onion, and garlic. Cook for about 20 minutes, until bones are thoroughly and darkly browned.

2 Add tomato paste, juniper berries, and red wine. Allow liquids to reduce by half.

3 Sprinkle flour into pot. Stir contents to brown flour lightly. Add a gallon of water and thoroughly stir contents of pot, scraping the bottom and sides of the pot as you do. Add thyme, marjoram, bay leaves, salt and pepper. Bring to a rapid boil for 10 minutes, then lower heat to medium-low. Simmer for an hour and fifteen minutes to an hour and a half, to reduce it by about one-third.

4 Strain stock through a sieve or china cap to remove bones, etc., then strain again to make smooth. Return sauce to medium heat and stir in currant jelly and sour cream until blended thoroughly. Adjust seasonings.

Makes 2½ qts. sauce.

Venison Medallions:

4 slices of sirloin of venison, 4-6 oz. each
1 Tbs. cottonseed oil
Salt and pepper to taste
1½ cups sauce, above

1 Place venison slices, one at a time, between two sheets of thick plastic (a food storage bag is perfect). Pound with the smooth side of a meat mallet until the venison approximately doubles in circumference. Salt and pepper lightly.

2 Heat the oil in a large skillet and saute the venison in hot oil for 45 seconds or so on each side. It cooks very quickly! Drain of excess oil.

3 Serve one slice of venison per person with four ounces of sauce.
Serves four.

Suggested wine: Brunello di Montalcino

Salsiccia Peperonata

Italian Sausage with Peppers

Loved in New Orleans as much as in its native Tuscany, this is a robust combination of flavors. Yet it's a relatively light dish. There is much controversy over what exactly constitutes "Italian" sausage. It's agreed that it's a pure pork sausage, about six inches long and an inch or so in diameter, inside a natural casing. The trouble begins when you try to say what seasonings go into it. In New Orleans, the most popular style of Italian sausage contains quite a bit of anise. On the other hand, one of our regular customers declares that there should be no anise at all! Please feel free to argue over this yourself while enthusiastically enjoying a big platter of the item in question.

2 green bell peppers
1 red bell pepper
1 yellow bell pepper
¾ cup extra virgin olive oil
4 cloves garlic
¼ tsp. crushed red pepper
2 lbs. Italian sausages
1 cup dry white wine
1 quart tomato juice
1 sprig fresh oregano
5 leaves fresh basil
½ tsp. salt
1/8 tsp. white pepper
4 sprigs Italian parsley

1 Slice peppers in half. Pull out the stem, seeds, and membranes inside. Slice peppers into strips.

2 Heat oil in a skillet until it just begins to smoke. Crush the garlic cloves and saute them with the crushed red peppers in the skillet until the garlic turns slightly brown. Add the pepper strips and saute until browned slightly on the edges. Remove peppers from skillet and reserve.

3 Add the sausages to the hot oil remaining in the pan. With a kitchen fork, prick the casings of the sausages about three times each. Saute the sausages over medium-high heat until the sausages are lightly browned all over.

4 Add wine and bring to boil. Stir in tomato juice and return to a boil. Add oregano, basil, salt and pepper. Put the skillet into a preheated 400-degree oven for ten minutes, or continue cooking over medium-low heat on the stovetop. (This allows the sausage to cook completely all over.)

5 Remove the sausages from the pan and return the sauce to the stovetop. Reduce over medium heat to half the original volume. Add the sausage and peppers. Warm through, then stir in the parsley.

Serves four.

Suggested wine: Barolo

191

Cotechino al Trentino

Rich Pork Sausage with Green Pepper Demi-Glace Sauce

Cotechino is a thick, large, rich-tasting pork sausage made from some odd parts of the pig—the ears, the tail, etc. It is very much loved in the northeast part of Italy, especially in Modena. As offbeat as it may sound, I think you will find it worthwhile to seek out a cotechino sausage (it is not the easiest thing in the world to find, although most good specialty meat markets have it). It has a fascinating taste all its own, and it's especially good during cold weather, served with a robust sauce and polenta, as below.

1 cotechino sausage, 1 to 1½ lbs.
¼ cup extra virgin olive oil
1 Tbs. chopped onions
1 tsp. chopped garlic
½ rib celery, cut up
½ red bell pepper, sliced
½ green bell pepper, sliced
1 green onion, cut up
4 sun-dried tomatoes, julienned
¼ cup dry red wine (preferably a Cabernet-Merlot from Trentino)
1 cup demi-glace
¼ tsp. chopped fresh basil leaves
¼ tsp. chopped fresh oregano
¼ tsp. chopped fresh rosemary leaves
Four wedges fried polenta (see **Risotto and Polenta***)*
½ Tbs. salt
¼ tsp. white pepper

1 Boil the cotechino sausage for two hours. Pierce it a few times with a fork to avoid major ruptures of the casing.

2 When sausage is cooked, heat the olive oil in a saute pan. Saute the the onions and garlic until light brown around the edges. Add the celery, bell pepper, green onion and sun-dried tomatoes. Saute until tender.

3 Add the red wine and bring to a boil. Stir in the demi-glace and return to a boil, then lower to a simmer. Add the basil, oregano, and rosemary, and cook for five minutes, until sauce is thickened.

4 Slice the cotechino about ¼ inch thick, and serve three or four slices with ¼ cup of the sauce and the polenta.

Serves four.

Suggested wine: Lambrusco

Salsiccia con Broccoli di Rape

Italian Sausage with Broccoli Leaves

Broccoli di rape (also known as broccoli raab) is a member of the cabbage family (as is the broccoli you're familiar with). Its leaves are used in a number of Italian dishes. While I have never seen real broccoli di rape in this country, the leaves of domestic broccoli have a taste and texture that is similar enough for this dish. You can use other greens, too: spinach, kale, turnip greens, or chard.

2 Tbs. extra virgin olive oil
2 Tbs. chopped onion
1 Tbs. chopped garlic
4 large links Italian sausage
1 lb. broccoli di rape
¼ tsp. crushed red pepper

Preheat oven to 400 degrees.

1 Heat the olive oil in a saute pan. Saute the onions and garlic until light brown around the edges. Put the sausage into the skillet and puncture the skins with a fork. Put the skillet into a preheated 400-degree oven. Cook for 10 minutes — until bottom of sausage has begun to brown.

2 Add ¼ cup water to the skillet, turn the sausage, and return to the oven for another eight minutes.

3 Meanwhile, wash the broccoli leaves well and drain. When sausages are cooked, remove skillet from oven and add broccoli leaves and crushed red pepper. Pour ¼ cup water over the greens and cook over medium heat until the greens wilt — about two minutes.

4 Serve one sausage and one-fourth of the broccoli di rape per person. Sprinkle with extra virgin olive oil and lemon juice at the table.

Serves four appetizers or two entrees.

Suggested wine: Barbaresco

Fegato Veneziana

Liver

It's a funny thing. There is no in-between when it comes to people's taste for liver. They either love it or hate it. I love it, and so do many of our regular diners, especially at lunch.

¼ cup vegetable oil
½ medium onion, sliced
1 Tbs. extra virgin olive oil
4 slices baby white veal liver, about 4 oz. each.
All-purpose flour
Salt and white pepper
1 tsp. chopped garlic
½ cup dry white wine
½ cup demi-glace
2 tsp. butter

1 Heat the oil in a skillet and saute the sliced onions until distinctly but lightly browned.

2 In a separate skillet, heat the olive oil very hot. Dust the liver very lightly with flour, salt and pepper. Cook the liver until browned—no more than about 30 seconds on each side. Remove the liver and keep warm.

3 In the same skillet in which you cooked the liver, saute the garlic until lightly browned. Add the wine, and bring it to a boil, then add the demi-glace and return to a boil. Reduce by about a third, then remove from the heat and dot with the butter.

4 Spoon the sauce onto the plate, put the liver on top, and cover with the grilled onions.

Serves two.

Suggested wine: Valpolicella

Fegato Saltati Maggiorana

Liver with Aromatic Brown Sauce

The first recipe was more or less classic. This one is a little different—lighter, for one thing.

2 slices baby white veal liver, sliced about ½ inch thick
Flour
Salt and pepper
1 Tbs. butter
2 Tbs. chopped onions
1 tsp. chopped garlic
2 Tbs. white vinegar
⅓ cup dry white wine
1 cup strong veal stock
½ tsp. marjoram
¼ tsp. salt
Pinch white pepper
1 Tbs. demi-glace

1 Dust the liver slices lightly with flour, salt and pepper. Heat the butter in a skillet and in it saute the onions and garlic until lightly browned. Sear the liver for 15 seconds on the first side, and about 30 seconds on the other. Remove the liver and keep warm.

2 To the same pan add vinegar, wine, veal stock, marjoram, salt, pepper and demi-glace. Bring to a boil and reduce by half.

3 Return the liver to the pan, and saute about another 30 seconds.

4 Nap the liver with the sauce and serve with mashed potatoes, spaetzle, or plain risotto.

Serves two.

Suggested wine: Valpolicella

Trippa

Tripe

Tripe definitely brings forth strong opinions from people. It is either loved or hated. We sell a good deal of it at lunchtime at Andrea's, but only to fans. In case you've never had the pleasure, tripe is the inner lining of the stomach of a cow. It's snow white and looks something like a honeycomb. It is essential that it be washed very well and then boiled for a long time before any dish with it is begun. In the process, it shrinks rather drastically.

3 lbs. tripe
1 lg. carrot, peeled and cut up
½ bunch parsley, chopped
3 ribs celery, chopped
1 sprig rosemary
1 lg. onion, cut up
4 bay leaves
1 Tbs. black peppercorns

1 Put all the ingredients into a stockpot with two gallons of water and bring to a boil. Boil for one hour and fifteen minutes. Remove the tripe from the pot and allow to cool.
2 Slice off the ends and spread the tripe out on a cutting board. Slice into strips about a quarter of an inch wide and two inches long.
3 Strain the stock in which the tripe was boiled and reserve.
   This will give you the basic tripe and stock used in the recipes below. You can freeze what you don't use right away; it's so much trouble to do the basic preparation of tripe that you'll find it handy to do a lot at one time.

Trippa Emiliana

Tripe with Demi-Glace Cream Sauce

The tripe is sauced with a beefy cream sauce with a faint taste of anise.

1 cup milk
1 cup whipping cream
1 pinch ground fennel seed
⅔ cup demi-glace
*1 cup tripe stock (see **Basic Tripe**, above)*
3 leaves fresh sage, chopped
*2 lbs. cooked, trimmed tripe (see **Basic Tripe**, above)*
½ tsp. salt
Pinch white pepper
4 portions cooked fettuccine

196

1 In a skillet, reduce the milk and cream over medium heat by half. Add fennel seed, demi-glace and tripe stock. Bring to a simmer for about three minutes, then add the tripe.

2 Simmer tripe in the sauce over medium-low heat for another 10 minutes, or until sauce is good and thick. Add the salt, pepper, and sage, and cook another minute. Serve over fettuccine.

Serves four.

Suggested wine: Bardolino Superiore

Trippa Regina

Tripe Stew with Tomatoes and Potatoes

The sauce is dominated by tomatoes and potatoes, which you can pronounce any way you want. This is one of my mother's favorites.

1 cup extra virgin olive oil
2 medium onions, sliced
2 leeks, sliced
2 ribs celery, chopped
1½ tsp. garlic, minced
2 cups dry white wine
2 cups canned chopped Italian plum tomatoes with lots of juice
2 cups tripe stock (see **Basic Tripe**, *above)*
1 tsp. crushed red pepper
2 potatoes, peeled and sliced
Salt and white pepper to taste
2 lb. cooked, trimmed tripe (see **Basic Tripe** *above)*

1 Heat olive oil in a large saucepan and in it saute the onions, leeks, and celery over medium-high heat until the vegetables are limp.

2 Add white wine, tomatoes, one cup of the tripe stock, crushed red pepper, salt, pepper and potatoes. Cook until potatoes are about halfway cooked—about 10 minutes—and then add the tripe and the second cup of tripe stock. Reduce heat to low and simmer until potatoes are completely tender.

Serves four.

Suggested wine: Bardolino Superiore

Carne

Trippa Milanese

Tripe with Red Wine Sauce and Rice

For this version, we make a thick, intense brown sauce with red wine.

1 Tbs. butter
⅓ cup chopped onions
½ Tbs. chopped garlic
1 Tbs. extra virgin olive oil
1 cup dry red wine
1/8 tsp. crushed red pepper
2 cups demi-glace
2 lbs. cooked, trimmed tripe (see **Basic Tripe***, above)*
1 Tbs. orange zest
1 Tbs. lemon zest
2 Tbs. chopped Italian parsley
½ tsp. salt
1/8 tsp. white pepper
4 cups cooked rice
Grated Parmesan cheese

1 Saute onions and garlic in butter over high heat until clear. Add olive oil and crushed red pepper and saute another minute. Add red wine and bring to a boil. Reduce liquid by half.

2 Add demi-glace and cook over medium-low heat until it returns to a boil. Add the tripe, orange and lemon zest, and the parsley. Cook for another five minutes, or until sauce thickens.

3 Serve over buttered rice with more Parmesan cheese than you might at first think reasonable.

Serves four.

Suggested wine: Refosco Del Pedunculo Rosso

Coda Coccodrillo

Alligator

The surprisingly tender, subtly-flavored meat of the ferocious, primitive alligator can be cooked in a lot of the same ways as veal. In South Louisiana, the gators are raised on farms, and people love to eat any dish made with this white meat.

4 slices alligator loin, 4-6 oz. each
Milk
Flour
¼ cup extra virgin olive oil
3 cloves garlic, crushed
½ Tbs. capers
1 rib celery, chopped
10 medium mushrooms, sliced
4 sprigs chopped Italian parsley
¼ cup lemon juice
4 drops Tabasco
¼ cup dry white wine
½ cup chicken stock
¼ cup butter
1 tsp. Worcestershire
Pinch cayenne

1 A few hours or the night before you're ready to cook, slice the alligator into ¼-inch-thick slices and submerge it in milk. This will tenderize the alligator.

2 When ready to cook, pound out the alligator slices to twice their original circumference. Dust the alligator scallops lightly with flour.

3 Heat the olive oil in a skillet until almost smoking hot. Cook the alligator until very lightly browned. Add the garlic, capers, celery, mushrooms, parsley, lemon juice, Tabasco, wine, and chicken stock. Cook until almost all the liquid is absorbed. Remove to a serving plate.

4 In the same skillet, heat the butter. Add the Worcestershire and cayenne and bring to a bubble. Pour sauce over alligator and serve.

Serves four.

Suggested wine: Pinot Grigio

Coccodrillo alla Creolaise

Alligator with Creole Sauce

Creole sauce, used in a number of very traditional New Orleans dishes, is a near-perfect match with alligator.

Creole sauce:
¼ cup olive oil
1 bell pepper, seeds and membrane removed, coarsely chopped
1 medium onion, sliced
2 ribs celery, coarsely chopped
1 tsp. chopped garlic
1 cup canned Italian plum tomatoes, chopped with lots of juice
1 Tbs. tomato puree
1 Tbs. tomato paste
2 bay leaves
1½ tsp. fresh thyme leaves
½ tsp. fresh rosemary leaves
½ tsp. salt
¼ tsp. black pepper
Pinch white pepper

4 alligator loin slices, about 6 oz. each
Milk
Flour
2 Tbs. extra virgin olive oil
4 sprigs chopped Italian parsley
Salt and white pepper

1 Make the sauce first. Heat the olive oil in a large skillet and in it saute the bell pepper, onion, celery and garlic until lightly browned. Add all the other ingredients and bring to a boil. Reduce heat to a simmer and cook for 10 minutes, or until thickened.

2 Slice, tenderize, pound out, and coat the alligator with flour, as for the recipe above.

3 Heat the olive oil in a skillet and saute the alligator until lightly browned. Add the Creole sauce and parsley, and bring to a boil. Adjust seasonings with salt and pepper and serve.

Serves four.

Suggested wine: Pinot Grigio

Coccodrillo Milanese

Panneed Alligator

This is the simplest alligator dish of all. Serve it with fettuccine Alfredo or risotto Milanese, with grated Parmesan cheese and lemon juice at the table.

4 slices alligator loin, 6 oz. each
Flour
Salt
White pepper
2 eggs, beaten
Bread crumbs
⅓ cup vegetable oil

Preheat oven to 400 degrees.

1 Pound out the alligator slices to double their original circumference. Dust alligator with flour, salt, and pepper. Pass alligator scallops through egg wash, then coat with bread crumbs.

2 Heat the vegetable oil in a skillet very hot. Saute the alligator on one side until lightly browned. Turn alligator and put the entire skillet into a preheated 400-degree oven for eight minutes—or continue cooking over medium-low heat on the stovetop for three more minutes..

3 Place alligator on plates and sprinkle with grated Parmesan cheese and Italian parsley.

Serves four.

Suggested wine: Pinot Grigio

Costata di Maiale Arrosto

Pork Rib Roast

Pork, after being largely ignored by first-class restaurants for years, has made a comeback. You will discover that its taste and texture are as fine as those of any other meat. And although it is necessary to cook pork all the way through, that doesn't mean that it has to be dried out.

1 pork rib roast, about 3 lbs.
4 whole cloves garlic
½ Tbs. fresh chopped rosemary
½ tsp. salt
Pinch white pepper

Sauce:
¼ cup vegetable oil
2 lbs. pork bones
1 medium carrot, cut up
1 medium onion, cut up
1 rib celery, cut up
2 cloves garlic, lightly crushed
¼ cup tomato paste
2 cups dry white wine
½ cup flour
3 bay leaves
8-10 parsley stems
1 Tbs. salt
Pinch white pepper

Preheat the oven to 450 degrees.

1 Trim the pork roast of all but a thin layer of fat on the back. Slit the thin layer of meat over the concave side of the bones.

2 Clean the handle of a wooden spoon and shove it through the entire roast, from one end to the other. In the hole that results, shove the garlic cloves alternately with generous pinches of the rosemary. Save a little rosemary to sprinkle on the outside of the roast, along with salt and pepper.

3 Heat the vegetable oil in a large saucepan or dutch oven till very hot. Put the pork roast in, fat side down, along with the pork bones, carrots, onions, celery and garlic. Brown everything, turning the roast once, for about five minutes.

4 Put the rib roast into a roasting pan and into a preheated 450-degree oven. After five minutes, pour one cup of the wine over the roast. Check the pan every ten minutes or so, basting when you do; if the liquid is almost gone, add a cup of water.

5 In the meantime, begin the sauce with what's left in that saucepan you used to brown the pork. Raise the heat to high and stir the tomato paste and one cup of the wine into the pan. Sprinkle the flour around the pan and stir well. When

202

browned, add a gallon of cold water and stir well. Scrape up all the burned parts that have stuck to the pan. Add bay leaves, parsley stems, salt and pepper. Bring the sauce to a boil, then reduce heat to a simmer.

6 The roast is done when a meat thermometer shoved into the middle of the roast (not touching bone!) registers 140 degrees. Remove from oven and cut off bones. Slice the roast ¼ to ½ inch thick.

7 The sauce is done after cooking for an hour, and reduced by one-half. Strain the sauce through a sieve and nap ⅓ cup over the slices of roast. Garnish with a sprig of fresh rosemary and a clove or two of lightly-crushed garlic fried till brown in hot olive oil.

Serves four.

Suggested wine: Refosco Grave del Friuli

Costolette di Maiale "Olivero"

Pork Chops with Herbs "Oliver"

I like to cook double pork chops—about an inch thick. Here are two recipes for them.

¼ cup olive oil
2 pork chops, about 10 oz. each
Salt and white pepper
1 clove garlic, sliced
¼ cup dry white wine
1 Tbs. chopped Italian parsley
¼ tsp. chopped fresh rosemary leaves
¼ cup pork sauce (from pork roast recipe) or demi-glace

Preheat oven to 450 degrees.

1 Sprinkle the pork chops with salt and pepper.

2 Heat the olive oil in a saute pan. Saute the pork chops until browned on both sides. Put the skillet into a preheated 450-degree oven for 15 minutes. Remove the pork chops and keep them warm.

3 Return the skillet to the stovetop over medium heat. Add the garlic and brown lightly. Add the white wine and bring to a boil. Add the parsley, rosemary, and pork sauce and return to a boil.

4 Reduce sauce for three minutes. Serve 2 Tbs. sauce with pork chops.
Serves two.

Suggested wine: Refosco Grave del Friuli

Costolette di Maiale alla Mostarda

Pork Chops with Mustard Sauce

What gives this its winning flavor is dill pickles — an under-appreciated ingredient in the cooking of meats. That flavor goes extremely well with pork.

¼ cup olive oil
2 pork chops, about 10 oz. each
Salt and pepper
2½ Tbs. chopped onions
½ tsp. chopped garlic
½ large dill pickle, julienned
¼ cup white wine
½ Tbs. Dijon mustard
¼ cup pork sauce (from pork roast recipe) or demi-glace

Preheat oven to 450 degrees.
1 Sprinkle the pork chops with peppered salt.
2 Heat the olive oil in a saute pan. Saute the pork chops until browned on both sides. Put the whole skillet into a preheated 450-degree oven for 10 minutes.
3 Remove the chops from the skillet and keep warm. Put the skillet on a medium heat, and in the pan juices saute the onions and garlic until light brown around the edges. Sprinkle in the flour and stir in well.
4 Add the white wine and bring to a boil. Stir in the Dijon mustard, pickles and pork sauce. Reduce by about one-fourth.
5 Spoon ¼ cup of the sauce, including lots of the pickles, over the pork chops on platters.
Serves two.

Suggested wine: Refosco del Pedunculo Rosso

Arista di Maiale ai Funghi

Pork Tenderloin with Chanterelle Sauce

Chanterelles are orange mushrooms that look like the bell of a trumpet. They used to be hard to find and expensive, and so it was with much joy that we discovered them growing wild, right under our noses here in New Orleans. Their nutty, earthy flavor is a fine foil to pork tenderloin—something else that's easier to find than it used to be.

Like many other recipes you are reading, this one was developed especially for this book. We were doubly happy that it turned out perfect the first time we tested it. It was the end of a very long day of cooking. Tom and I drank a bottle of Moet et Chandon White Star to celebrate the success of this dish. It was our last dish for the cookbook, ending a year of creating, testing, re-working and discovery.

1 pork tenderloin, about 10 oz.
1 Tbs. extra virgin olive oil
¼ cup dry white wine

Sauce:
1 Tbs. extra virgin olive oil
2 cups fresh chanterelle mushrooms
1 Tbs. chopped onions
1 tsp. chopped garlic
1 cup pork sauce (from pork roast recipe) or demi-glace
½ tsp. salt
Pinch white pepper
½ tsp. chopped fresh sage

Preheat oven to 450 degrees.
1 Heat the olive oil in a saute pan. Saute the the pork tenderloin, turning every minute or so, until browned on the outside. Add the wine and ½ cup water and bring to a boil. Then put the skillet into a preheated 450-degree oven.

2 Meanwhile, make the sauce. Heat the olive oil in a saute pan. Saute the onions and garlic until light brown around the edges. Add the chanterelles and saute until the mushrooms become tender on the outside—which happens in less than a minute over high heat.

3 Add the pork stock to the sauce skillet and toss with the mushrooms to coat. Bring to a boil, then add the sage.

4 The pork tenderloin is done when a meat thermometer pushed into the center registers 140 degrees. Slice the pork tenderloin diagonally into slices about ¼ inch thick.

5 Serve four slices of pork per person, napped with about ¼ cup of the sauce. *Serves two.*

Suggested wine: Chianti Classico

Pollo, Anatra, Altri Ucelli

Chickens, Ducks, And Other Birds

I am very proud of the poultry and game birds we serve in our restaurant, but for a variety of reasons. Every Monday, we feature our Pollo Al Forno Della Nonna (the first recipe in this chapter) as a lunch special, and it is very rare that we have any left at the end of the meal, no matter how many we cook. Whenever I hear that somebody has ordered a duck, I view it as a new challenge — only serious eaters order duck, and they usually love ours. I look forward to the Christmas season so that I can roast some geese. And no pheasant is safe around here.

Pollo al Forno Della Nonna

Grandmother's Baked Chicken

Roast chicken is such a simple, homely thing that I believe many people forget just how delicious it is. Our roast chicken, fragrant with herbs, moist and juicy, with a tantalizing crisp skin, is one of our guests' favorite entrees at lunch. It's something I love so much that we prepared it on our very first session of recipe testing—mainly so we could eat it afterwards.

2 whole chickens, 2 to 2½ lbs. each
½ large onion
½ large carrot
1 rib celery
2 sprigs fresh rosemary
Salt and white pepper
¼ cup olive oil
½ tsp. chopped fresh garlic
¼ cup dry white wine
2 cups chicken stock
4 medium-large mushrooms

Preheat oven to 450 degrees.

1 Remove gizzards and giblets from chickens. Wash chickens well and pat dry. Chop onion, carrot and celery into large chunks (about an inch long). Reserve two or three pieces of each; chop these into slivers. Stuff remainder of vegetables and rosemary inside cavity of chickens. With string, tie up wings and legs to make the chicken a tight package. Dust lightly with salt, pepper, and a little rosemary.

2 In a large, heavy skillet, heat olive oil over high heat. When surface of oil begins to ripple when you shake it slightly, put chickens in (one at a time, if necessary), stomach side down. Cook for one to two minutes, until lightly browned. Turn chickens and brown lightly on all sides. Then put skillet with chickens into the oven. Every five minutes or so, baste chickens with drippings in skillet.

3 After 30-35 minutes, turn bottom side up and continue to roast, basting as before. After 20-25 more minutes, prick the thigh deeply with a kitchen fork. When juices run clear, chicken is completely cooked. Remove chickens from oven.

4 Untie chickens and remove vegetables from inside. Drain most (but not all) of the oil and drippings from skillet. Put vegetables in skillet, along with garlic, white wine, chicken stock, and a pinch of salt and pepper.

5 Cook for about two minutes, then remove vegetables and puree in food processor or blender. Meanwhile, reduce liquid in skillet to about half. Return puree to skillet and stir in. Then add slivered fresh vegetables reserved earlier and quartered mushrooms; cook about two minutes, leaving vegetables crisp. Your sauce is now complete.

6 Put two or three pats of butter on top of each chicken and return to oven for three to five minutes longer. Remove from oven. Slice chickens in half top to bottom; remove backbone and rib cage.

Serves four. Suggested wine: Merlot Colli Berici

Pollo alla Cacciatore

Hunter's Chicken

This is one of the most famous and best-loved dishes in all the Italian cuisine. A hearty platter of chicken with a robust tomato sauce, it is joyful—if sometimes a little messy—eating.

2 cups flour
1 Tbs. salt
¼ tsp. white pepper
1 whole chicken, 2 to 2½ lbs., cut up
1 cup olive oil
½ cup chopped onion
1 tsp. chopped garlic
2 sprigs fresh rosemary (leaves only)
½ tsp. crushed red pepper
1 cup dry white wine
6 cups canned Italian plum tomatoes
2 cups juice from canned tomatoes
2 bay leaves
16 medium fresh mushrooms
1 tsp. chopped Italian parsley

Preheat oven to 450 degrees.

1 In a bowl, mix flour, salt and pepper and coat chicken with it.

2 In a large skillet, heat olive oil very hot and in it cook chicken pieces for three to five minutes on each side, until lightly browned. Remove chicken and keep warm.

3 In the oil in which the chicken was browned, add the onion, garlic, rosemary, and crushed red pepper. Saute until onions turn blond. Add wine and bring to a light boil.

4 With clean hands, squeeze tomatoes through fingers into the saucepan with the extra juice. Bring sauce back to a boil and add chicken pieces. Add salt and white pepper to taste and bay leaves. Return to a boil, then put entire saucepan into a preheated 450-degree oven. Cook for about 45 minutes, until chicken is tender and starting to fall off the bones.

5 Take saucepan from oven, and remove chicken. Stir mushrooms and parsley into sauce and cook over medium heat until both are incorporated into sauce— about two minutes. Serve immediately.

Serves eight.

Suggested wine: Ciro Rosso from Calabria

208

Pollo con Salsa Bianca

Chicken with White Sauce

Here is a very subtly-flavored dish that has a certain polish. What you taste is chicken, and what you see is whiteness.

1 whole chicken, 2½ lbs., cleaned, giblets reserved
1 medium onion, cut up
1 stalk celery, cut up
3 bay leaves
1 Tbs. butter
3 Tbs. all-purpose flour
½ tsp. salt
2 Tbs. whipping cream
½ leek, white part only, chopped
¼ red bell pepper, sliced

1 Put the chicken in a saucepan with enough cold water to cover. Bring to a boil, then boil chicken 35 minutes. Remove from water and cool.

2 When cool enough to handle, pull chicken apart to remove the backbone, rib cages and wing tips. Return these to the saucepan and bring to a boil. Reduce water to one-quarter its original volume. Strain the stock.

3 In a skillet, make a blond roux with the butter and flour. Add the stock to the roux and briskly whisk. Reduce by about one-third.

4 Meanwhile, remove the skin from the chicken pieces. Add the chicken to the sauce and simmer until it's heated through.

5 Strain off 1½ cups of the reduced chicken sauce. Add salt. Heat it in a skillet till bubbling, then add the cream and the leek. Saute until the leek is tender. Nap over the chicken. Garnish with strips of red bell pepper.

Serves four.

Suggested wine: Chianti Classico

Pollo Valdostana

Chicken Valdostana

Here is a greatly-improved version of the basic pan-sauteed chicken stuffed with ham and cheese. The spinach and herbs add accents to the chicken, and the tangy, buttery sauce sharpens it into irresistability.

10 large leaves fresh spinach
2 chicken breasts
4 slices prosciutto
4 slices mozzarella
2 fresh basil leaves
Flour
Pinch salt
Pinch white pepper
1 egg, beaten
Bread crumbs
¼ cup vegetable oil

Sauce:
1 Tbs. olive oil
1 tsp. chopped onion
½ tsp. chopped garlic
¼ tsp. fresh rosemary leaves
Pinch salt
Pinch white pepper
2 Tbs. dry white wine
¼ cup chicken stock
1 Tbs. butter, softened
¼ tsp. chopped Italian parsley

Preheat oven to 400 degrees.

1 Bring a pot of water to a boil and briefly poach the spinach leaves—no more than 30 seconds—and plunge them into cold water. Pat the spinach leaves dry.

2 Skin and debone the chicken breasts and pound them out to uniform thickness. Cover the surface of the chicken with spinach leaves. Top that with mozzarella, prosciutto, and basil. Fold the chicken breast over in thirds.

3 Dust these chicken "packages" with a little flour, salt and pepper. Pass them through the egg, then coat lightly with bread crumbs.

4 Heat the oil very hot in a skillet. Saute the chicken on one side for about a minute, until it lightly browns. Turn the chicken and put the entire skillet into the oven for 10 minutes.

5 Meanwhile, prepare the sauce. In a skillet, heat the olive oil over medium heat. Saute the onions and garlic until blond. Add the rosemary, salt, pepper, wine and chicken stock, and bring to a boil. Reduce by half, then take the pan off the stove. Whisk the butter into the sauce.

6 Spoon the sauce over the chicken and top with parsley. *Serves two.*

210

Quaglie Principessa

Quail "Princess Anne"

This is one of several dishes I created for Princess Anne of England in 1984, when she was a guest in the home of Mr. James Coleman. It is a fairly complicated recipe, but you can be sure that none of your guests have ever had it before. A small serving provides an enormous amount of flavor.

3 oz. baby white veal leg, cubed
3 oz. pork tenderloin, cubed
½ tsp. four-spice powder ("Quatre Epices," Bovida brand)
1 Tbs. foie gras
½ tsp. garlic, minced
1 egg yolk
1 Tbs. brandy
1 Tbs. Madeira
2 Tbs. whipping cream
½ tsp. salt
Pinch white pepper
1 tsp. chopped black truffles
1 Tbs. pistachio nuts
4 quails, washed and split, with backbone and ribcages removed
4 thin slices pork fat, about two inches on a side
4 slices bacon
¼ cup vegetable oil

Sauce:
½ cup red wine
1 cup demi-glace
½ tsp. salt
Pinch white pepper
1 Tbs. pate de foie gras

Preheat oven to 450 degrees.
1 Put the veal, pork, four-spice powder, foie gras, garlic, egg yolk, brandy, Madeira and whipping cream into a food processor and process until mixture is well blended. Add salt and pepper to taste. (It is helpful to pinch off a small "meatball" of the stuffing and cook it in a little olive oil, just to sample the taste so you can adjust the seasonings.)

2 Spoon into a bowl and add truffles and pistachios, and stir in well.

3 Load mixture into a pastry bag with a large opening and squeeze mixture inside the cavity of the quails. (The effect will be something like inflating the quails.)

4 Top each quail with squares of thinly-sliced pork fat. Wrap a slice of bacon around each quail, from the front to the back, and secure with a toothpick.

5 Heat the oil in a skillet and put the quails in breast down. Cook over high heat for about two minutes, turn the quails, and put the skillet into a 450-degree oven for 18-20 minutes, or until quails feel firm when squeezed with thumb and forefinger at the sides. Remove pork fat and bacon.

6 Now make the sauce. In a skillet, reduce red wine by about half, then add demi-glace. Bring to a simmer. Whisk in salt and pepper and pate de foie gras until the latter is completely incorporated into the sauce. Spoon 1 Tbs. of sauce on plate, place quail on top, and serve.

Serves four.

Suggested wine: Barbaresco

Oca al Forno Andrea

Roast Goose Andrea

I think it's unfortunate that we only get geese in the market around Christmas time. But I look forward to getting it then, when we make this intensely flavorful fowl as part of holiday feasting.

1 4- to 6-lb. fresh goose
1 rib celery, cut up
1 medium peeled carrot, cut up
1 medium peeled onion, cut up
2 cloves garlic, sliced in half
½ orange, cut up
1 apple, cut up
½ pear, cut up
3 oz. cottonseed oil
6 oz. pork fat
2 oz. Calvados brandy
4 oz. white wine
2 qts. chicken stock
1 fresh leek, cut up
Salt and pepper to taste

Sacchetto: Put these dry seasonings into a small cheesecloth bag:
2 bay leaves
½ tsp. whole black peppercorns
1 tsp. rosemary
1 tsp. sage
1 tsp. marjoram

Preheat oven to 425 degrees.
1 Save the neck and the gizzard of the goose. Wash and dry the goose very well.
2 Stuff the cavity of the goose with the celery, carrot, onion, garlic, orange,

212

apple and pear, each chopped into big pieces. Close cavity and tie goose with a string. Heat oil in roasting pan. Place goose in roasting pan and cover with foil. Place in oven at 425 degrees.

3 Baste every 10 to 15 minutes. Roast for 1½ to 2 hours, checking that the goose doesn't get too brown. When you prick the thigh with a skewer and juices run clear, the goose is cooked. Remove goose from oven. Split the goose in half and remove the backbone and breastbone. Keep the rest of the goose covered and warm.

4 Use the drippings from the roasting pan to begin the sauce. Add the neck, gizzards, backbone, and breastbone to the saucepan, along with the fruit and vegetables from inside the goose and the pork fat. Stir continuously over medium-low heat.

6 Add Calvados, and flame until alcohol has evaporated. Add the wine and bring it to a boil. Cook three minutes longer.

7 Add chicken stock, leek, salt, pepper and sacchetto. Bring to a boil and let simmer until sauce has been reduced by half. Remove the gizzards, bones, sacchetto and orange. Strain the rest of the sauce through a sieve into a saucepan.

8 Put the solid ingredients from the sieve into a food processor and puree. Stir the puree into the sauce and heat through. Serve the goose with the sauce.
Serves two.

Suggested wine: Runchet Valtellina

Anatra

Duck

Duck is one of the most interesting meats in the world to me. We serve it five different ways to the command of our guests daily, and we have some other ways to prepare it when we're in the mood.

More than any other dish, duck inspires anecdotes around Andrea's. We still scratch our heads over what possible response we could have made to the lady who sent two ducks in a row back to the kitchen. She said we had removed the breasts. "There's no white meat!" she complained. We apologized for this and let her learn from somebody else that there is no white meat in a duck.

Then there was the man who had an interesting test to determine whether a fresh duck was a Long Island duck. If I ever have the pleasure of knowing you personally, I will tell you this story over a few glasses of grappa. I don't think I can get away with printing it.

My basic technique of roasting a duck is to cook it very fast and hot at the beginning to seal in the juices, slow in the middle to keep it moist, and fast and hot again at the end to crisp the skin.

1 duckling, about 4 ½ lbs.
1 medium carrot, cut up
1 medium onion, cut up
1 rib celery, cut up
1 small orange, cut in eighths
1 sprig fresh rosemary
2 Tbs. salt
¼ tsp. white pepper
¼ cup vegetable oil
1 tsp. black peppercorns
2 large bay leaves

Preheat oven to 500 degrees.

1 Remove and reserve the gizzards, liver, etc. Wash the duck well. With a meat cleaver, cut off the last two sections of the wings. Stuff the cavity of the duck with the carrots, onions, celery, orange and rosemary. Sprinkle half the salt and pepper inside the cavity and the rest on the outside of the duck.

2 Tie up the duck securely with butcher string to close the cavity and hold the legs and wings against the body.

3 Heat the oil in a large skillet until almost smoking. Put the duck in the skillet breast side down over high heat, turning every three minutes or so until entire exterior is browned lightly.

4 Add the duck neck and wing tips to the skillet, and put the whole skillet into a preheated 500-degree oven. Baste the duck with the pan juices every 15 minutes or so.

5 After 30 minutes, take the skillet out of the oven and remove the duck to a roasting pan with a wire rack. Turn the duck upright to allow the juices to drain out of the interior. Pour the drippings from the original skillet over the duck. Lower the oven to 450 degrees, and return the duck to the oven in the roasting pan.

6 After 45 more minutes (during which you should continue to baste every 15 minutes), lower the oven to 400 degrees.

7 After yet another 30 minutes (this is a total of 1 hour and 45 minutes roasting time), remove the duck from the oven.

8 With a serrated knife, cut through the breast of the duck to the backbone, front to back. Remove all the vegetables from the inside of the duck. Cut the backbone out. Reserve everything.

9 Turn the duck halves inside up and pull out the rib cages. Twist out the drumsticks.

10 Put all the bones, along with the vegetables from the inside of the duck, the neck, and the wing tips, into a large saucepan with one gallon of water. Add the peppercorns and bay leaves and bring to a boil.

11 Reduce stock to ½ gallon of liquid. Strain through a sieve. You now have a duck stock for making the sauces for duck which follow.

12 Just before you're ready to serve, put the duck halves on ovenproof plates and put them into a preheated broiler, about three inches from the heat. Broil for about three minutes, or until crisp, dark brown areas form on the high spots. Serve as is, or with one of the sauces below.

Serves two.

Suggested wine: Marzemino

Anatra ai Lamponi

Raspberry Sauce for Duck

The duck lovers who come to Andrea's are not in agreement as to whether this is the most delicious of our sauces for duck. Some love it, some prefer other sauces. But they all admit that it is the prettiest to look at on the plate.

1 Tbs. sugar
1 Tbs. brown sugar
¼ tsp. white vinegar
¼ cup framboise (raspberry liqueur)
2 cups duck stock (from roast duck recipe, above)
1 cup fresh raspberries
½ cup demi-glace
½ Tbs. butter, softened
½ Tbs. flour
½ tsp. salt
Pinch white pepper

1 In a hot skillet, melt the sugars. Keep stirring to avoid burning.

2 Add the vinegar to the skillet and blend with sugar. Add the framboise and allow alcohol to evaporate.

3 Add the duck stock and bring to a boil. Add the raspberries and stir in, breaking them up a little but not too much. Add the demi-glace and bring all to a gentle boil.

4 Reduce sauce by half, then strain—preferably through a food mill, which will squeeze out more of the fresh fruit essence.

5 Return the sauce to the skillet. Make a white roux with the butter and flour and whisk it in. Reduce until you like the consistency as a sauce for duck. Then use it that way.

Makes one cup of sauce, enough for one duck.

Suggested wine: Moscato Nero

Anatra con Prugne

Plum Sauce for Duck

I think this is my favorite duck dish, and it's the one we have been serving at Andrea's since we opened. When fresh plums are in season, there is nothing better.

½ cup sugar
1 cup prune juice
2 cups duck stock (or chicken stock)
Six fresh plums, pitted and sliced, plus two more for garnish
Salt and white pepper to taste
½ cup Mirabelle plum liqueur
2 Tbs. butter, softened

216

1 Stir 1 Tbs. water into the sugar to form a slurry. In a medium saucepan, cook the sugar over low heat until it melts and browns lightly. Be careful not to brown it too much. Add the prune juice to stop the browning.

2 Add the duck stock and bring to a boil. Add the plums (except the two for garnish) and simmer for one hour, until sauce is reduced by about half. Add salt and white pepper to taste.

3 Strain the sauce through a food mill. Rinse the saucepan and return the sauce to it. Add the Mirabelle and carefully flame it in the sauce. Simmer another ten minutes to eliminate all the alcohol. Chip in the butter and whisk into the sauce.

4 Serve about two ounces of the sauce with the roasted duck, as above. Garnish the plate with half a fresh plum, fanned out.

Serves four.

Suggested wine: Lacrima Christi

Anatra all'Aranci

Orange Sauce for Duck

Duck a l'orange (to use the familiar French name) is probably the most famous European duck dish there is. If you think you've had all the duck a l'orange you ever needed, I think our version will change your mind. And remember: nothing in the world rhymes with orange.

2 Tbs. sugar
1 Tbs. brown sugar
1 oz. Cointreau
1 oz. Grand Marnier
½ Tbs. butter, softened
½ Tbs. flour
1 cup orange juice
2 cups duck stock
½ tsp. salt
Pinch white pepper
1½ Tbs. orange zest (finely grated rind, colored part only)

1 In a hot skillet, melt the sugars. Keep stirring to avoid burning.

2 Add the Cointreau and Grand Marnier to the skillet and carefully flame. Make a white roux with the butter and the flour and whisk it into the skillet, along with the orange juice, duck stock, salt and pepper and bring to a boil.

3 Reduce the sauce by two-thirds. When it gets close to that, boil the orange zest in a little water for one minute, then put it into the sauce. Cook for another two minutes and serve.

Makes enough sauce for one duck.

Suggested wine: Lacrima Christi

Piccioni con Lamponi e Morene

Squab with Berries

Squabs are young pigeons. Pigeon breeders harvest squabs right before they take their first flight. These birds have been so fattened up by their parents that they are bigger than they will ever be again in their lives. (Flying must be good exercise.) It is a delicious, under-appreciated bird. Its meat is dark and red, yet delicate and pure in flavor. It can fool some people into thinking they are eating beef.

1 pint cranberries (or whatever other berry is in season)
1 tsp. butter
1 Tbs. flour
⅓ cup sugar
⅓ cup raspberry vinegar
⅓ cup duck or chicken stock
½ tsp. salt
Pinch white pepper
4 squabs
Salt and white pepper
½ cup olive oil

Preheat oven to 450 degrees.

1 Start the sauce first. Put the cranberries in a small saucepan with enough cold water to cover. Bring to a boil and cook until the berries are soft. (This step is not necessary for raspberries, blueberries, or other soft berries.) Save a few berries for garnish. Put the rest through a food mill. Take ¼ cup of the resulting puree and reserve the rest for other recipes.

2 Blend the butter and the flour well with your fingers to form what the French call "buerre maniere" ("hand butter").

3 In a skillet over medium heat, melt and brown the sugar lightly. Add the raspberry vinegar and bring to a boil. Whisk in duck stock, buerre maniere, salt and pepper. Lower the heat and simmer for 25 minutes, or until sauce is suitably thick.

4 Wash and trim the squabs. With a sharp knife, cut the squabs open at the backbone and remove the backbone and the rib cage. Dust with salt and pepper inside and outside.

5 Heat the olive oil in a saute pan. Saute the the squabs until outsides are browned all over. Then put the entire skillet in a preheated 450-degree oven for 15 minutes. Squabs are done when juices from thigh run clear when pricked with a skewer.

6 Spoon 4 oz. of the sauce on a platter. Serve one squab per person, along with wild rice, vegetables, and a garnish of rosemary.

Serves four.

Suggested wine: Inferno

218

Pizza

If you think that pizza is too frivolous a food for an ambitious, first-class restaurant, then you've never had a great pizza before. We don't have pizza on our menu, but we do wind up making quite a few of them. It's my fault. Every now and then I get in a mood to make pizza and I offer it to a regular customer. Once they taste it, they want it almost every time they come in.

Most restaurants that make pizza in the United States have the wrong idea about it. They think of it as something like lasagne, as a bunch of cheese, sauce, and meat. The essence of a pizza, however, is that it's a bread. And if the crust doesn't give you a thrill with its freshly-baked aroma and its toasty crust, then the pizza is a failure. If you make a great crust—as you will if you follow the recipe below—it almost doesn't make any difference what you put on top of the pizza.

Pizza

1 Tbs. active dry yeast
1 lb. bread flour
1 Tbs. extra virgin olive oil
½ tsp. salt
Olive oil for pan coating
Semolina flour or corn meal

Preheat oven to 400 degrees.

1 In a bowl, mix yeast into 1 cup of lukewarm water. Stir well. Let sit for five minutes.

2 Meanwhile, pile the flour on a clean table or cutting board. Make a well in the center of the flour and add olive oil and salt. After yeast begins to foam, pour water with yeast into flour and begin mixing everything into a dough. Knead well, adding warm water a little at a time as needed to keep the dough moist as you go. (When we tested this recipe, we used about 1¼ cups of water, in addition to what we started with. But the humidity and temperature of your kitchen will dictate the amount of water you'll need.)

3 Sprinkle the dough occasionally with flour to keep it from getting too sticky. Roll dough ball away from you while, with the same motion, tearing it in half. Put it back together and repeat this again and again, slapping and pounding the dough to get a uniform texture.

4 When dough is fully formed and springy to the touch, sprinkle with flour and tear pieces off about half the size of a tennis ball. Flatten these slightly, sprinkle with flour, and cover with a cloth. Set aside in a warm, moist place to rise for 30 minutes. When dough has risen, pat each ball out into a disk, and then roll out to the thickness of two stacked quarters.

5 It is not necessary to throw the dough such as one sees pizza-makers in pizzerias do. But if you want to indulge in this, be ready to drop a few of them onto the floor until you get the hang of it. The technique is to pick up the rolled-out dough by placing a couple of knuckles underneath its center and letting the dough drape down. Toss the dough with a twist of the wrist, so that centrifugal action makes the dough spread out and get even thinner.

6 You can use any kind of metal pan to bake the pizza; often we place several on a sheet pan. Coat the pans lightly with olive oil, then sprinkle with semolina flour. Place the dough on pans, and let it rise again in a warm, moist place for 15 minutes. The outside will get a thin, slightly dry surface.

7 Put pans with the pizzas in a 400-degree oven for 10 minutes. Remove them at that point and add the toppings of your choice (see below). Return the pizza to the oven for another 10-15 minutes, or until crust begins to brown.

8 To achieve the crusty bottom that a pizza crust would get from the brick bottom of a real pizza oven, use this trick. While the pizzas are in the oven, heat up your griddle or a large black iron skillet as hot as you can get it. Right after you take the pizza out of the oven, put it right on the superheated surface until you get a few spots of dark brown on the bottom. Serve immediately.

Makes six pizza crusts.

220

Salsa Classica

Tomato Sauce With Herbs For Pizza

There are three words to describe the kinds of foods you can put on top of a pizza: Anything, anything, and anything. But let's start with a classic pizza sauce. The secret of our pizza sauce is that it is not cooked when it's spread on the pizza. I feel this is where most American pizzerias go wrong. When the sauce is cooked ahead of time, it loses the fresh taste that a great pizza should have.

1 cup canned Italian plum tomatoes, chopped, with a good bit of juice
½ tsp. crushed red pepper
2 tsp. chopped garlic
Pinch salt
Pinch pepper
4 leaves chopped fresh basil
1 sprig chopped fresh oregano leaves
½ Tbs. extra virgin olive oil

Combine all ingredients and mix well. No cooking required.
Makes enough sauce for six six-inch pizzas.

Suggested wine with pizzas: Capri Rosso

Pizza Andrea

This is my favorite pizza. You can scatter all the ingredients across the top of the pizza, or place them so that each slice has different tastes.

Two six-inch pizza crusts, partially baked
½ cup pizza sauce
½ cup shredded mozzarella
1 tsp. capers
1 slice boiled ham, chopped
2 chopped anchovies
2 strips each red and green bell pepper
2 Tbs. grated Parmesan cheese
2 tsp. extra virgin olive oil

1 Spread the sauce on the two partially baked pizza crusts. Top with all other ingredients in order listed.
2 Return the pizza to the oven and finish as per the instructions for pizza crust.
Serves two entrees or four appetizers.

Pizza Quattro Stagioni

Four Seasons Pizza

One of my favorite ways to build a pizza is to make each slice different on a single pizza. The four quadrants of this pizza, each a different color, are supposed to remind you of the seasons of the year.

2 six-inch pizza crusts, partially baked
½ cup classic pizza sauce
4 mushrooms, sliced thin
1 large slice ham, chopped
⅓ cup black olives, sliced
4 artichoke hearts, cut into quarters
⅓ cup red and green bell pepper, coarsely chopped
2 Tbs. grated Parmesan cheese
2 tsp. extra virgin olive oil

1 Spread the sauce on each of the pizza crusts. Then top the pizza with different ingredients in each quadrant:
Spring — Artichokes
Summer — Ham and olives
Fall — Red and green peppers
Winter — Mushrooms
2 Top each pizza with the olive oil and grated Parmesan, then finish as above.
Serves two entrees or four appetizers.

Pizza alla California

Anything that has avocados on it, by international treaty, must be referred to as a "California" whatever.

1 nine-inch or 2 six-inch pizza crusts
1 tsp. extra virgin olive oil
1 Tbs. sun-dried tomatoes, julienne sliced
½ avocado, sliced thin
½ cup mushrooms, sliced
1 tsp. fresh chopped oregano
1 tsp. chopped fresh basil leaves
2 Tbs. goat cheese
1 Tbs. ricotta cheese
1½ Tbs. shredded mozzarella
2 anchovies, chopped
4 black olives, chopped coarsely
¼ roasted red bell pepper (see **Basics***)*
1 Tbs. grated Parmesan cheese

1 Brush the pizza crusts with the olive oil, and make wedges of each of the other ingredients except the Parmesan cheese on top of the crusts. Sprinkle Parmesan cheese over the top.

2 Finish the pizza as per the instructions for pizza crust.

Serves two entrees or four appetizers.

Calzone con Salsiccia

Italian Turnover Pastry with Sausage

A calzone is an inside-out pizza. The crust is folded over the sauce, meats, and cheeses involved. The only possible problem is that the inside will have a lava-like heat when the calzone comes out of the oven, so it's probably a good idea to let them cool a few minutes before you serve them. Given the irresistable aroma, your guests may not be able to work up such forebearance.

2 large Italian sausages
1 tsp. chopped garlic
Pinch crushed red pepper
20 leaves fresh spinach, well washed and picked of stems
10 oz. pizza dough
1 tsp. extra virgin olive oil

Herbed Cheese Stuffing:
4 oz. mozzarella cheese
1 oz. goat cheese
3/4 oz. mascarpone
½ cup grated Parmesan cheese
½ cup ricotta cheese
1 tsp. chopped fresh oregano
1 tsp. chopped fresh basil
1 large leaf fresh sage, chopped
Pinch nutmeg

   Preheat oven to 475 degrees.
   1 In a skillet, brown the sausages over medium-low heat to near-crispness on two sides. Remove from skillet and keep warm.
   2 In the same skillet, saute the chopped garlic until light brown around the edges. Add the crushed red pepper, the spinach, and 1 Tbs. water. Saute until spinach is limp and remove from heat.
   3 On a floured board, pat out half of the pizza dough into the usual pizza shape, about nine inches across. Lay out half the spinach in the center of the dough. Brush the olive oil over the spinach.
   4 Combine all the ingredients of the herbed cheese stuffing and mix well. Spread 5 Tbs. of the mixture on top of the spinach. Put one sausage on top of that.
   5 Fold the pizza dough over and crimp the edges with a fork. Cut the edges round with a serrated pastry wheel.
   6 Coat the bottom of a pie pan or pizza pan with shortening. Place the pastry on it and bake in a preheated 475-degree oven for 20-25 minutes, until golden brown.
   Warning! Allow to cool a few minutes before eating!
   Makes two entrees or four to six appetizers.

224

Calzone Primavera

Springtime Calzone

This is a lighter calzone, with a great variety of different flavors in each bite.

10 oz. pizza dough
¼ cup tomato basil sauce (see **Sauces***)*
8 pitted black olives, chopped coarsely
1 Tbs. capers
4 thin slices ham
12 leaves spinach, washed well and trimmed
4 anchovies, chopped
2 large mushrooms, sliced
2 Tbs. grated Parmesan cheese
½ roasted red bell pepper, cut into strips (see **Basics***)*
8 fresh basil leaves, sliced
2 oz. mozzarella cheese, shredded
2 Tbs. ricotta cheese

The procedure is the same as for the sausage calzone. Just spread the tomato sauce on the two crusts, and top with all the other ingredients. Fold, crimp, trim, and bake.

Makes two entrees or four to six appetizers.

Pane

Pane Nero Knisley

Whole Wheat Bread

The baskets of bread we bring to our tables at Andrea's contain two kinds of bread: small French loaves, which we have baked for us by a local French bakery, and whole wheat bread, which our master baker Lonnie Knisley bakes daily. At almost every table, the whole wheat bread disappears faster. In fact, we can hardly keep up with the demand for it. This recipe makes enough to keep you in these rolls all week. They're great toasted for breakfast with butter and cane syrup or jam.

1 oz. dry yeast
1 lb. bread flour
2½ lbs. whole wheat flour
10 oz. milk
3 oz. brown sugar
1½ Tbs. salt
¼ lb. butter
½ cup molasses

1 Dissolve the yeast in one cup warm water and set aside.

2 Sift the two flours together in a bowl.

3 Bring the milk to a boil, then remove from the heat. Stir in the brown sugar, salt, butter, and molasses until completely dissolved.

4 Add the milk mixture to the flours and work in. (If you have a strong mixer with a dough hook, that's the easiest way to do it; run the mixer on slow speed.)

5 When all the milk is worked into the flour, add the yeast and the water it was dissolved in. Then add, a little at a time, up to 2 cups more water. Use only enough to get a smooth, workable dough. (The amount of water varies greatly with the temperature and humidity of your kitchen.)

6 Knead and pound the dough for 15 minutes. Then put it into a lightly-greased bowl and cover it with a cloth. Put it in a warm, moist place to rise for 30 minutes, until doubled in volume.

7 Punch down the dough. Cut off pieces somewhat smaller than the size loaves you want to bake. Place these on a lightly-greased baking sheet and let the loaves rise in a warm, moist place for 15 to 20 minutes.

Preheat the oven to 375 degrees.

8 After the loaves rise, bake them in the preheated 375-degree oven for 15-20 minutes, until crusty.

Makes three dozen small rolls or six French loaves.

Contorni

Vegetables

No entree goes out to the table at Andrea's without at least two fresh vegetables. Not only do I like the taste, I also love the feeling of abundance that the vegetables lend to a plate. But vegetables are not consigned entirely to the side-dish role in our restaurant. Some of what follows can make a whole meal. And several of them serve well as antipasti.

Melanzane Parmigiana

Eggplant Casserole with Tomato Sauce and Cheese

Here is a dish that we literally cannot keep in our kitchen. The staff gobbles it up as fast as we can make it. When by some miracle enough has been saved for our dining room patrons, they also like it a lot. This comes out looking almost like lasagne.

3 lbs. medium eggplants
1 Tbs. olive oil
3 cups tomato basil sauce (see **Sauces***)*
1 lb. grated Parmesan cheese
2 lbs. shredded mozzarella
¼ cup chopped fresh oregano
¾ cup chopped fresh basil leaves

Preheat oven to 450 degrees.

1 Peel the eggplants and slice them about two quarters' thickness. Sprinkle liberally with salt and place in a pan with enough of a weight on top of the eggplants that the water in them will drip out. (See **Basics**.) After 30 minutes weighted down, wash the eggplant slices well and drain. Coat with flour.

2 Heat the olive oil in a saute pan over medium heat. Saute the eggplant until light brown around the edges. Drain the excess oil. Saute only one layer of eggplant in the pan at a time.

3 Coat the bottom of a 10" x 12" pan with the olive oil, and pour in 8 oz. of the tomato basil sauce. Put down a layer of the eggplant. Ladle on another 8 oz. of the sauce. Sprinkle on enough Parmesan cheese to cover, then about one-fourth of the mozzarella. Sprinkle lightly with the basil and oregano.

4 Lay down another layer of eggplant, and cover it in turn with sauce, Parmesan, mozzarella and herbs in the same proportions as above. Continue making layers until you run out of materials.

5 Finish the top of the pan with a generous layer of Parmesan cheese. Then put the pan into a preheated 450-degree oven for 45 minutes.

7 Allow to cool for at least 30 minutes before attempting to slice or serve. This is actually better the second day. It can be refrigerated and served either cold or at room temperature. It will still have a great flavor and a surprisingly light texture.

Serves 12 entrees or 24 side dishes.

Melanzane alla Giardiniera

Eggplant with Garden Vegetables

A superb, very full-flavored vegetable side dish. It's particularly good when the weather is cold out, for some reason.

1 medium eggplant, cut into large cubes
½ Tbs. salt

⅓ cup olive oil
1 zucchini, cut into large dice
1 yellow squash, cut into large dice
1 green and 1 red bell pepper, stems and seeds removed, cut into large dice
1 cup sliced fresh mushrooms

Sauce:
1 Tbs. extra virgin olive oil
½ onion, cut up
½ Tbs. chopped garlic
5 canned Italian plum tomatoes, chopped
½ cup juice from tomatoes
10 chopped fresh basil leaves
4 sprigs oregano leaves, chopped
1 bay leaf, broken
1 tsp. salt
¼ tsp. white pepper

1 Coat the eggplant cubes with salt and squeeze out the bitter water. (See **Basics**.) Wash the salt off and pat the eggplant dry.

2 Heat the olive oil in a saute pan. Saute the squash, zucchini, eggplant and bell peppers separately until light brown around the edges. Saute the mushrooms until tender. It will speed things along to use two skillets, each with ⅓ cup olive oil. The reason you must saute the vegetables separately is that they cook at different rates. The eggplant will take the longest. Drain the excess oil from the vegetables as you remove them from the pan.

3 Heat the extra virgin olive oil in a saute pan over medium heat. Saute the onions and garlic until blond. Add the tomatoes, juice, basil, oregano, bay leaf, salt and pepper and bring to a boil.

4 Add all the vegetables except mushrooms to the sauce. Cook until tender on the outside but still quite firm within. Add the mushrooms. Add a bit of water if needed to keep a steaming effect going in the skillet.

Serve ½ cup as a vegetable side dish. Serves 12.

Carciofini Francesca

Artichokes Francesca

Save this recipe for the day you find some especially tender, fresh baby artichokes. When the leaves are tender enough to eat without even trimming, that's when this recipe is best. It's good either as a side dish or as an antipasto.

6 tender baby artichokes
2 Tbs. lemon juice
2 eggs
¼ cup grated Parmesan cheese
½ tsp. salt
Pinch white pepper
All-purpose flour
⅓ cup olive oil

1 Bring ½ gallon of cold water with lemon juice to a boil. Meanwhile, trim points and tough outer leaves from artichokes. When water comes to a boil, put the artichokes in and cook them for 30 minutes. Drain artichokes and cut into quarters from top to bottom.

2 Beat the eggs in a bowl and then beat in the Parmesan cheese.

3 Sprinkle the salt and pepper over the artichokes and then lightly dust them with flour. Put the artichokes into the bowl of egg and cheese, and toss to coat.

4 Heat the olive oil in a saute pan. Saute the artichokes, cut side down, until golden brown. Turn and saute another two minutes or so until browned all over.

5 Remove and drain artichokes. Sprinkle with grated Parmesan cheese and chopped Italian parsley.

Serves six.

Riso e Fagioli

Red Beans and Rice Capri Style

In New Orleans, everybody eats red beans and rice for lunch—usually on Mondays. I was delighted to discover this when I first moved to town, because I grew up eating red beans almost exactly the same way in my native Capri. The difference between my style of red beans and the New Orleans style is that I don't cook the beans as long (so they're a little firmer) and I add the rice directly into the pot of beans instead of serving it on the side. Italians also like to put a teaspoon or so of extra virgin olive oil and a sprinkling of Parmesan cheese on top of the plate of beans. Orleanians would find this a little peculiar—despite the fact that many of them top their beans with anything from pickle relish to catsup.

1 lb. red beans
1 lb. hamhocks (with bones)
4 sprigs Italian parsley
4 sprigs celery leaves
4 sprigs fresh oregano
2 tsp. salt
½ tsp. white pepper
1 white onion, chopped coarsely
2 sprigs celery, chopped coarsely
1½ Tbs. chopped garlic
½ cup extra virgin olive oil
½ tsp. crushed red pepper
1½ cups Arborio or long-grain rice

1 The night before you want to serve red beans, pick through the beans to remove dirt, rocks, misshapen beans, etc. Soak the remaining beans overnight in cold water.

2 The next morning, drain the beans and put them into a large pot with a gallon of cold water. Bring the pot to a boil. Lower to a simmer and add the hamhocks, parsley, celery leaves, oregano, salt and pepper.

3 After the beans have simmered for an hour and a half, heat the olive oil in a second large saucepan over medium heat. Saute the chopped onion, celery, garlic and crushed red pepper. When the vegetables are tender and have just begun to brown, pour the contents of the bean pot in with the sauteed onions and celery. Add the rice right into the pot and cook until the rice is tender.

The beans need to cook at least two hours. They get better, however, the longer you simmer them—all day, even. It may be necessary to stir in additional water to keep the texture of the beans loose.

Serves six.

Suggested Wine: Vernaccia Di San Gimignano

Fagiolini Saltati in Olio Virgine d'Oliva

Sauteed Green Beans with Olive Oil and Garlic

This dish comes out with the brilliant green color and fresh snap of green beans, but with a mouthful of flavor. Extra virgin olive oil strikes again.

½ lb. fresh green beans
¼ tsp. baking soda
¼ tsp. salt
1 Tbs. extra virgin olive oil
1 Tbs. chopped onions
½ tsp. chopped garlic
1 pinch crushed red pepper
Juice of 1 medium lemon
3 sprigs Italian parsley, chopped
Salt and white pepper to taste

1 Bring a pan of water to a boil and add the green beans, baking soda and salt. When the water returns to a boil, boil for 12 minutes, until the beans are cooked al dente.

2 Remove the beans to a bowl of ice and chill them to retain the flavor and color.

3 Heat the olive oil in a skillet, and saute the onions and garlic until lightly browned. Add crushed red pepper, lemon juice, parsley, half the beans, and a tablespoon of water. Toss the beans in the pan for about one minute, then add the rest of the beans. Cook while agitating the pan to toss beans until the beans are heated all the way through. Add salt and pepper to taste.

Serves four as a side dish.

Fagiolini Carnivale

Green Beans Carnival

This colorful dish puts us in mind of Mardi Gras.

½ lbs. fresh green beans
¼ tsp. baking soda
¼ tsp. salt
¼ cup extra virgin olive oil
1 Tbs. chopped onion
1 tsp. chopped garlic
1 pinch crushed red pepper
4 canned Italian plum tomatoes, chopped
1½ tsp. chopped fresh oregano
½ tsp. salt
Pinch white pepper

1 Bring a pan of water to a boil and add the green beans, baking soda and salt. When the water returns to a boil, boil for 12 minutes, until the beans are cooked al dente.

2 Heat the olive oil and saute the onions and garlic until onions are translucent. Add the crushed red pepper, tomato, and oregano and heat to boiling. Add the green beans and saute until beans are heated all the way through. Add salt and white pepper to taste.

Serves four.

Cavolo Rosso

Red Cabbage

Here is the ideal accompaniment to venison, duck, or any other kind of game.
I picked up the recipe during the time I spent as a chef in Germany.

5 oz. pork fat
¼ cup vegetable oil
1 medium onion, sliced
1 large red cabbage
3 cups dry red wine
½ cup red wine vinegar
6 crushed juniper berries
2 bay leaves
1 Tbs. salt
½ tsp. white pepper
3 apples, peeled and cored
1 potato, peeled
2 Tbs. sugar

Preheat oven to 450 degrees.

1 Fry the pork fat in the oil until the amount of oil in the pan approximately doubles. Then add onions and saute until they begin to brown.

2 Cut the red cabbage in half, then cut out the core. Chop as if you were making cole slaw. Add it to the pot and cook for five minutes over medium heat.

3 Add red wine, vinegar, juniper berries, bay leaves, salt and pepper. Cook another five minutes. Cover saucepan and place in preheated 450-degree oven.

4 Cut up the apples and potato and process into a coarse puree in a food processor or blender. After cabbage has been in the oven for 30 minutes, stir in the apple-potato puree.

5 Continue to cook in the oven for 35 minutes, covered, stirring every five minutes or so. The cabbage is ready when it has the consistency of al dente pasta. Add sugar and stir in thoroughly.

Serves eight.

234

Asparagi Bianchi

White Asparagus

The arrival of fresh asparagus is always a time of rejoicing at Andrea's. We love to offer it to our guests—especially when we have fresh white asparagus. White asparagus are raised by keeping mounds of soil around the spears as they grow. This involves a lot of hand work, so they are very expensive—but the taste is mellow and outstanding.

The first step with all asparagus except the very smallest kind is to strip off the woody exterior skin. This can be done with single strokes of a potato peeler. It's time-consuming and seems to generate a lot of waste (especially given the price of asparagus!), but it does greatly improve the texture.

Depending on the length of the asparagus you have on hand, you should cut off the bottoms of the stems so that you have only fresh, tender tissues inside. Save these bottoms for making soup. (There's a recipe in the **Soups** chapter.) Tie the asparagus in a bundle with butcher string and stand the bundle up in a pan of boiling water. Cook for four to seven minutes, depending on the size of the asparagus. They should give to a squeeze, but still be springy and firm and not wrinkled. As soon as you remove the asparagus from the water, plunge them into ice water and cut the string off.

At Andrea's, we serve asparagus four different ways. The first two are appetizers, the second two are side dishes.

1 Squeeze the juice of ½ lemon and drizzle 1 tsp. extra virgin olive oil over four chilled spears per person.

2 Nap 1 Tbs. of vinaigrette sauce (see **Salads**) over four chilled spears per person.

3 Pour 1 Tbs. hollandaise sauce (see **Sauces**) over four spears per person, and run them under a hot broiler or toaster oven until the sauce browns lightly.

4 Spoon 1 tsp. melted butter and 1 tsp. grated Parmesan cheese over the spears. Run the asparagus under a hot broiler or toaster oven until the butter lightly browns.

Suggested Wine: Gavi di Gavi

Puré di Patate

Mashed Potatoes

Although it may seem odd to include something as everyday as mashed potatoes in a gourmet Italian cookbook, in Italy mashed potatoes are prized and frequently found in the best restaurants. When made properly, without shortcuts, these mashed potatoes will proclaim their specialness through their terrific taste and texture.

4 large Idaho potatoes, peeled and cut up into cubes
1 Tbs. butter
¼ cup whipping cream
Pinch nutmeg
1 tsp. salt
¼ tsp. white pepper

1 Put the potatoes in a saucepan with enough cold water to cover and bring to a boil. Once the water starts boiling, boil the potatoes for 20 minutes.

2 Drain the water. Mash the potatoes in a food mill. (You can use a food processor or mash the potatoes by hand, but a food mill gives a much nicer texture and strains out any pieces of skin or other foreign matter.)

3 After mashing the potatoes, add the salt, pepper, nutmeg, butter and whipping cream while stirring briskly to incorporate everything into what will almost seem like a dough. Serve hot and in large quantity.

Serves four.

Patate alla Campagnola

Country-Style Potatoes

Here's a great-tasting, robust potato side dish that you'd better make plenty of. When we make it for our staff specials, everyone looks at everyone else's plate to see if he can grab any extra potatoes.

2 lbs. red new potatoes
1 cup vegetable oil
⅓ cup olive oil
½ medium onion, sliced
¼ cup chopped red and green bell pepper
¼ cup pitted, sliced black olives
1 Tbs. fresh rosemary leaves
½ tsp. salt
Pinch white pepper
1 sprig Italian parsley, chopped

Preheat oven to 400 degrees.
1 Bring two quarts of water to a boil in a large saucepan.
2 Wash the potatoes well. Pare off any bad parts, then slice each potato into six wedges.
3 Boil the potato wedges for six minutes. (Make sure that there is not so much water in the pot that the potatoes are more than ½ inch under, otherwise the water will not return to the boil fast enough and the potatoes will not have a good texture.) Remove the potatoes and drain well for five minutes.
4 Meanwhile, heat the vegetable oil in a skillet. Making sure not to get any water into the skillet, put the potatoes in. Saute them until they begin to brown here and there. Put the entire skillet into a preheated 400-degree oven for seven minutes. Remove from the skillet and drain on paper towels.
5 In a skillet, heat the olive oil over medium heat. Saute the onions until blond. Add the bell peppers. When peppers are tender, add the olives and the rosemary and saute for another minute.
6 Add the potatoes, salt and pepper and toss well. Garnish with chopped Italian parsley.
Serves six to eight.

Patate Rissolate

Crispy Sauteed Potatoes with Garlic

The Italian answer to brabant potatoes. When we made up a batch of these to test the recipe, the entire pan disappeared within minutes as everybody in the kitchen popped one in his mouth—and then came back and ate two or three more.

4 medium Idaho potatoes, washed, peeled, and cut into large cubes
1 tsp. salt
1 cup vegetable oil
1 Tbs. extra virgin olive oil
1 tsp. chopped garlic
1 Tbs. chopped onion
½ sprig chopped fresh rosemary
½ tsp. paprika
Salt and pepper to taste

Preheat oven to 450 degrees.

1 Boil a quart of water. Put the potato cubes into the water. There should be just enough water to not quite cover all the potato chunks. Add the salt.

2 As soon as the water returns to a boil, take the pan off the stove, pour off the water, and let the potato chunks cool in a single layer. Dry the potatoes with a towel.

3 Heat the vegetable oil in a large skillet (preferably cast iron) and fry the potatoes in one layer. We fry them on top of the stove until they get white around the edges, then put them into a 450-degree oven until they're light brown. But you can do the entire procedure on top of the stove. Remove the potatoes and drain excess oil.

4 While the potatoes are frying, heat the olive oil in a skillet over medium heat. In it saute the onions, garlic, rosemary and paprika until the onions are blond.

5 Toss the potatoes in the skillet with the onions, etc., until the potatoes are uniformly seasoned. Sprinkle on salt and pepper to taste and serve hot.

Serves four.

Patate Gratinate Milanese

Potato Casserole with Cheese

These are the potatoes we most often serve at Andrea's—mainly because regular customers get upset if they don't find them on their plates.

½ gallon milk
6 medium Idaho white potatoes, peeled
⅓ cup butter
½ onion, chopped coarsely
1 tsp. chopped garlic
¼ tsp. nutmeg
1 tsp. salt
¼ tsp. white pepper
1 cup coarsely grated Swiss cheese
½ cup finely grated Parmesan cheese

Preheat oven to 400 degrees.
1 Bring the milk to a simmer in a large saucepan.
2 Slice the potatoes into coins about ¼-inch thick.
3 Heat the butter in a saucepan over medium-low heat until it bubbles. Saute onions and garlic in it until tender and translucent.
4 Add the potatoes and cook, tossing with the butter, until they just start to turn starchy at the edges—about three minutes.
5 Add the boiling milk, nutmeg, salt and pepper and return to a boil.
6 When the saucepan returns to a boil, remove it from the heat and stir in the cheeses. Pour the potatoes into a casserole or baking dish coated lightly with butter, and bake it in a preheated 400-degree oven for 40 minutes—until a nice brown crust forms over the top of the pan.
7 Cover the pan with aluminum foil and continue baking for 20 minutes. Potatoes are done when all the liquid has been absorbed and the potatoes at the bottom are soft.
Serves eight to twelve.

Croquette di Patate

Potato Croquettes

Small nuggets of well-seasoned potatoes with an interesting, slightly crusty exterior. The basic item is pretty straightforward, but the variations can be exciting.

2 lbs. white potatoes, peeled
Pinch nutmeg
2 tsp. salt
¼ tsp. white pepper
2 egg yolks
Cornstarch
All-purpose flour
2 egg yolks, beaten
Bread crumbs
Vegetable oil for frying

Preheat oven to 400 degrees.
1 Cut the potatoes into large dice and put in a saucepan with enough water to cover. Bring to a boil.
2 After potatoes have boiled for 15 minutes, drain the water and put the potatoes into a pan. Put the pan into a preheated 400-degree oven for five minutes.
3 Mash the potatoes in a food mill or processor. Stir in salt, pepper and nutmeg. Quickly stir in the egg yolks, one at a time. Don't stop stirring until the egg has been completely incorporated, or the heat of the potatoes will cook the egg into curdles.
4 Coat a clean counter space lightly with cornstarch. Load the potatoes into a pastry bag and squeeze out tubes about a half-inch in diameter onto the counter. Roll these "worms" in the cornstarch, then slice them into 1½-inch lengths.
5 Dust the potato segments with flour, pass through beaten egg, then coat with bread crumbs. Roll the croquettes on the counter to shape and smooth the exteriors.
6 Heat the oil in a saucepan to about 425 degrees. Fry the croquettes about eight at a time until golden brown—about four minutes. Allow the oil to recover in temperature before putting in the next batch. Drain them as they're finished and keep warm until serving.
Serves six to ten.

Croquette di Patate al Tartufo

Berny Potatoes with Truffles

The earthy, nutty, indescribable taste of truffles turn this into a startlingly interesting side dish.

2 lbs. Idaho white potatoes, peeled
Pinch nutmeg

240

Pasta Salad

Cotechino Sausage with Green Pepper Demi-Glace

Tripe Regina

Gnocchi alla Romana

Zuppa Inglese

Cannoli

Tirami Su

Josephine Pastry

2 tsp. salt
½ tsp. white pepper
2 egg yolks
Cornstarch
All-purpose flour
2 egg yolks, beaten
8 oz. almonds, finely chopped
1 medium fresh truffle

1 Prepare the potatoes as for the croquettes above through Step 3.

2 Coat the countertop with cornstarch. With a spoon, scoop out balls of the potato mixture about the size of a cherry tomato. Roll then into uniform shape.

3 Slice the truffle into pieces about the size of your little fingernail. Push the truffles into the center of each potato ball.

4 Dust the potato balls with flour, pass through egg wash, then coat with crumbled almonds. Fry in vegetable oil, six at a time. Use enough oil and a large enough pot so that the balls will be surrounded by and submerged in oil.

Serves six to eight.

Patate Regina

Potato Croquettes with Salami and Mozzarella

I named this stuffed potato croquette for my mother, a beautiful lady who never thought that any dish was too much work as long as it made her family happy. These serve well as a side dish, as an appetizer, or as a cocktail party tidbit.

2 lbs. Idaho white potatoes, peeled
Pinch nutmeg
2 tsp. salt
½ tsp. white pepper
2 egg yolks
Cornstarch
All-purpose flour
2 egg yolks, beaten
4 slices salami
4 slices mozzarella
18 small fresh basil leaves

1 Prepare the croquette dough as in the basic recipe above through Step 3. Dust the countertop with cornstarch and flatten out the dough to about ¼ inch thick. Cut the dough into squares about 1½ inches on a side.

2 Slice the salami and mozzarella into thumbnail-size pieces. Put a few of these onto each potato pad, along with a basil leaf. Roll up into croquettes.

3 Coat with flour, dip in beaten egg, then coat with bread crumbs. Deep-fry as in the basic recipe above. Drain and serve two per person.

Serves six to eight.

Insalata

Salads

When you finally make it to Italy, make sure you eat as many salads as you can. Just go to the marketplace in whatever city or town you find yourself and look over the vegetables available. You'll quickly realize why many authorities have said that Italian salads are the best in the world. The raw materials are outstanding; if you buy a bunch of arugula, you may find yourself eating a lot of it raw on the way home.

We make many, many varieties of salad at Andrea's. (Some of them can be found in the **Antipasto** chapter.) Here are a few of our best salad concoctions, followed by eight of the dressings we make from scratch every day.

Insalata di Pasta Quattro Stagione

Pasta Salad

Pasta salads have become very popular in recent years. The contrast in textures between the soft pasta and the crunchy vegetables makes them very interesting to eat. And, like anything involving pasta, there's endless variety in the ways you can make it. Here's ours.

3 cups rotelli (corkscrew) pasta (1 cup each white, red, and green, if possible)
⅓ head cauliflower florets
⅓ each red and green bell peppers, seeded and cut into strips
4 mushrooms, sliced
3 cloves garlic, pressed
1 Tbs. capers, crushed
¼ small onion, sliced
2 sprigs fresh oregano
6 leaves chopped fresh basil
4 cherry tomatoes, quartered
8 pitted black olives, sliced
1 tsp. salt
¼ tsp. white pepper
1 green onion, chopped
3 sprigs Italian parsley, chopped
1 slice Provolone cheese
2 Tbs. grated Parmesan cheese
½ cup extra virgin olive oil
1 Tbs. balsamic vinegar
2 steamed baby artichoke hearts (canned is okay), cut into quarters
2 radishes, sliced
¼ cucumber, sliced
½ fennel bulb, coarsely chopped

1 Cook the pasta al dente, then plunge it into ice water. Drain very well and put into a large bowl.

2 Using the same water you cooked the pasta in, boil the cauliflower for eight minutes. Remove, rinse with cold water, and add to the bowl with the pasta. Add peppers and mushrooms.

3 Crush the garlic in a garlic press. (Or sprinkle it with salt, and render it into a near-paste by working it on you cutting board with the back of a heavy kitchen spoon.) Add garlic and capers to bowl.

4 Add all the other ingredients except the lettuce leaves and toss well. There should be no runoff of liquid at the bottom of the bowl, but all parts of the salad should be well-coated with the oil and vinegar.

5 Place four lettuce leaves in the bottoms of four glass bowls. Serve two cups of pasta salad per person as a luncheon entree. Garnish with fresh basil.

Serves four entrees or six first courses.

Insalata di Frutti di Mare Portofino

Seafood Salad Portofino

Portofino is a seaport city on the western coast of Italy. They love seafood there — as much as we do in New Orleans. This seafood salad is especially refreshing during the warmer months. It makes an excellent antipasto at any time.

½ lb. scallops
1 lb. squid, cleaned
1 lb. shrimp, peeled and deveined
1 lb. red snapper fillets
1½ lbs. mussels, in shell
1½ lbs. clams, in shell
½ lb. lump crabmeat
1 Tbs. vinegar
2 bay leaves
¼ cup extra virgin olive oil
2 tsp. chopped onions
1 tsp. chopped garlic
¼ tsp. crushed red pepper
½ tsp. salt
¼ tsp. white pepper
½ cup dry white wine

Sauce:
1 cup extra virgin olive oil
¼ cup lemon juice
½ cup dry white wine
½ Tbs. Worcestershire
¼ cup chopped Italian parsley
1½ tsp. chopped garlic
2 tsp. chopped onion
Romaine or Bibb lettuce

1 Wash all the seafoods, one at a time.

2 Bring a gallon of water to a boil with the vinegar and the bay leaves. Poach the scallops, squid, shrimp, and snapper, one seafood at a time, for five minutes each, or until water returns to a boil after the seafood is added. Remove the seafood, drain, and refrigerate.

3 To cook the mussels and clams, heat the ¼ cup of olive oil in a large skillet until very hot. Saute the onions and garlic until lightly browned. Add crushed red pepper, salt and pepper. Put the mussels into the pan and pour the wine over them. Bring the wine to a boil and cover the pan. Cook the mussels until they gape open—about five minutes.

4 Remove the mussels from the pan and repeat the procedure above with the clams. Refrigerate the mussels and clams until cold. Remove about half of the clams and mussels from shells, and chop them coarsely.

(Crabmeat does not require any preparation before going into the salad.)

5 Whisk together all the sauce ingredients in a large bowl. Add all the seafoods and toss lightly with the sauce until well coated. Serve the seafood atop the lettuce, surrounded by mussels and clams in the shells.

Serves six.

Suggested wine: Vernaccia di San Gimignano

Insalata di Spinaci Agrodolce

Sweet and Sour Spinach Salad

Spinach makes a different kind of salad than any other green. For one thing, a spinach salad is not usually crisp. Second, it has an aroma—a very appetizing aroma, especially if it's prepared in the dining room, as we sometimes do. Be extra careful about washing and trimming the spinach leaves.

1 Tbs. extra virgin olive oil
4 slices bacon, chopped
½ small onion, sliced julienne
½ Tbs. chopped garlic
1½ Tbs. brown sugar
2 Tbs. balsamic vinegar
1 Tbs. white vinegar
1 tsp. honey
1 tsp. Dijon mustard
1 lb. fresh spinach, washed and trimmed
Salt and pepper to taste

1 Heat olive oil in a skillet. Saute the the bacon until translucent.

2 Add the onions and garlic and saute until light brown at the edges.

3 Add the brown sugar, vinegars, 1 Tbs. cold water, honey, and Dijon mustard. Cook until everything in the pan is about the color of coffee.

4 Remove the skillet from the heat and add the spinach. With a fork, toss the spinach with the sauce until all the leaves are coated. Be careful not to get the spinach too hot. You want it slightly warm, but still firm. Season with salt and pepper and serve warm.

If by mistake you overcook this until the leaves are limp, just call it a side vegetable. It may not qualify as salad, but it still tastes great.

Serves four.

Insalata d'Anatra

Duck Salad

Duck is a popular entree at Andrea's, and they take so long to cook that we have to roast a lot of them ahead of time. We occasionally have a duck or two left over at the end of the night, which actually makes me happy. It means that I can chill the meat and make this great salad the next day.

½ *roasted duckling (see* **Chickens, Ducks, And Other Birds***)*
2 Tbs. balsamic vinegar
½ *cup extra virgin olive oil*
1 Tbs. Dijon mustard
½ *cup chopped apples*
½ *Tbs. honey*
¼ *cup sun-dried tomato, cut into strips*
2 Tbs. roasted pine nuts
1 Tbs. chopped onions
1 Tbs. chopped garlic
2 sprigs celery leaves, chopped
¼ *cup Major Grey's chutney*
½ *tsp. salt*
¼ *tsp. white pepper*
¼ *tsp. soy sauce*
Juice of ½ *lemon*

1 Remove bones and skin from duck. With the smooth side of a meat mallet, smack the pieces of duck meat to flatten them somewhat. This will make it easy to slice thinly.
2 Mix the vinegar, mustard and oil in a large bowl. Stir in the duck strips and all the other ingredients, one at a time in order.
3 Serve the duck mixture atop crisp, cold leaves of romaine and Boston lettuce, or chop lettuce coarsely and toss with duck.
Serves two entrees or four appetizers.

Suggested wine: Marzemino

Insalata di Pollo Livornese

Chicken Breast Salad Livornese

This is an admirable use of all that chicken that results from making chicken stock. It's a light salad with a lot of flavor and protein but very little fat or calories.

2 cups cooked chicken breast, cut into medium dice
1 Tbs. chopped onion
½ Tbs. chopped garlic
6 pitted black olives
1 medium tomato, cut up
1 Tbs. sun-dried tomatoes, sliced julienne
6 medium mushrooms, sliced
½ Tbs. capers
3 anchovy fillets
¼ cup extra virgin olive oil
½ tsp. salt
1/8 tsp. Tabasco
4 chopped fresh basil leaves
1 sprig fresh oregano leaves
1 head romaine lettuce, washed, outer leaves removed
2 Tbs. balsamic vinegar
¼ cup extra virgin olive oil

1 Put the chopped onion and chopped garlic on a chopping board, sprinkle with a pinch of salt, and, with the back of a heavy spoon, squeeze it into a semi-paste. Do the same thing with the anchovies. (This can also be done with a garlic press.)

2 Combine all ingredients in a bowl and toss well.

3 Slice the romaine crosswise about an inch wide. Toss it with the balsamic vinegar and extra virgin olive oil. Divide it on plates and spoon the chicken mixture equally and place half atop each salad.

Serves two entrees or four to six appetizers.

Suggested wine: Orvieto

Insalata Luigi Veronelli

Arugula, Endive, and Radicchio Salad

Maestro Veronelli is a master of cuisine in Verona. I created this salad in his honor. If you serve it it will be the most beautiful course in the meal.

1 head Belgian endive
1 head radicchio
40 leaves of arugula (approximately 2 cups), large stems removed
*⅓ cup toasted pine nuts (see **Basics**)*
1 Tbs. Dijon mustard
1 Tbs. balsamic vinegar
1 cup extra virgin olive oil
½ tsp. salt
Pinch white pepper

1 Arrange four endive leaves into an X on a large plate. Place three leaves of radicchio on top in the center. Place arugula leaves in between the endive leaves. Top each salad with toasted pine nuts.

2 Combine mustard and vinegar. Add olive oil in a small stream while stirring briskly—in one circular direction only! (It helps greatly to have one person pour while the other person stirs.) Stir in the water, salt and pepper.

3 Sauce each salad with 2 oz. of the dressing and serve.
Serves four.

Insalata d'Indivia Belga "Aurora"

Belgian Endive Salad Aurora

In Belgium, they eat so much of this hybrid variety of lettuce that they have four different names for it. I like it for its crispness and slight bitterness, which awaken the palate. I also like the way the knife-shaped, greenish-white leaves look.

3 heads Belgian endive
1 cup freshly-made mayonnaise (see **Sauces***)*
½ tsp. Worcestershire sauce
¼ tsp. Tabasco
½ Tbs. brandy
¼ tsp. salt
1 Tbs. catsup
Lettuce leaves and red bell pepper for garnish

1 Pull off the discolored or damaged outer leaves of the endives. Slice the heads of endive from top to bottom. With a sharp, tapered knife, cut out the stem core. Pull the endive halves apart and wash well. Dry the leaves inside a towel or with a salad spinner. Reserve 16 of the best-looking leaves. Cut the rest of the leaves across into five or so pieces.

2 Arrange four of the nice, whole leaves in an X on the plate.

3 In a large bowl, combine the mayonnaise, Worcestershire, Tabasco, brandy, salt and catsup and mix well. Put the cut-up endives into the sauce and toss. It will seem like there is way too much dressing, but the residue will drip down onto the whole endive leaves on the plate. Spoon the sauce-coated endives onto the center. Garnish with small leaves of green lettuce and strips of red bell pepper.
Serves four.

Suggested Wine: Fiano Di Avellino

Insalata Andrea

Andrea Salad

I created this salad, with its unique pastry "bag" of cheese, for a dinner given in conjunction with the Sun King Exhibit that came to New Orleans in 1984. Since then I have presented it at many gourmet society banquets and private dinners; it has always received raves. It's a combination salad and cheese course; the cheese comes as a surprise to some, since it's baked inside a bag of flaky pastry.

2 oz. Fontina cheese
1 oz. Bel Paese cheese
1 oz. Swiss cheese
2 oz. Gorgonzola cheese
2 oz. goat cheese
1 oz. sour cream
1 oz. mascarpone cream cheese
¼ cup Reggiano Parmigiano cheese, grated
12 leaves fresh basil, chopped
2 sprigs fresh oregano leaves, chopped
2 tsp. chopped garlic
Phyllo pastry dough
Butter
2 heads radicchio
2 heads Belgian endive
4 cups arugula leaves, loosely packed
½ cup toasted pine nuts (see **Basics***)*

1 Start with all the cheeses at room temperature. Blend them with the basil, oregano, and garlic in a food processor until you have a paste. Spoon this cheese mixture into a bowl and work it with the back of a wooden spoon until it's smooth. Firm the cheese mixture in the refrigerator for 30 minutes.
Preheat oven to 400 degrees.
2 Cut phyllo dough into squares about eight inches on a side. Place 1 Tbs. of the cheese mixture in the center of a square of dough. Separate three thicknesses of the dough and make it into a little bag around the cheese. Put the bag into a porcelain or Pyrex baking cup coated with a little butter. Tie the tops of the bags loosely with string.
3 Put the cups on a baking pan and put the pan into a preheated 400 degree oven for five to seven minutes—until tops of bags are lightly browned. Remove from the oven and allow to cool for ten minutes.
4 Untie the bags and place them aside a salad of radicchio, Belgian endive, and arugula—or whatever greens you like. Serve with extra virgin olive oil, balsamic vinegar, and toasted pine nuts. Tell your guests that it's cheese in the bag, not lemon—as many of our guests have supposed!
Serves 10.

250

Salsa Fredda al Balsamico

Andrea's House Salad Dressing

This is a satisfyingly rich salad dressing that we make in enormous quantities for use with our house salads. It is essentially a freshly-made mayonnaise with a lot of other flavorings. So the technique for making it is like that for mayonnaise: you have to watch it. This dressing will keep well for several days at least, so you cam make a lot of it at once. It comes out better when made in good-size batches.

5 eggs
1 Tbs. balsamic vinegar
1 Tbs. white vinegar
¼ cup Cremona mustard
1 Tbs. lemon juice
2 cups olive oil
1 cup extra virgin olive oil
2 cups vegetable oil
1 tsp. black pepper
½ tsp. white pepper
½ tsp. sugar
1½ tsp. salt
½ tsp. white pepper
½ Tbs. dry mustard, mixed with a little water into a paste
½ tsp. Tabasco
½ tsp. Worcestershire
¼ cup chopped fresh garlic
¼ cup whipping cream
¼ cup half-and-half cream

1 In a mixer bowl with the mixer running slowly, combine the eggs, vinegars, mustard, and lemon juice.

2 Add the olive oils and vegetable oil, in a slow dribble at first. When the sauce starts to "take" and become fluffy, you can add the oils faster.

3 Add each of the other ingredients in turn, allowing time for each to blend in.
Makes about six cups—enough for about 18 salads.

Salsa Olio e Aceto

Italian Vinaigrette

Here is our version of the ubiquitous "Italian" salad dressing. I think you'll find it a little better than the stuff in the bottles.

2 Tbs. chopped onions
1 Tbs. chopped garlic
2 Tbs. chopped fresh basil leaves
1 Tbs. chopped fresh oregano
1 Tbs. capers
1 cup olive oil
1 cup extra virgin olive oil
1 Tbs. balsamic vinegar
2 Tbs. red wine vinegar
1 Tbs. lemon juice
½ tsp. black pepper

Put the first five ingredients into a food processor or blender and chop them very fine—but not to where it becomes a mush. Add the olive oils, vinegars, lemon juice, and pepper and blend well.
Makes enough for eight small salads.

Salsa alla Mostarda

Mustard Vinaigrette

This is a zippy version of the traditional French vinaigrette. Jennifer Connell, one of our copy editors, says it's even better when you use half Dijon mustard and half Creole mustard.

¼ cup Dijon mustard
¼ cup white wine vinegar
¼ tsp. sugar
¾ cup olive oil
Salt and white pepper to taste

Blend first three ingredients plus 1 tsp. cold water with a whisk in a bowl. Then whisk in olive oil slowly. Add salt and pepper.
Makes enough for four small salads.

Salsa al Gorgonzola e Roquefort

The blue cheeses have a powerful, distinctive taste, and people either love it or hate it. For those who love it, we have two different blue cheese dressings. Both of them are superb with ripe tomato slices or with fresh asparagus.

Gorgonzola Dressing

Gorgonzola is the blue cheese of Italy. The smooth taste and light crunchiness of the pine nuts gives this some interesting contrasts.

½ cup softened Gorgonzola cheese
1 cup freshly-made mayonnaise (see **Sauces***)*
¼ cup dry white wine
½ Tbs. balsamic vinegar
4 drops Tabasco
½ Tbs. Dijon mustard
½ Tbs. lemon juice
¼ cup toasted pine nuts, chopped (see **Basics***)*

With the side of a large knife on a cutting board, work the Gorgonzola until it's smooth. Blend with the mayonnaise, wine, vinegar, Tabasco, mustard, lemon juice and 1 Tbs. water. Sprinkle the pine nuts atop the salad after the dressing.
Makes enough for about six salads.

Roquefort Dressing

Roquefort is the most famous of the blue cheeses. It's made from sheep's milk and aged in caves in Roquefort, France. It's quite rich and salty, so a little of it goes a long way.

1 cup Roquefort cheese, softened
1 Tbs. Dijon mustard
1 cup freshly-made mayonnaise (see **Sauces***)*
½ Tbs. Worcestershire
½ tsp. Tabasco
1 Tbs. balsamic vinegar
2 Tbs. red wine vinegar
½ tsp. salt
¼ tsp. black pepper

With the back of a large spoon on a cutting board, work the Roquefort until smooth. Whisk cheese and all other ingredients together.
Makes enough for about six salads.

Salsa Vino Bianco

Chablis Dressing

This has a sharpness that makes it superb on any salad with a mellow taste, like Bibb lettuce, watercress, or avocados.

1 small onion, chopped
½ cup freshly-made mayonnaise
1½ Tbs. Cremona mustard (or Dijon)
¼ tsp. Tabasco
¼ tsp. Worcestershire
1 Tbs. brandy
1½ Tbs. lemon juice
2 Tbs. white vinegar
¼ cup Chablis
¼ tsp. salt
Pinch white pepper

Put the chopped onion into a cheesecloth bag and squeeze it to extract the juice. Whisk this and all other ingredients in a bowl.
Makes enough for six small salads.

Salsa Europa

This is for people who like thousand-island dressing. It's an elegant version, with the islands left out. It is also very good on cold boiled shrimp or crabmeat as a cocktail sauce.

¼ cup mayonnaise
1½ Tbs. Cremona mustard
¼ tsp. Tabasco
¼ tsp. Worcestershire
1 Tbs. brandy
2 Tbs. catsup
2 tsp. lemon juice
1/8 tsp. salt
Pinch white pepper

Whisk the ingredients together in a bowl.
Makes about ⅔ cup—enough for four salads.

Salsa Agrodolce

Sweet and Sour Dressing

This is great on a spinach salad.

6 Tbs. freshly-made mayonnaise (see **Sauces***)*
1 Tbs. honey
1 Tbs. apple juice
1 Tbs. pineapple juice
¼ cup whipping cream
1/8 tsp. Worcestershire
4 drops Tabasco
1 Tbs. white vinegar
1/8 tsp. salt
Sprinkle of black pepper

Whisk all ingredients together.
Makes enough for four small salads.

Dolci

Desserts

One part of our kitchen that sets Andrea's apart from most restaurants is our bake shop. Only the food service operations of major hotels can rival our in-house production of pastries, cakes, tartes, mousses, and other desserts. Our baker, Lonnie Knisley, has worked with me since before we even opened Andrea's. He is a master baker of unusual talent, and has provided us with many spectacular recipes. We are very pleased to be able to present them here, along with a few of our own.

It's very important to keep in mind that baking, unlike other kinds of cooking, requires faithfulness to the recipe. You cannot add a little more of this or that later while baking. Measurements—some by weight, some by volume in this chapter—are critical.

Torta di Mandorle

Flourless Almond and Chocolate Cake

This is a delightful light, crumbly chocolate cake with almonds that my mother made for us when we were children. (She still does.) It is delicious with ice cream, zabaglione, or whipped cream. We have made our recipe for two cakes so that you will be able to enjoy a slice for breakfast. (Roberto and I eat more torta di mandorle in the morning with coffee than at any other time.)

1 cup semi-sweet chocolate morsels
½ cup butter
½ lb. sugar
¼ oz. amaretto
¾ cup cocoa powder
1½ tsp. baking powder
3 Tbs. cornstarch
1 lb. finely crushed almonds
8 eggs, separated
Powdered sugar

Preheat the oven to 275 degrees.
1 Melt the chocolate in a double boiler over medium-low heat.
2 While the chocolate is heating, cream the butter and sugar together in a powerful electric mixer with a paddle attachment. (It may be necessary to do this by hand with a wooden spoon if your mixer doesn't have a lot of oomph.) You want this mixture to have as little graininess as possible; well-creamed sugar and butter will have a very pale color.
3 Add the amaretto to the mixer bowl with the creamed butter and sugar. Sift the cocoa powder, baking powder and cornstarch together. Add to the mixer bowl.
4 Grind the almonds to a fine powder in a food processor. Add that to the mixer bowl with the egg yolks.
5 When all the ingredients are well blended, scrape down the bowl. While running the mixer on medium speed, slowly add the chocolate. Continue to mix until blended, then stop the mixer.
6 In a separate bowl, whip the egg whites until stiff but not dry. Fold this with a wooden spoon into the other bowl carefully. (Your bare hands will do an even better job of this.) Keep in mind that you are using the egg-white meringue—which contains a lot of air—to fluff up the batter. The more you handle it, the more air escapes, and the heavier the cake will be.
7 Coat two nine-inch pie pans with shortening and load them with the batter almost to the top.
8 Bake in a preheated 275-300 degree oven for one hour. Cakes are done when the top starts to show cracks and fissures.
9 Allow cakes to cool. Turn pans over onto plates. Dust the tops of the cakes with powdered sugar.
Serves twelve.

Zabaglione

Marsala and Egg Sauce

Zabaglione is a familiar and much-loved flavor in Italian desserts. We use it at Andrea's in a wide variety of desserts. There are many Italians who believe that it is an aphrodisiac. I'm not sure about that, but just in case I eat zabaglione whenever possible.

3 egg yolks
1 Tbs. dry Marsala wine
1 Tbs. sugar
1 Tbs. dry white wine
2 Tbs. freshly squeezed orange juice
Juice of 1 small lemon
1 cup whipping cream, chilled

1 Whisk together the egg yolks, Marsala, sugar and white wine in the top of a double boiler over low heat. Do not let the temperature of the mixture rise much above lukewarm. (Pull top part of double boiler out if it gets too hot.) Whisk until the mixture is frothy.

2 Whisk in the orange and lemon juices.

3 Whip the whipping cream (it must be cold) until peaks form. Fold whipped cream into egg mixture carefully, with a rubber spatula. Refrigerate at least one hour.

Note: This zabaglione will fall apart if it is held too long. If you need it to hold up more than a few hours, dissolve ½ tsp. plain gelatin into 1 Tbs. water. Whisk that into the egg mixture before you combine it with the whipped cream.

Makes about four cups.

Panna Montata

Whipped Cream

Whipped cream is an ingredient in many of the desserts to follow. There is no reason why you should use some fake product instead of whipping your own cream. It's not too difficult, and the taste is incomparably better. Here are the things you need to know before you whip cream:

1 The cream you should start with is whipping cream or heavy cream — two names for essentially the same thing. There are substitutes, but no good ones.

2 The cream must be cold. If your kitchen is hot, you may have to whip the cream in a bowl placed atop a pan of ice. If the cream is too warm, it will suddenly turn to butter and whey instead of whipped cream.

3 Start out whipping the cream with the medium-high speed on your electric mixer. (Blenders, by the way, don't do the job.) When it starts to get thick, lower the speed and watch carefully. When the cream starts to form soft peaks when you spoon through it, it's ready. It should still be wet-looking. Don't overwhip cream — it will break!

258

Sfogliata ai Lamponi "Josephine"

Josephine Pastry

My idea with this delicate raspberry dessert was to make something like the classic French Napoleon pastry, but with fresh raspberries. After playing around with this for awhile, it didn't look much like a Napoleon—but we named it Josephine anyway.

One sheet of puff pastry dough, 18 x 12 inches
3 cups fresh raspberries
4 cups whipped zabaglione
2 tsp. confectioner's sugar

Raspberry sauce:
1 tsp. sugar
1 oz. Kirschwasser
1 cup raspberries (frozen can be used)

Preheat oven to 375 degrees.

1 Use a pizza cutter to cut eight pieces of puff pastry dough about two inches by six inches. Coat a baking pan with shortening and place the pastry pieces in the pan. Bake at 375 degrees for 45 minutes. If the top starts to get brown, cover with parchment paper. Remove from oven and allow to cool. Separate the puff pastry to get a top and a bottom.

2 For the raspberry sauce, blend 3 oz. water, sugar, and Kirschwasser and bring to a boil. Add raspberries and cook for 10-15 minutes over low flame. Cool and put into a food processor until you have a very smooth sauce. Remove seeds by straining.

3 To serve, place two tablespoons of raspberry sauce onto a plate. Put a bottom part of the puff pastry on the sauce. Spoon two tablespoons of the zabaglione atop the pastry. Top with a layer of fresh raspberries. Place top of pastry on top of berries and sprinkle confectioner's sugar over pastry. Refrigerate and serve chilled.

Serves twelve.

Suggested wine: Marsala Amabile

Torta al Formaggio

Cheesecake

Everybody loves a good cheesecake, but most people are afraid to bake one—
probably because it involves a special piece of equipment, the springform pan.
Don't be intimidated. Springform pans are nothing more than baking pans with
removable sides, and they're not necessarily even expensive. The most important
thing to remember about baking cheesecakes is that they must be heated and then
cooled gradually, without being subjected to blasts of heat or drastic changes of
temperature.

At Andrea's, we make a praline cheesecake that has the richness of a New York-
style cheesecake with the nutty goodness of the New Orleans praline flavor.

1½ lbs. cream cheese
1 cup sugar
1 cup sour cream
3 eggs
½ pint half & half cream
1 Tbs. vanilla
1 Tbs. lemon juice

Crust:
2 cups graham cracker crumbs
¼ cup sugar
4 oz. melted butter
Pinch of cinnamon

Praline topping:
½ cup praline or hazelnut paste
½ cup toasted pecans

1 Combine cheese and sugar in a mixing bowl with a paddle attachment on an
electric mixer. Whip until light—about 15 minutes on medium speed.

2 Add sour cream and let it whip in for five minutes. As you add this and the
other ingredients, remember to scrape down the bowl after every ingredient addition. This is critical to keep lumps or streaks from forming later.

3 Add eggs one at a time. (Break them into a cup first, to avoid the possibility
of discovering a bad egg too late.) Add the half-and-half, then the vanilla and lemon
juice. Continue to mix and scrape down the bowl as you go until all the ingredients are blended together smoothly.

Preheat the oven to 325 degrees.

4 Now begin the crust. Combine all crust ingredients in a mixer.

5 Coat nine-inch springform pan with shortening. Pack the graham cracker mixture into the pan around the sides and the bottom between 1/8 and ¼ inch
thick. Make sure that the joint between the bottom and the sides is completely
sealed with crust—perhaps using a little extra there. This will keep water from

seeping in during the baking.

6 Pour the cheese mixture into the crust. Put the springform pan into a larger pan of warm water. The water should come up the side of the springform pan less than one inch. Put the pans into the 325-degree preheated oven. Bake for about one hour. The cake is ready when the filling has risen and begun to brown lightly at the top.

Note: The drier, heavier New York-style cheesecake can be made by baking at 275 degrees for 1½ hours.

7 After the cake is baked, remove the springform pan from the pan of water and put it nack into the oven. Turn the oven off and let the cake cool for one hour inside the oven. This will keep the top from cracking.

8 Remove the sides of the springform pan. Put the cheesecake into the refrigerator until cool all the way through—three to five hours, minimum.

9 For a praline cheesecake, melt the hazlenut paste in a double boiler until smooth. Toast the pecans in the oven until darkish brown. Pour the melted praline paste over the chilled cheesecake and cover with chopped pecans quickly, before the praline paste sets (which it will quite quickly on that cold cheesecake). Return the cheesecake to the refrigerator.

Serves eight to twelve.

Suggested wine: Vin Santo

Crema Pasticciera

Pastry Cream

Pastry cream is one of the most useful basic items in baking. It can be used as a starting point for many pastries, or as a finishing touch—a filling or a topping—for others.

2 quarts milk
6 oz. cornstarch
5 eggs
¼ lb. butter
1 lb. sugar
1 Tbs. vanilla

1 Mix 2 cups of milk with the cornstarch and the eggs and set aside.

2 Mix the rest of the milk and the butter and sugar in a saucepan over high heat and bring to a rolling boil. Add the cornstarch-milk-egg mixture and the vanilla to the pot and whisk in vigorously. Return the pot to a boil and then take it off the heat.

3 Since pastry cream is one of the most bacteria-prone concoctions in the kitchen, it is essential to cool it as quickly as possible. We spread it out on sheet pan, cover it with plastic film, then cool it rapidly in the refrigerator.

Makes three quarts pastry cream.

Pan di Spagna

Basic Genoise (Sponge Cake)

We bake all our own cakes at Andrea's, and this is the one we probably bake most often. It is the basis for our tirami su, our strawberry cake (recipes for both follow) and a few others.

5 eggs
2 egg yolks
6 ½ oz. sugar
1 tsp. vanilla
6 ½ oz. cake flour
¼ tsp. cornstarch
Pinch salt

Preheat the oven to 350 degrees.

1 Blend the eggs, egg yolks, and sugar in a mixer bowl with a wire whip attachment until the mixture doubles in volume—about 15 minutes on high speed. Just before stopping the mixer, add the vanilla and mix in.

2 Sift together the cake flour, cornstarch and salt. Fold dry mixture into egg mixture with a wooden spoon or rubber spatula, just until blended.

3 Coat two 10-inch round cake pans with shortening. Pour the batter into the pans and put them immediately into a preheated 350-degree oven. Bake until tops are springy to the touch—about 45-50 minutes.

4 Remove the cakes from the pans and cool on a wire rack. When cool, use a long serrated knife to slice off the tops of the cakes. For tirami su or other layer cakes, divide each cake into three uniform layers with a serrated knife.

Makes two cakes.

Suggested wine: Passito del Santo

Tirami Su

"Pick-Me-Up" Cake

This is a relatively new Italian dessert that is all the rage in Italy and New York. The original version was made with lady fingers, and was scooped out in the manner of an English trifle. We took a fresh approach to it by substituting sponge cake for the lady fingers. It is so light that you don't eat it—you inhale it.

Filling:
2 egg yolks
½ cup sugar
1 cup mascarpone cheese
1 pint whipping cream, chilled
1 tsp. vanilla

1 genoise (sponge) cake, sliced into three layers
¼ cup sugar
¾ cup espresso or strong coffee
1 oz. rum
2 Tbs. cocoa powder

1 Whisk egg yolks and ¼ cup sugar together. Whisk in the mascarpone cheese.

2 In a separate bowl, whip the cream, the rest of the sugar, and the vanilla until almost stiff—no peaks.

3 Fold the mascarpone cheese mixture into the whipped cream and continue to whip, until stiff. Set aside.

4 Make a fully-dissolved syrup with ¼ cup sugar, 2 Tbs. water, espresso and rum.

5 Brush a layer of the sponge cake with espresso mixture. With a spatula, smooth about a half-inch-thick layer of the mascarpone cheese mixture on top. Brush the second cake layer with espresso, and place it espresso side down on the first layer. Brush the top with espresso. Spread on another half-inch of the mascarpone cheese mixture. Repeat the procedure with the third layer of cake. Cover the top and sides of the cake with a thin layer of mascarpone filling.

6 With a sieve and a spoon, sprinkle the top of the cake with cocoa powder. Cover the sides of the cake with chocolate shavings. Refrigerate at least three hours. This cake does not hold up well when exposed to any heat, so keep it cool.
Serves eight.

Torta alle Fragole

Strawberry Cake

For some reason nobody quite understands, this has become known around the restaurant as a strawberry shortcake. It's not a shortcake at all, but a genoise layer cake. It is beautiful both to the eye and to the palate — especially when Louisiana strawberries are in season, in the spring.

1 pint strawberries
½ cup sugar
1 oz. Kirschwasser (a cherry brandy)
¾ cup whipped cream
1 genoise cake, cut into three layers

1 Wash the strawberries. Cut off the leaves and the white part right next to the leaves. Slice the strawberries about ¼ inch thick, slicing from top to bottom. Set aside the end slices for garnishing the top.

2 Make a simple syrup by dissolving the sugar in ¼ cup of warm water. Stir in the Kirschwasser.

3 Brush the top of the bottom third of the genoise with the Kirschwasser syrup. With a spatula, spread about ½ inch of whipped cream on top. Place strawberries generously on top of the whipped cream.

4 Brush one side of another genoise layer with the Kirschwasser syrup and place it on top of the first. Brush the top with syrup, then lay down another layer of whipped cream and strawberries. Repeat the procedure for the third layer. Smooth whipped cream around the sides and top. Use the round-end strawberries to decorate the top.

Serves eight to ten.

Suggested wine: Asti Spumante

Zuppa Inglese

Italian Trifle

This is a lovely dessert made with fresh fruit, cake and liqueur. It requires no cooking, but it does need to marinate in the refrigerator for at least a day so the flavors can come together. One of the many things I like about this cake is that it gives us a use for all the perfectly good tops of the sponge cakes we bake for tirami su, which would otherwise go to waste.

1 nine-inch sponge cake, or six tops from sponge cakes
1 cup Kirschwasser
3 cups pastry cream (see recipe in this chapter)
3 cups fresh ripe strawberries, sliced
3 bananas, sliced
3 cups whipped cream
½ cup candied fruit (such as is found in fruitcake)
1 cup crushed pistachio nuts

You will be making layers of all the ingredients in a glass bowl. The bowl should have a capacity of about a gallon. Each layer should use about one-third of the quantity given for each ingredient. Here are the layers, starting from the bottom of the bowl:

1 A ½-inch-thick layer of sponge cake, moistened with Kirschwasser.
2 Pastry cream, spread uniformly with a spatula.
3 Strawberries.
4 Bananas.
5 Whipped cream.
6 Candied fruits and pistachios.
7 Two more layers each of all of the above ingredients, in the same order. Finish off the top with a very smooth later of whipped cream studded with a few of the candied fruits and pistachios. Place the bowl into the refrigerator to chill.

Serve by slicing, so each guest gets the full impact of all the layers.
Serves twelve.

Budino di Cioccolato

Chocolate Mousse

I must give credit where credit is due. This recipe was originally developed at the Royal Orleans Hotel, where I was executive chef before we opened Andrea's. It makes the best chocolate mousse I have ever tasted—and that's an opinion shared by a number of New Orleans food writers and other chocolate mousse fans.

12 oz. top-quality semi-sweet chocolate (the better the chocolate, the better the mousse)
1 cup whipping cream
¼ cup coffee
3 egg yolks, beaten
1 tsp. vanilla
5 egg whites
⅓ cup sugar

1 Melt the chocolate in a double boiler over medium-low heat. It's a good idea to stand over the chocolate while it's melting and stir it until it's completely melted, then take it off the heat immediately.

2 Whip the cream and set aside. (See tips on whipping cream earlier in this chapter.)

3 Pour the hot coffee and ¼ cup hot water slowly into a bowl with the egg yolks, whisking briskly as you go until completely mixed.

4 Whisk in the melted chocolate. Keep whisking even after the mixture is completely combined; this will help cool the chocolate. Whisk in the vanilla.

5 Whip the egg whites and the sugar until peaking but not dry.

6 Fold the egg-white meringue into the chocolate mixture carefully with a wooden spoon.

7 Fold in the whipped cream. This is the most critical part of the recipe. The key to a great chocolate mousse is that you can't incorporate hot melted chocolate into whipped cream. The chocolate mixture must be cool to the touch or the whipped cream will break. Lightly blend the two mixtures until uniform.

8 The mousse is actually at its best cloudlike texture right now. But we pipe it into the dish-shaped "Champagne" glasses, sprinkle chocolate shavings and powdered sugar over the top, and refrigerate. This causes the mousse to set, which will give it a different, heavier texture.

Serves twelve.

Budino di Cioccolato Bianco

White Chocolate Mousse

White chocolate is not really chocolate at all, but cocoa butter with the cocoa liquor left out. At Andrea's, we serve it in a chocolate cup in a pool of raspberry sauce.

1 lb. white chocolate
1 cup whipping cream
3 eggs, separated
¼ cup brandy
¼ cup hot water
1 Tbs. vanilla
2 oz. sugar

The procedure is the same as for the dark chocolate mousse, except substitute the brandy for the coffee, and add the vanilla to the egg whites and sugar as you beat them.
Serves twelve.

Pera Affogata con Zabaglione

Poached Pears with Zabaglione Sauce

Wait until late summer and early fall, when pears are at their peak, to serve this intensely delightful dessert.

4 ripe pears, peeled and cored
⅓ cup lemon juice
⅓ cup dry white wine
4 oz. semi-sweet chocolate
1 cup zabaglione

1 Put the pears in a bowl with ½ gallon cold water and half of the lemon juice. This will keep the pears from browning as you continue.

2 Bring ½ gal. cold water to a boil. Put the pears in as soon as the water starts to roll, along with the rest of the lemon juice and the wine. Boil for 20 minutes, then turn off the heat but leave pears in the hot water.

3 Meanwhile, melt the chocolate in a double boiler over medium-low heat. Pour the chocolate into a measuring cup set in a pan of hot water to keep it warm.

4 After the pears have cooled to lukewarm, dry them and dip them, top down, into the hot melted chocolate in the cup. After the chocolate sets, coat the bottom halves of the pears with chocolate. Refrigerate.

Note: Make sure the pears are very dry before you dip them. Even a small amount of water will cause melted chocolate to start lumping up.

5 Serve on a plate with 2 Tbs. zabaglione. Garnish with mint.
Serves four.

267

Sorbetto al Limone

Lemon Sorbet

Few things could be more refreshing on a summer day than this tart, light ice. It also makes a terrific palate refresher in the middle of a large meal.

Juice of 12 medium lemons
1 Tbs. lemon zest*
2 cups sugar dissolved in 2 cups water

Load all the ingredients into an ice cream freezer and run it for 20-30 minutes, until you have a thick, thoroughly frozen slurry. Scoop the slurry into a plastic container and put into your freezer until frozen hard.
Makes one quart.

*Lemon zest is made by running an inexpensive tool called a "zester" across the skin of the fruit. Don't go into the white part of the skin when doing this; all the oils are in the colored exterior.

Sorbetto al Calvados

Calvados Sorbet

Calvados is the famous brandy made from apples in the Normandy region of France. Many formal dinners serve a shot of Calvados at mid-meal, in order to create what the French call *le trou Normande* ("the Norman hole") in your stomach. Then, it is alleged, you can eat more. We thought it would be interesting to incorporate the Calvados into a refreshing sorbet.

1 sweet, ripe apple, peeled and cored
¼ cup Calvados
2 cups sugar dissolved into 2 cups water

Cut up the apple and puree in a food processor. Combine with other ingredients and proceed as for the lemon sorbet, above.
Makes about a quart.

Gelato al Tartufo

Ice Cream Pastry

This is a combination of ice cream and cake in a delightful confection flavored with liqueur.

1 pint each vanilla and chocolate ice cream
Squares of sponge cake
Mozart chocolate liqueur
Amaretto liqueur

1 Use glass, metal or porcelain cups measuring about 1 cup each. (Custard cups, or something in that shape, are perfect.) Freeze the cups for a few hours before starting the recipe.

2 Put about 3 Tbs. vanilla ice cream into each cup, pressing it with a spoon along the sides of the cup to leave a deep depression. Return the cups to the freezer so the ice cream will freeze in place.

3 While waiting, cut sponge cake into squares about an inch on a side. Spoon a bit of the two liqueurs onto each piece of cake.

4 When the ice cream cups are frozen, put about 2 Tbs. of chocolate ice cream into the depressions in the vanilla ice cream. Top that with a square of liqueur-soaked sponge cake. Cover the cake with chocolate ice cream to the top of the cup. Smooth the ice cream down on top. Return to the freezer until frozen hard.

5 Unmold the tartufi by running warm water on the outside of the cup until the ice cream drops out onto a plate. Spoon ½ tsp. Amaretto over each cup. Return to the freezer once more to freeze hard, and serve.

Serves six.

Torta Nunziale

Wedding Cake

We have been pleased to host many weddings and wedding receptions at Andrea's. We always encourage the bride to let us bake the wedding cake. They are never sorry. We include this cake recipe at the insistence of co-author Tom Fitzmorris, whose wedding reception we catered and who enjoyed this cake very much.

⅔ cups shortening
1⅔ cups sugar
2¼ cups all-purpose flour
3 ½ tsp. baking powder
1 tsp. salt
1¼ cups milk
1 tsp. vanilla
½ tsp. almond extract
5 egg whites

Preheat the oven to 350 degrees.

1 Cream the shortening and sugar together in a mixer bowl. Sift the dry ingredients together and add them to the mixer bowl about one-fourth at a time, alternating with one-fourth of the milk, while continuing to run the mixer on medium speed. Add vanilla and almond extract.

2 Beat egg whites in a separate, grease-free bowl till stiff but not dry.

3 Fold the beaten egg whites into the cake batter with a spatula or (most effective) with your fingers. Do not overmix; try to retain the fluffiness of the egg whites.

4 Spoon the batter into cake pans of appropriate size to your idea of a wedding cake. Bake the cakes in a preheated 350-degree oven for 45 minutes, until springy. Or until a cake tester inserted into the middle comes out clean.

5 Slice off the tops of the cakes, and then slice the cakes into three layers with a long serrated knife. Spread raspberry marmalade between the layers.

We finish our cakes with sheets of fondant—a thick, commercially prepared, flexible sugar wrap. You can make your own fondant if you are daring, or you can ice the cake in the traditional ways. We leave that up to you. However, here is a great variation using almond butter cream as the frosting:

Almond butter cream:
½ cup sugar
2 oz. Amaretto
1 lb. butter, softened
½ lb. shortening
1 lb., 2 oz. confectioner's sugar
1 tsp. vanilla
¼ tsp. almond extract

1 Dissolve the sugar in ¼ cup of warm water to make a simple syrup. Add the Amaretto.

270

2 Combine the butter and the shortening and beat it with an electric mixer on medium speed until light in texture. Add the powdered sugar, a little at a time, and continue to beat to spreading consistency. Beat in the vanilla and almond extract.

3 Proceed with the cake through all the steps up to the point where you begin assembling the cake. Leave out the raspberry marmalade. Brush each side of each layer of the cake with the Amaretto syrup, and spread about one-eighth inch of the almond butter cream between each layer as you go up. Coat the sides and the top with the butter cream with a spatula and decorate according to your whim.

This makes a wedding cake big enough for about 50 people.

Suggested wine: Picolit

Torta al Lime

Key Lime Pie

There is nothing Italian about this. It's a rich, tart pie that hails originally from Key West, Florida, where they grow the distinctive key limes. These are almost impossible to find in stores, but regular limes offer plenty enough sacrifice in the amount of time it takes to juice them out. (That's why we use half fresh lime juice, half bottled.)

Juice and pulp of 5 limes
Zest of 2 limes
5 whole eggs
5 egg yolks
1½ cups sugar
3 oz. reconstituted lime juice
2 oz. melted butter
10-inch pre-baked pie shell

1 Combine all ingredients except the pie shell and the butter in a double boiler over lightly-boiling water. Whisk briskly until the mixture thickens and becomes fluffy—about 10-15 minutes.

2 When the mixture has reached the desired thickness, whisk in the melted (but not hot!) butter.

3 Pour the mixture into the pie shell. Put the pie into the refrigerator to set for about two hours.

4 Decorate pies with shaved chocolate, whipped cream, or lime slices.
Serves eight to ten.

Crema Caramellata

Caramel Custard

The custard part is easy. The caramel part is a little trickier, involving split-second timing at one point. The result is one of the most popular restaurant desserts there is.

Caramel:
1 cup sugar
¼ cup or less water
Pinch cream of tartar

Custard:
1 quart milk
1 lb. sugar
10 eggs

1 Dissolve the sugar and cream of tartar in just enough water to suspend all the sugar.

2 Put the sugar slurry into a small saucepan with a very smooth surface. With a wet brush, clean all the sugar crystals off the side of the pan. If the mixture has any place where crystals can begin to form, it will granulate again—and you don't want that to happen.

3 Bring the slurry to a boil over high heat and cook until you see the first bit of browning. The sugar is now extremely hot—about 350 degrees—so be careful. It can burn very quickly. Lower the heat and continue to cook, flowing it around a bit, until the center of the pan is light brown. The sugar will continue to cook from its own heat, so remove it from the fire.

4 Quickly pour about ½ tsp. of the sauce into the bottoms of 6- to 8-ounce custard cups and set aside.

Preheat the oven to 325 degrees.

5 To make the custard, combine all custard ingredients in mixer bowl and beat on slow speed with balloon whisk until mixed well—about five minutes. Strain the mixture.

6 Pour into custard cups over caramel sauce.

7 Put the custard cups into a pan of hot water and allow the contents of the cups to become warm.

8 Put the entire pan into a preheated 300-325 degree oven. Bake for 30 minutes, or until the custard has set and is clearly no longer liquid. The tops should brown only slightly. Remove from oven and allow to cool at room temperature for about 15 minutes, then refrigerate.

Serves eight.

Suggested wine: Marsala

Cannoli

Cannoli are crisp pastry tubes filled with a sweet filling of ricotta cheese and flavorings. They are made outstandingly well at Angelo Brocato's in New Orleans. But we make our own, and so can you. The shells are the hard part. Preparation of cannoli shells requires a special form used for nothing else in the kitchen: metal pipes about six inches long and a half-inch to an inch in diameter. We use the latter. Six-inch pieces of broomstick also work well.

Shells:
1¼ cup all-purpose flour
5 Tbs. Marsala wine
1 Tbs. sugar
Pinch of cocoa powder
Pinch cinnamon
Pinch salt
Vegetable oil for frying

Filling:
1 lb. ricotta cheese
1 cup sugar
½ cup mixed jellied fruit (as for fruitcake)
2 Tbs. chocolate chips
1 Tbs. vanilla
½ oz. triple sec liqueur

1 Mix all the dry ingredients in a bowl, then add Marsala and stir with a fork until the mixture turns crumbly.

2 With your hands, knead the dough until it forms a gritty ball. Roll it out on a board to smooth it out, but don't overwork.

3 Using a pasta machine, run about one-fifth of the dough, flattened out into a disc, through the sheet-making apparatus on the number one (thickest) setting. Double the dough over and run it through again. Increase the setting to number three and run the dough through twice more, folding it over between pressings. Increase the setting to number five and repeat the procedure. Run it through one final time on the number six setting. The dough should now be about as thick as a lasagne noodle.

4 Cut out 4-inch-wide discs of the dough with a cookie-cutter or a knife. Wrap them around the cannoli forms.

5 Heat vegetable oil to 375 degrees. Deep-fry the dough on its forms until crisp—about five minutes. Remove from the oil and drain. Remove the forms, and allow the shells to cool.

6 Meanwhile, make the filling by mixing all the ingredients until well blended. When the shells are cool, fill them using a pastry bag with a large tip. Dip ends of cannoli in pistachio nuts or melted chocolate, and dust with powdered sugar.
Makes 18-24 cannoli.

Index